The Prison of Time

The Prison of Time

*Stanley Kubrick, Adrian Lyne,
Michael Bay and Quentin Tarantino*

Elisa Pezzotta

BLOOMSBURY ACADEMIC
NEW YORK • LONDON • OXFORD • NEW DELHI • SYDNEY

BLOOMSBURY ACADEMIC
Bloomsbury Publishing Inc
1385 Broadway, New York, NY 10018, USA
50 Bedford Square, London, WC1B 3DP, UK
29 Earlsfort Terrace, Dublin 2, Ireland

BLOOMSBURY, BLOOMSBURY ACADEMIC and the Diana logo are trademarks
of Bloomsbury Publishing Plc

First published in the United States of America 2023
Paperback edition published 2024

For legal purposes the Acknowledgements on p. xii constitute an extension
of this copyright page.

Cover design: Eleanor Rose
Cover image: *The Killing*, 1956, Dir. Stanley Kubrick. Still © Photofest Digital

Library of Congress Cataloging-in-Publication Data
Names: Pezzotta, Elisa, author.
Title: The prison of time : Stanley Kubrick, Adrian Lyne, Michael Bay and Quentin Tarantino /
Elisa Pezzotta.
Description: New York : Bloomsbury Academic, 2022. | Includes bibliographical references
and index. | Summary: "This book focuses on the representation of time in cinema, by
focusing on four filmmakers: Stanley Kubrick, Quentin Tarantino, Adrian Lyne,
and Michael Bay"– Provided by publisher.
Identifiers: LCCN 2022008932 (print) | LCCN 2022008933 (ebook) |
ISBN 9781501380600 (hardback) | ISBN 9781501380570 (paperback) |
ISBN 9781501380594 (epub) | ISBN 9781501380587 (pdf) | ISBN 9781501380563
Subjects: LCSH: Time in motion pictures. | Kubrick, Stanley–Criticism and interpretation. |
Tarantino, Quentin–Criticism and interpretation. | Lyne, Adrian–Criticism and interpretation. |
Bay, Michael, 1964– Criticism and interpretation.
Classification: LCC PN1995.9.T55 P49 2022 (print) | LCC PN1995.9.T55 (ebook) |
DDC 791.43/684—dc23/eng/20220418
LC record available at https://lccn.loc.gov/2022008932
LC ebook record available at https://lccn.loc.gov/2022008933

ISBN: HB: 978-1-5013-8060-0
       PB: 978-1-5013-8057-0
       ePDF: 978-1-5013-8058-7
       eBook: 978-1-5013-8059-4

Typeset by RefineCatch Limited, Bungay, Suffolk

To find out more about our authors and books visit www.bloomsbury.com
and sign up for our newsletters.

Contents

Illustrations

Figures

Tables

Acknowledgements

Sed fugit interea,
fugit inreparabile
tempus

Virgil (Georgics, III, verse 284)

I have always been fascinated by the concept of time. As a little girl, I looked at shadows that changed directions and length. I did not know this was due to circadian rhythms. I went to my relatives' funerals, 'from ashes to ashes and dust to dust'. I knew we have a beginning and an end, but I did not strictly link them to time. Time is that invisible friend and enemy that walks with us, sometimes silently on tiptoe, other times so loudly that we can listen to its persistent ticking. In films, as well as in our lives, it shortens or lengthens, it mixes with past memories and fantasies, with an unknown future that is often dreamt and with a present that perhaps does not even exist. I love time and all its meanings, and I thank all the experts who dedicated their time, which is so precious, to this book. Thank you to all the great scholars, whom I esteem so much, who read my manuscript and gave me useful suggestions: Mick Broderick, Ruggero Eugeni, James Fenwick and Jeremi Szaniawski. Thanks to all the Kubrick scholars who accepted me in their community and have always been ready to involve me in their interesting projects, I learnt a lot from their conferences and papers.

Thanks to Robert Armstrong, who first revised and corrected my manuscript.

Thank you to all the editorial staff at Bloomsbury and RefineCatch at Bloomsbury, especially Katie Gallof, Stephanie Grace-Petinos, Mervyn Honeywood, Jonathan Nash and Roza I. M. El-Eini.

I would like to underline that if there are mistakes or forgetfulness, it is not the fault of the experts who helped me, but mine because I am so headstrong that sometimes I do not follow the others' suggestions, and pursue my way.

I am especially grateful to my parents, Ulisse and Patrizia, who helped me with my two daughters, Anna and Linda, allowing me to complete this text in what has been one of the more difficult periods in my life.

I dedicate this book to them as well as to those who love, live and feel time and films.

Introduction

Stanley Kubrick's *Killer's Kiss* (1955) opens with the protagonist Davey Gordon (Jamie Smith) waiting at the train station to go back to his uncle's farmhouse. It is the end of his career in New York City as a boxer, and probably the end of his love story with Gloria Price (Irene Kane), a taxi dancer whom he saved from her boss and former lover, Vinnie Rapallo (Frank Silvera). During the film, which is mainly a flashback about the protagonist's last two days, Davey appears more than once at the station while his voice-over explains fragments of his thoughts and life. The protagonist's waiting seems endless because he walks to and fro, while he rethinks his experiences and hopes to see Gloria coming and jumping on the train with him. He lives three different times simultaneously. On the one hand, the train timetable which is measurable. On the other, those of his memories and the waiting for Gloria's appearance, times that cannot be quantified. We, spectators, experience also the screen time, which is the same for all of us, and a time that changes according to our involvement in what is happing on the screen. An important question spontaneously arises and inspires this book.

Does time exist? In quantum mechanics, we do not need time to describe the world, but variables that we can observe and feel, and possibly measure. The basic equations of gravitational theory do not comprehend a variable called 'time', but outline the world through the possible relations among variable quantities: not how things evolve in time, but how they change in relation to each other (Rovelli 2017: 102–4). If the time variable does not necessarily describe our world, neither should we need it to analyse narrative films that are personal representations and visions of the world conveyed to us through the cinematic medium. On the other hand, the concept of time imbues our thoughts, and every representation and vision is sustained by an ensemble of ideas that cannot avoid bearing the traces of time.

To resolve this paradox, it is useful to refer to Conceptual Metaphor Theory (CMT), according to which we understand abstract concepts in terms of concrete concepts by a process of conceptual correspondence. For example, spatial metaphors are mainly based on spatial orientation, i.e. on concrete concepts such as up-down, in-out, ahead-behind, deep-superficial, central-peripheral, etc., deriving from how the human body is made and interacts with our physical environment (Lakoff and Johnson 1998: 33). Spatial metaphors are rooted in our physical and cultural experiences, thus they are not arbitrarily established (37). Our abstract idea of time is structured through the mappings – set of correspondences – of attributes and relations from bodily based sensory-motor source domain space onto abstract target domain time. Where 'domain is a mini-scenario consisting of semantic roles and relations' (Moore 2014: 5), and source and target domain are, respectively, 'the frame from which the metaphorical vocabulary comes from' and 'the frame that has as roles the concepts actually being talked about' (9). Thus, the experience of time is almost entirely understood metaphorically through the spacialization of time (Lakoff and Johnson 1998: 151).

George Lakoff and Mark Johnson go so far as to claim that metaphors can create realities for us, and guide our future actions that will correspond to these metaphors. These actions will, in turn, strengthen the power of metaphors in giving coherence to our experiences. This loop leads to the fascinating conclusion that metaphors can be self-determining prophecies (193). Given the fact that in quantum mechanics we do not need time to describe our world, could time be a self-determining prophecy? Surprisingly, cognitive linguistics and quantum mechanics seem to reach similar conclusions. According to Lakoff and Johnson, the target domain – time – is understood through properties of interaction because the source domain – space – derives from our relations with other people and the environment. Similarly, the physicist Carlo Rovelli claims that we need to discuss how things change in relation to each other in order to describe our world.

I will not dwell on these questions, but I am aware that time can be tentatively defined as a metaphor of change among things and their relations, I would like to focus on how films convey these transformations through narrative and stylistic technique. In particular, how each film, and often how films of the same genre or directed by the same filmmaker, transmit a peculiar idea of time that is not only experienced by the audience, but also envelops and imprisons the whole film, as it were, as it does our own lives. I am particularly interested in those moments during which we, as spectators – as well as spectators of our own world – feel a suspension in the incessant flow of time, a fleeting escape from this overwhelming and powerful metaphor.

In Chapter 1, I discuss some concepts of time in the cinematic medium borrowed from literary theory, especially formalism and structuralism, and from the second generation of cognitive film studies, in particular its notions of embodied extension and cognitive linguistics. Formalism and structuralism, together with some basic notions of mathematical analysis, will assist me to define ideas that are necessary for the close analysis of film time: I will show that some concepts, that are taken for granted, are useless, and I will introduce new notions. Cognitive film theory will instead be adopted to discuss how the audience experiences time while watching a film. These approaches, that would seem to differ widely from one another, will be blended during close analyses and together will shed light on how the time that dominates a particular film is created, or on how, conversely, narrative and stylistic features create a peculiar time, how this 'ruling' time is sometimes changed and disrupted, and on the spectator's experiences in both of these cases. The very mix of these approaches should offer a new perspective.

The notions proposed in Chapter 1 will be applied in subsequent chapters to different directors: Stanley Kubrick, Chapter 2; Adrian Lyne, Chapter 3; Michael Bay, Chapter 4; and Quentin Tarantino, Chapter 5. Whereas scholarly literature is abundant in the cases of Kubrick and Tarantino, it is almost non-existent in the case of, respectively, Lyne and Bay, although some of their films are well known and have achieved cult status – hence, these latter case studies distinguish my book from other texts. As will be obvious in subsequent chapters, I have chosen these four directors, rather than others, because, in each of their oeuvres, time is very different, offering an interesting and wide range of examples, but remaining within the context of films, in which we are always able to understand narration and find a particular point of view from which we can interpret events, empathizing with a character or group of characters and experiencing their time – unlike in art cinema and impossible puzzle films as defined by Miklós Kiss and Steven Willemsen (2017), in which we are often left alone, unable to share a character's point of view.

Of times

Temporalities

Neither memory nor anticipation is much interested in Father Time, and all dreamers, artists and lovers are partially delivered from this tyranny; he can kill them, but he cannot secure their attention, and at the very moment of doom, when the clock collected in the tower its strength and struck, they may be looking the other way.

E. M. Forster (1927: 49)

1.1 Fabula, sujet, story and plot

We adopt distinctions between story and plot, and fabula and sujet, to discuss narration, independently of the medium and often confusing story with fabula, and plot with sujet. On the one hand, these well-known, shared notions speed up the discussion of several narrations, on the other they overshadow the analysis of specific aspects of narration, such as time, blurring, for example, the distinction between chronological and causal succession. At the heart of this clutter, there are translations from one language to another – Russian to English – and from one medium to another – the written to the cinematic.

Regarding the first problem, Meir Sternberg notes: 'Lenon and Reis, in their English translation of Boris Tomashevsky's essay, have given currency to the rendering of the Russian terms fabula and sujet as "story" and "plot," thus clearly suggesting that the former distinction is identical to that proposed by E.M. Forster in *Aspects of the Novel*' (1978: 10). Before introducing the distinction between *fabula* and *sujet*, Tomashevsky defines the theme and motifs of a literary work. The former is the common idea of a literary work, what is discussed in the work that results from the unity of the meanings of all the single elements into which the work can be divided. Through a breakdown of the literary work into parts that maintain a signified, it is possible to obtain segments characterized by thematic unity and constituted by propositions, which are the smallest elements that retain a meaning called 'motif'. From this division there follow two distinctions. One between literary works in which motifs are linked by causal and temporal bonds – e.g. novels, short stories and epic poems – or those in which they are ordered in a structure that does not imply causality – e.g. lyric, educational and descriptive poetry. In the former case, literary works are characterized by a fabula, whereas in the latter they are not. The second differentiation is between fabula and sujet. Whereas fabula is an abstraction of the literary work constructed in the reader's mind and constituted by the set of motifs ordered in their causal and temporal relations, in which it does not matter when and how readers come to know about an event, the sujet is the concrete literary work, in which motifs succeed one another linked by different relations, in which it is of the utmost importance when and how readers are told about an episode. The fabula is not only the sujet 're-edited' following a causal and temporal order, but it is also a 'synopsis' of it. To better define the fabula, Tomashevsky classifies motifs according to their functions in the temporal and causal development of the action. They are free if they can be omitted without destroying the causal and temporal chain of events, and bound if they cannot be left out; they are static if they do not cause any change, whereas they are dynamic if they transform a situation. Only bound and dynamic motifs are important in the fabula, while free and static motifs may be more significant than others for the development of the sujet (Tomaševskij 1968 [1925]: 311–18). While I believe that all the propositions in a literary work, combined according to their motifs, constitute a structure held together by a theme, and that the theme is the ensemble of all the motifs is a tautology, in my work motifs and the differences among them will be useful for the discussion of time.

Unlike Tomashevsky, writing in 1925 and attempting to distinguish between fabula and sujet, in 1927 Forster defines story and plot as a narrative of events arranged chronologically in the former case and causally in the latter. He takes the well-known example:

1. 'The king died and then the queen died' is a story because the proposition (a) 'the king died' is written before the proposition (b) 'the queen died' and (a) happens, in the characters' world, before (b);
2. 'The king died and then the queen died of grief' is a plot because the complement 'of grief' transforms (a) and (b) into a cause and an effect respectively, introducing a causal relation between them alongside the temporal relation;
3. 'The queen died, no one knew why, until it was discovered that it was through grief at the death of the king' is a plot enriched with curiosity because (b), the effect, is narrated before (a), the cause, which is delayed through the propositions 'no one knew why' and 'until it was discovered'.

Whereas a story answers the question 'and then?', the plot focuses upon 'why?' (Forster 1927: 130). Let us analyse the three sentences according to Tomashevsky's definition of fabula and sujet. Analysing sentence (3), (b) 'the queen died' and 'through grief at the death of the king' are bound and dynamic motifs; 'no one knew why' and 'until it was discovered' are instead free and static motifs because if they are omitted they do not damage the causal and temporal chain of events, and they do not change the situation, that is to say neither the death of the king nor that of the queen. Thus, if (3) is a sujet, (2) is its fabula because it is constituted only by the bound and dynamic motifs in their chronological and causal relation. On the other hand, (1) is another fabula because (a) and (b) are presented in their temporal order but they are not linked by an explicit cause-and-effect chain: we cannot know either what is the cause of the queen's death or if it is linked to her husband's death. Without incurring what Roland Barthes calls an ontological merger between the temporal and logical succession of events, a fusion between before/after and because of/therefore, summarized in the fallacy *post hoc, ergo propter hoc*, a mistake in the philosophical reasoning already denounced by scholasticism (Barthes 1994: 105), fabula, as defined by Tomashevsky, is for my purposes a more useful and accurate instrument to compare narrations and discuss their time.

According to Forster, the only merit of the story is 'that of making the audience want to know what happens next', and its only fault is: 'that of making the audience not want to know what happens next' (Forster 1927: 47). Sternberg would claim that a story may only arouse suspense in its readers, neither curiosity nor surprise. 'When we isolate the story like this from the nobler aspects through which it moves, and hold it out on the forceps – wriggling and interminable, the naked worm of time – it presents an appearance that is both unlovely and dull' (Forster 1927: 48). Similarly, 'Daily-life is also full of the time-sense' (48), but beyond it there is 'value' which escapes time and is measured by 'intensity' rather than clock time:

> so that when we look at our past it does not stretch back evenly but piles up into a few notable pinnacles, and when we look at the future it seems sometimes a wall, sometimes a cloud, sometimes a sun, but never a chronological chart [...] So daily life, whatever it may be really, is practically composed of two lives – the life in time and the life by values – and our conduct reveals a double allegiance.
>
> 48–9

In summary, life in time is to story what life by values is to plot, and whereas life in time and story can be measured through clock time, life by values and plot can be measured by intensity. As we cannot live without time – although 'it is always possible for you or me in daily life to deny that time exists and act accordingly even if we become unintelligible and are sent by our fellow citizens to what they choose to call a lunatic asylum' (50) – plot cannot do without story, although both life and plot are able to shape time. 'A plot cannot be told to a gaping audience of cave men or to a tyrannical sultan or to their modern descendant movie-public' (130) because it demands intelligence and memory. Despite the low opinion of filmgoers, Forster, introducing the importance of the reader's active role in the comprehension of plots, and stressing the importance of their intelligence and memory, foretells David Bordwell's cognitive emphasis on the role of the audience's hypotheses.

The American film scholar distinguishes between story and plot. The latter is 'everything visibly and audibly present in the film before us' (Bordwell and Thompson 2001: 61), the ensemble of the diegetic and non-diegetic material – 'The total world of the story action is sometimes called the film's diegesis (the Greek word for "recounted story")' (61). The story is the sum of the diegetic episodes and the events presumed by the audience, i.e. 'The set of all the events in a narrative, both the ones explicitly presented and those that the viewer infers' (61). The plot being the film and its definition does not imply a relation between it and its spectators; its story is the sequence of the events shown, and those deduced by the audience in their temporal and causal succession. For Bordwell and Tomashevsky alike, the story/fabula is the temporal and causal succession of diegetic episodes, although the American scholar adds to the story the events presumed and inferred by the audience, while the Russian formalist includes in the story only the propositions that convey dynamic and bound motifs. On the other hand, for Forster, the story is the temporal succession of events (Table 1.1).

The memory and intelligence of the reader/spectator are already necessary in the reconstruction of Tomashevsky's fabula and Bordwell's story, whereas in the case of Forster's theory they play a role only in understanding the plot because it is only in the plot that the cause-and-effect chain dominates the structure of a literary work. According to the different definitions of story, fabula, plot and sujet, it seems that the causal sequence of events is one of the more important, if not the most relevant, variable in discussing narrative films and novels. But the 'naked worm of time' can track a sinuous path, stretch and shorten its body, remain still or change the speed at which it crawls. In the sentence, 'The king died and then the queen died,' the two propositions are explicitly linked in a temporal sequence, but the conjunction 'and' implicitly raises the question: why did the queen die? Moreover, the sentence seems to begin *in medias res*, implying another question: why did the king die? Both the first and second propositions, as well as their temporal succession, arouse curiosity.

I wonder whether in film studies we really need the distinction between story and plot or fabula and sujet to analyse a film and, as regards my specific work on time, if these notions are not, on the contrary, misleading. The problem of the translation of fabula and sujet, and story and plot from the written to the cinematic medium leads to the wide field of adaptation studies and, in particular, to the approach that I call elsewhere 'fidelity', according to which scholars strive to adapt ideas and concepts that have proven to be useful for the study of novels to the discussion of narrative films (Pezzotta 2013: 4–9). If the sentence, 'The king died and then the queen died,' was

Table 1.1 Summary of the differences between story and fabula, plot and sujet in Tomashevsky, Forster and Bordwell.

	Tomashevsky	Forster	Bordwell
Story/Fabula	Fabula: Temporal and causal succession of bound and dynamic motifs	Story: Narrative of events in their time sequence	Story: Temporal and causal succession of diegetic events, and of episodes presumed and inferred by the audience
Plot/Sujet	Sujet: Literary work, succession of all the motifs in the order in which they are presented to the reader	Plot: Narrative of events in their causal sequence	Plot: Everything visibly and audibly present in the film, diegetic and non-diegetic material

adapted from the written to the cinematic medium, maintaining the curiosity about the causes of the couple's death – hypothesizing that they are husband and wife – we would be shown at least two shots: the first and the second during which a king and his queen are, respectively, shown dead in their coffins or already buried. In the absence of titles and other characters, such as loyal and grieving subjects, costume, make-up and *mise-en-scène* should help us to understand that the dead are royals. The two shots could be of different or the same length, and edited together through a cut, a fade to and from black, a fade in and out with different durations, etc., and there could be camera movements during the shots or zooming in or out from the royals' close-ups, or the camera could remain still. With only two shots and no soundtrack, there are countless possibilities of adapting a sentence constituted by two propositions that succeed one another temporally. After having watched the two shots, depending upon their style, we may no longer be curious about the cause of the royals' death and the link between the two events, and the sentence, 'The king died and then the queen died,' may no longer be suitable to describe them. Moreover, rethinking the shots, we may not even evoke the sentence, but simply images or shots.

Furthermore, in my example, I hypothesize that each proposition corresponds to a shot, but can the segmentation of sentences into propositions that still maintain meaning be compared with the division of a film into shots or scenes? Can the study of syntax, adopted for the written medium, be equated to the analysis of editing in the cinematic medium?[1] According to a neuropsychological approach, when we watch a film, its segmentation into events not only, or better, does not necessarily, depend upon montage, but on diegetic elements. 'Segmentation is an automatic memory updating that runs when prediction error occurs,' i.e. 'when we perceive (unpredictable) changes or discontinuities in the situation depicted in the film'. When our expectations about what will be shown are frustrated, we experience 'an event boundary that is manifested both in' our: 'neuronal activation and conscious awareness'. 'Viewers tend to identify event boundaries at point of change in the stimulus, ranging from physical changes, such as changes in the movements of actors, to conceptual changes, such as changes in the goal or causes' (D'Aloia and Eugeni 2016). Thus, we can easily recognize and isolate those segments of the film that develop bound and dynamic motifs because the boundaries of the former motifs are identified by causal and temporal changes, whereas those of the latter are bound by any type of change in the diegetic situation. From a neuropsychological point of view, the concept of motif, consequently that of a fabula constituted by bound and dynamic motifs, can be adapted from the written to the cinematic medium, although the processes adopted to define and find them cannot be compared, that is to say the analysis of syntax cannot be equated to the segmentation of a film.

In order to study narrative structures, I will adopt the notion of the fabula, as defined by Tomashevsky, as well as his concepts of bound and free, dynamic and static motifs and, rather than using the idea of sujet or plot, I will either simply refer to the

---

[1] Cf. Metz (1989).

film or to the notion of image schema. As regards narrative structures, I believe that it exists only the film, as it is presented to us, whereas in our mind and memory there remain only abstractions of it: its fabula, punctuated, enriched with some shots or scenes, and its image schemas. The latter are structures 'for organizing our experience and comprehension, where the basic frames for this structuring activity are derived from our habitualised bodily engagement with the physical world', i.e. they are: 'cognitive shortcuts to understanding' (Kiss 2015: 47).

> Proprioception describes one's feeling and understanding of one's own specific, bodily determined existence, allowing for grasping basic spatial relations (like 'back-front', 'centre-periphery', 'part-whole', 'inside-outside', and so on). [...] 'exteroception' refers to one's awareness of one's own environmental situatedness, which is a bodily understanding of the actual environment's physical limitations, allowing for understanding elementary spatial affordances (such as 'up-down', 'links', 'paths', 'forces', and so on).
>
> Kiss and Willemsen 2017: 32–3

Proprioceptive and exteroceptive: 'explorations mentally solidify as CONTAINER, SOURCE-PATH-GOAL, LINK, FORCE, BALANCE, UP-DOWN, FRONT-BACK, PART-WHOLE and CENTRE-PERIPHERY image schema constructions' (34, original capitals). These basic structures can be extended and elaborated metaphorically to link different aspects of conceptual meaning: 'are *blended* [...], *binded* [...] or *transfigured* [...] into narrative schemas' (34, original italics). For example, the source-path-goal schema 'is grounded in our real-world experience of bodily movement from one point to another, along a path in a certain direction' (Kiss 2015: 55), and through it we understand classical narrative schemas, in which the events develop from a beginning to an end, following a chronological and causal progression. The part-whole schema 'solidifies from the habitualised perception of our bodies as wholes made up of its parts' (56), as much as films are wholes constituted by shots, scenes, sequences, etc., 'where some of these parts function as necessary while others as optional in relation to some narrative minimum' (56), thus bound and dynamic motifs can be considered necessary for the whole, whereas free and static ones are optional. The container schema 'arises from our body awareness, characterized by the iterated perception of the inside, outside, and boundary', and thanks to it we understand embedded narrative structures, and transgressions among different diegetic, extra-diegetic and intra-diegetic levels (57).

1.2 The order of the film and chronological order of diegetic events

When I watch a narrative film, my first concern is to understand what I am shown: the questions Who are the characters and what are their aims? can be primarily deduced from the sequence of the events. When the scenes are not edited following a chronological order, I 're-edit' the film in my mind, following the temporal order of the diegetic episodes. If we hypothesize a film consisting of three scenes, e_1 e_2 e_3, in which, according to diegetic time, e_2 follows or occurs at the same time as e_1, and e_3 follows or occurs at the same time as e_2, and we discuss the re-edited film, there are three possibilities in the sequence of scenes.

First, succession or *post hoc* when an event follows another – e_1 then e_2 then e_3.

Second, simultaneity, when an episode occurs in the same diegetic time as another or other events – e_1 and then e_2 e_3 that take place in the same time, or e_1 e_2 that occur simultaneously and then e_3, or e_1 e_2 e_3 that take place at the same time. When two or more actions occur simultaneously and each one involves a different character or group of characters, events can take place in different spaces and end in the same place or not. Widespread examples are those of chases and phone calls. In polyphonic or ensemble plots, several characters – 'each of whom has an individual goal, but none of these characters' goals becomes the featured goal of the film, the narrative's organizing principle' (Ramírez Berg 2006: 16) – act in the same time and in neighbouring places and their lives may intertwine or not (e.g. *Magnolia*, Paul Thomas Anderson, 1999; *Sin City*, Robert Rodriguez, 2005). Similarly, in parallel plots, characters have different aims and can act at the same time but, unlike in polyphonic or ensemble plots, their lives play out in different, not contiguous, places (e.g. *Syriana*, Stephen Gaghan, 2005; *Traffic*, Steven Soderbergh, 2000; Ramírez Berg 2006: 18–19). Moreover, a film can show simultaneous actions that involve the same characters and occur in the same place but are shown from different characters' points of view – e.g. the robbery at the racetrack in *The Killing* (Stanley Kubrick, 1956), or the exchange of money at the mall in *Jackie Brown* (Quentin Tarantino, 1997). In the repeated event plot, as in *Jackie Brown*, 'one action is seen from multiple characters' perspective' (Ramírez Berg 2006: 33), and in the hub-and-spoke plot, as in *The Killing*: 'multiple characters' story lines intersect decisively at one time and place'. Unlike in the repeated event plot, in the hub-and-spoke plot, the repeated event: 'is the narrative's dramatic fulcrum and its organizing principle [. . .] the narrative follows characters before and after they converge at the axis point. Like the polyphonic plot, its multiple protagonists occupy the same space and time, have different goals, and are more or less equal in narrative stature' (39).

So far, I have discussed simultaneity in cases in which films show us one diegetic world, but a character or group of characters can be shown in two or more different parallel realities that develop simultaneously. The multiple personality or branched plot is a variant of the parallel and polyphonic or ensemble plot, 'in which the multiple protagonists are the same person, or different versions of the same person' (19), and in which the alter egos may live in different realities that occupy the same time (20).[2] For example, in *Sliding Doors* (Peter Howitt, 1998), the life of the protagonist (Gwyneth Paltrow) takes two different paths, depending upon whether she manages to get on the

---

[2] Bordwell calls branched plots 'forking-path narratives' (Bordwell 2002). Edward Branigan adopts the same nomenclature, adding that forking-path narratives are a subset of multiple draft narratives, in which: 'the relationship among parallels and alternatives is ambiguous or indeterminate, as if the parallels were seen in parallax' (Branigan 2002: 107).

train or not. These two possibilities develop at the same time, but in two parallel realities. The narrative structure of branched plots – i.e. the different versions of the protagonist live in different realities that occupy the same time – is based on simultaneity thus, although these films may be considered more complex than those described above, they are not because the cinematic techniques used to create them are the same as those adopted to show simultaneity in one diegetic reality. Indeed, actions that take place at the same time and in the same or different realities can be edited one after the other, or shots of an event can be alternated with those of another or other events – i.e. parallel editing or cross-cutting. This technique is frequently used in some action films, such as in the series of *Transformer* films (Michael Bay) which are almost entirely constructed through cross-cutting of fights or chases among different groups of characters. Furthermore, simultaneous actions can be shown together through a split screen, that is to say the frame can be divided into two or more parts that show different events, or superimpositions.[3]

It is interesting to compare time travel and branched plots with repeated action plots in which the protagonist relives the same diegetic time twice or more (e.g. *The Butterfly Effect*, Eric Bress and J. Mackye Gruber, 2004) and *Groundhog Day* (Harold Ramis, 1993; Ramírez Berg 2006: 30). As in time travel narratives in which the traveller can go back and forth in time, entering into his younger or older self, in repeated action plots the protagonist finds himself back in time, in his younger self, aware that he has to go through the same diegetic time whereas all the other characters are unaware of this jump in time. Unlike in branched plots in which each alter ego inhabits a parallel reality and is unaware of the existence of other worlds and versions of himself, in repeated action plots different versions of the same reality are presented in temporal succession and the protagonist, aware of the possible future effects of his actions, strives to improve his behaviour and free himself from the temporal loop. In repeated action plots, the same diegetic time is repeated, much like in branched plots, but in the former the protagonist is aware that he is back in time – and we, as spectators, share his knowledge – and to free himself from the loop of time he has to improve his relations with himself and other characters, so we do not experience diegetic time as a repetition of the diegetic past, but as an improvement within the succession of time. 'Like most other classical plots, they [repeated action plots] present their protagonists with a series of character-building obstacles, only in this case the trials are all variations of the same one. Other than the repetition, then, structurally they are identical with a well-known classical narration trope: the grow-by-enlightenment character' (Ramírez Berg 2006: 30). Thus, I do not include repeated action plots among those films that present a narrative structure or part of it based on simultaneity (Table 1.2).

Third, apart from succession and simultaneity, if the sequence of scenes in our film e_1 e_2 e_3 is not altered, it presents a third possibility: permanent gaps when one of the

---

[3]   Simultaneity is also discussed in Chapter 4 through the introduction of two other variables, causality and character knowledge; whereas Chapter 5 analyses cross-cutting of events that occur at different times.

Table 1.2 Differences among scenes, sequences, and narrative structures based on simultaneity.

Possible features in two or more simultaneous shots or scenes: →	Characters	Space	Characters' points of view	Parallel-worlds
Chases and phone calls	Different characters or groups of characters	Different spaces, but during chases, the different actions usually end in the same place	–	–
Polyphonic or ensemble plots	Different characters or groups of characters, each of whom has an individual aim	Neighbouring spaces	–	–
Parallel plots	Different characters or groups of characters, each of whom has an individual aim	Different spaces	–	–
Repeated event and hub-and-spoke plots	Same characters	Same space	Different characters' points of view	–
Branched plots	Different versions of the same character	–	–	Parallel-worlds

three episodes is missing – $e_2 e_3$ or $e_1 e_3$ or $e_1 e_2$. This type of ellipsis gives rise to questions that will never receive answers, remaining open and generating enigmas, although spectators can, having watched the whole film, advance hypotheses and fill them with their interpretations. So, 'permanent gaps are located both in the fabula and the sujet, "they result" already from the process of selection that produces the fabula' (Sternberg 1978: 51). Permanent gaps are ellipses that cannot be filled in through re-editing of the film according to the temporal sequence of diegetic events.

In this imaginary film constituted by the three scenes $e_1 e_2 e_3$ in which, according to diegetic time, e_2 follows e_1 and e_3 follows e_2, the scenes can be edited in six different orders. In general, given a film consisting of n scenes, the number of all possible permutations, that is to say the act of arranging them into some order, is n! – i.e. n factorial, n!= 1 x 2 x 3 x ... (n-1) x n, the product of all integers less than or equal to n. In the case of my film, any order different from $e_1 e_2 e_3$ produces either a flashforward, or one or two flashbacks, consequently, one or two temporary gaps. There is a flashback or analepsis when we are shown a scene that occurred in the diegetic past, and a flashforward or prolepsis when we watch a scene that will take place in the diegetic future (Genette 1986: 88–9). I have used the verbs 'to show' and 'to watch' because in this work I call a scene or a shot that took place in the diegetic past or will happen in the diegetic future 'flashback' and 'flashforward', respectively, only when they are shown, that is to say when there is enactment, when actions are shown as if they occurred at the moment we watch them. Whereas I specify that an analepsis or prolepsis is recounted when characters or a narrator give information about prior or future events, and enacted recounting when prior or future events are shown while a character's or narrator's voice-over relates them (Bordwell 2001: 77–8). If my film has a structure – e_2 **e1** e_3 or e_2 e_3 **e1** or e_3 **e1** e_2 – the flashback is in all cases **e1**, and if the scenes appear in the order e_1 e_3 **e2** the analepsis is **e2**: in the former and latter cases **e1** and **e2** are respectively shown later in the film, even if they occurred before in the context of the temporal sequence of diegetic time. If the scenes are instead shown in the order e_3 **e2 e1**, there are two flashbacks, **e2** and **e1**. On the other hand, in e_1 e3 e_2, the second scene e3 is a prolepsis because it is shown before e_2, but will occur after it in diegetic time (Table 1.3).

The sequence e_2 e_1 e_3, e_2 e_3 e_1, e_3 e_1 e_2 and e_3 e_2 e_1 begin with a scene that will occur in the diegetic future, but is shown before events that precede it in the temporal order of the diegetic episodes. In general, when a film does not begin with the first event that takes place in the diegetic chronological sequence of episodes, it begins *in medias res*. Sternberg, writing about literary works, explains: '*In medias res* logically denotes no more than a certain deformation of the chronological sequence. Though it often coincides with a plunge into a scenic occasion and the delay of most antecedents, it necessarily involves only the preclusion of identical starting points for fabula and sujet' (1978: 40). A film begins *in medias res* whenever its first scene is not the first episode that occurs in the diegetic world, but an event that will take place in the diegetic future. I do not consider the episode that opens a narration *in medias res* a flashforward – thus, in e_2 e_1 e_3 and e_2 e_3 e_1, I do not call e_2 a 'flashforward', and, in e_3 e_1 e_2 and e_3 e_2 e_1, I do not consider e_3 a prolepsis – because at the very beginning of a narration, spectators are not yet provided with a temporal point of reference to understand what the diegetic present is, what diegetic time the characters consider their present.

The presence of a flashback or a flashforward is a sufficient condition for the creation of a temporary gap that: 'the work opens at some point upon the continuum of the text only to fill it in explicitly and satisfactorily itself – or at least enable the

Table 1.3 The presence of flashbacks (bold) and flashforwards (underlined), in a film consisting of three events, e_1 e_2 e_3, according to the order in which they are presented to the audience.

Neither flashback nor flashforward	One flashback *In Medias Res*	Two flashbacks *In Medias Res*	One flashforward and one flashback
e_1 e_2 e_3	e_2**e1** e_3	e_3**e2e1**	e_1 e3**e2**
	e_2 e_3**e1**		
	e_3**e1** e_2		

reader to do so with ease – at a subsequent stage' (51). Sternberg claims that the opening of both a permanent and a temporary gap 'and the explicit filling in of a temporary gap necessarily involve a deformation of the chronological order of presentation' (51), but I do not believe that a gap necessarily implies a distortion of the temporal sequence of diegetic events. It is simply the result of the omission of diegetic material. Whereas permanent gaps generate questions that cannot be answered with certainty and confidence, not even when we have watched and rewatched and closely analysed the whole film, temporary gaps, 'being "artificially" created and sustained through temporal manipulations of some perfectly straightforward and coherent segment or segments of the fabula' (51), can be filled in as soon as the temporarily omitted material is revealed to the audience. It is interesting to note that for spectators there is no difference between permanent and temporary gaps until the end of the film, when they are sure about which gaps have been filled in:

> For as long as the withheld information is not authoritatively communicated [...] any gap must for the time being be regarded as virtually permanent. The more so since, if the reader is to make sense of what is happening he cannot forgo gap-filling even when fairly convinced that the text will sooner or later double back to dispel its referential ambiguities. Accordingly, the reader cannot but construct different hypotheses and revise, rearrange or replace them.
>
> Ibid., 238

Whereas temporary gaps are a feature of films that are edited in a different order from that of the temporal development of the diegetic events, both permanent and temporary gaps can be present in any film, independently of the order of presentation of its scenes. For example, in *Pulp Fiction* (Quentin Tarantino, 1994), we are never shown what is inside the briefcase that Vincent (John Travolta) and Jules (Samuel L. Jackson) take at the boys' apartment and that two robbers try to steal at a diner. In *Eyes Wide Shut* (Stanley Kubrick, 1999), the true identity of the woman who sacrifices herself at the orgy to save the protagonist Bill (Tom Cruise) is never revealed because, although Victor (Sidney Pollack) claims that she is Mandy (Julienne Davis), and at the morgue Bill sees her corpse, at the orgy the character is played by another actress (Abigail Good). These permanent gaps are created by stylistic techniques that do not involve editing.

The distinction between temporary and permanent gaps becomes a distinction between the main features used by Miklós Kiss and Steven Willemsen to distinguish between disorienting but solvable puzzle films and impossible puzzle films. According to the two scholars: '*narrative complexity is a trend in contemporary cinema and television.* [...] *a kind of structural-constructional complexity in storytelling logic*' (2017: 10, original italics). Narrative complexity was a characteristic of the complicated causality of films noirs of the 1940s, and of the loosening or suppression of cause-and-effect chains in European modernist art cinema of the 1950s, 1960s and 1970s. This trend re-emerged in the mid-1990s, following the success of *Pulp Fiction*, and is still present in the mainstream. Indeed, unlike in noirs and, especially, in art films, narrative complexity, since the mid-1990s: 'seems to be significantly more pervasive and widespread [...] manifesting itself across multiple genres and platforms, and in both national and international cinemas' (12). Kiss and Willemsen call complex or puzzle or complex puzzle films all those that can be included in the trend discussed above, thus all the complex post-classical films, i.e. all those released from the mid-1990s that: 'evoke temporary or enduring cognitive puzzlement in the viewer' (52). Among complex puzzle films, Kiss and Willemsen distinguish disorienting but solvable puzzle films, e.g. *Jacob's Ladder* (Adrian Lyne, 1990), *Inception* (Christopher Nolan, 2010), from impossible puzzle films, e.g. *Inland Empire* (David Lynch, 2006), *Donnie Darko* (Richard Kelly, 2001). The former are characterized by temporary gaps that spectators strive to fill in with more or less confidence and that, at the end of the film, or after having rewatched it one or several times, they are able to fill in for certain. By contrast, in impossible puzzle films, there are one or more permanent gaps which raise questions that remain unanswered even when it is possible to order their scenes in a chronological succession. Moreover, one of the peculiarities of these films is that they often cannot be re-edited in a temporal order (Kiss and Willemsen 2017: 52). Permanent gaps are present both in art cinema, thanks to open ends and the loosening or suppression of causal links, and in impossible puzzle films. What changes are the various audience strategies to formulate hypotheses to explain the presence of gaps and try to fill them in. According to Torben Grodal, spectators at an art film, unable to find an explanation for what they are shown in the succession of actions and events, adopt a different, abstract interpretive strategy that develops beyond the concreteness of the diegetic world to formulate poetical, lyrical or allegorical readings. The audience: 'suspends the mimetic make-believe in the storyworld, and exchanges it for a more interpretive apprehension, a shift that ultimately justifies the categorization of these experiences under a reception-defined label of art film, which, according to Grodal, is "a subcategory within film art in general"' (Grodal quoted in Kiss and Willemsen 2017: 128). On the other hand, without distinguishing among different films and spectators: 'impossible puzzle films are characterised by a striking balance between offering viewers challenging incongruities on the level of narrative on the one hand, while maintaining their immersion and willingness to engage in interpretive and analytic operations on the other' (139). That is, 'viewers tend to persistently approach impossible puzzle films using classical narrativising and rational sense-making strategies', they: 'keep trying to make sense of these films on the diegetic, intratextual and often immersed level' (163). The audience is less concerned with what the films signify, with their 'thematic, psychological, symbolical, allegorical or meta-fictional meaning', than with how they work (163). Spectators usually strive to find a key to decipher them, believing that a secret code is hidden in their very structure and style. This audience's interpretive behaviour is encouraged by how the films are constructed. Indeed, while their complexity derives both from contemporary complex puzzle films, which broadly subscribe to a classical Hollywood style and structure, and from the European modernist films released between the 1950s and 1970s, they: 'tend to remain primarily rooted in the classical narrative system by relying on rather classical presentation modes and viewing routines' (143).

Let us suppose that our imaginary film is constituted by four scenes, e_1 e_2 e_3 e_4, and that e_2 follows e_1, e_3 follows e_2 and e_4 follows e_3 in diegetic time. The scenes can be edited in $4! = 4 \times 3 \times 2 \times 1 = 24$ different orders reported in Table 1.4, in which the flashforwards are underlined and the flashbacks are in bold type, as in Table 1.3. To distinguish analepsis and prolepsis, I have to look at subscript numbers that indicate in which temporal sequence the scenes follow one another according to diegetic time. Let us imagine that n and m are two subscript numbers and that, obviously, n and m are whole numbers, n≠m, n>0 and m>0. We can obtain two general rules to understand when there is a flashback or a flashforward. If n<m, e_n is a flashback, it follows e_m in the order of montage. If m>n+1 and e_m is neither the first scene nor the last in the series, e_m is a flashforward if it precedes e_n in the order of montage, and is followed by at least one analepsis.

The rules to obtain a flashforward are more complicated than those to obtain a flashback for several reasons. First of all, whereas to obtain a flashback it is sufficient to invert the order of two consecutive scenes, e_2 **e1** instead of e_1 e_2; to be a flashforward, a scene must not only follow a scene that immediately precedes it in diegetic time, as in e_1 e_2 – otherwise there would be neither a flashback nor a flashforward – but must also leave a gap, as in e_1 <u>e3</u> **e2**. Indeed, even if in e_1 e_2, e_2 follows e_1, e_2 cannot be considered a flashforward because it immediately follows e_1 in diegetic time. In e_2 **e1** e_3, **e1** is a flashback because it is shown after e_2 even if in diegetic time it occurred before, but e_3 is not a flashforward, even if it is presented immediately after e_1, because e_2 has already been presented and e_3 does not leave any gap open. Similarly, in the example e_2 **e1** e_3 e_4: **e1** is a flashback because it occurs before e_2 in diegetic time and is shown after it in the film; e_3 cannot be considered a flashforward because, although it is presented after **e1**, it is followed by e_4, the scene that immediately succeeds it in diegetic time and the one that closes the sequence. If the sequence had been e_4 **e1** <u>e3</u> **e2**, <u>e3</u> would have been a flashforward because it would have been followed by the flashback **e2**. Consequently,

Table 1.4 The presence of flashbacks (bold) and flashforwards (underlined) in a film consisting of four events, e_1 e_2 e_3 e_4, according to the order in which they are presented to the audience

	First column e_1 **is the first episode**	**Second column** e_2 **is the first episode**	**Third column** e_3 **is the first episode**	**Fourth column** e_4 **is the first episode**
First row	e_1 e_2 e_3 e_4	e_2 **e1** e_3 e_4	e_3 **e1** e_2 e_4	e_4 **e1** e_2 e_3
Second row	e_1 e_2 <u>e4</u> **e3**	e_2 **e1** <u>e4</u> **e3**	e_3 **e1** <u>e4</u> **e2**	e_4 **e1** <u>e3</u> **e2**
Third row	e_1 <u>e3</u> **e2** e_4	e_2 e_3 **e1** e_4	e_3 **e2** **e1** e_4	e_4 **e2** **e1** e_3
Fourth row	e_1 <u>e3</u> e_4 **e2**	e_2 e_3 e_4 **e1**	e_3 **e2** <u>e4</u> **e1**	e_4 **e2** e_3 **e1**
Fifth row	e_1 <u>e4</u> **e3** **e2**	e_2 <u>e4</u> **e3** **e1**	e_3 e_4 **e1** e_2	e_4 **e3** **e1** e_2
Sixth row	e_1 <u>e4</u> **e2** e_3	e_2 <u>e4</u> **e1** e_3	e_3 e_4 **e2** **e1**	e_4 **e3** **e2** **e1**

each flashforward implies a flashback. Thus, there are more possibilities to create flashbacks than flashforwards.

Moreover, if I take a closer look at Tables 1.3 and 1.4, if a film begins *ab ovo*, there are more possibilities to create flashforwards; whereas if it begins *in medias res*, there are more chances of encountering flashbacks, and the more it begins near the end of the diegetic order, the more the possibilities of creating flashbacks increase, until the maximum possible number of flashbacks of the backwards plot is achieved. A film with a backwards plot presents its scenes or sequences inverting their diegetic order, thus each scene or sequence follows that which precedes it in diegetic time, so that the film begins with the last diegetic scene and ends with the first diegetic scene – e_3 **e2 e1**, e_4 **e3 e2 e1**, e.g. *5x2* (François Ozon, 2004) and *Irréversible* (Gaspar Noé, 2002; Ramírez Berg 2006: 27–30). Many scholars claim that authors privilege flashbacks rather than flashforwards. Sternberg, more accurately, writes that prolepsis: 'is an optional device rather than a necessary compositional condition [...] for to present some future development as a foregone conclusion is to produce a gap subsuming all that intervenes' (1978: 164). I have argued that the possibilities to create flashbacks are more numerous than those to create flashforwards and that each prolepsis, to be called such, must be followed by an analepsis, thus it may be true that authors give priority to flashbacks, but it is also true that they have more probabilities to create analepses than prolepses.

I have discussed time first given a re-edited film that follows the temporal sequence of diegetic events, and then given a film as it is presented to the audience. If I compare the film with its re-edited version, I find what I experience while I watch and try to understand a film reordering its scenes in a temporal and causal succession, making hypotheses about past episodes – thus striving to fill in gaps – and hoping for better and fearing the worst for future outcomes. Let us take once more our imaginary film consisting of three scenes and the six different possibilities of editing it. If I draw a Cartesian coordinate plane with the time of the re-edited film on the x-axis and the time of the film on the y-axis and, for simplicity, I do not consider either the duration of diegetic or screening time – which I will define and discuss later – but only their order, I obtain the six graphics shown in Figure 1.1, one for each of the editing possibilities. The abscissas of the scenes are obviously always the same in each graphic because they represent their sequence in the re-edited film, whereas their ordinates change because they are edited differently in each of the six cases.[4]

A Euclidean vector is a geometric object that has a length and a direction, and is represented by a line segment with a definite direction, and graphically as an arrow connecting an initial with a terminal point. If I draw a vector that links a scene to the subsequent one, that is to say to the scene that succeeds it following the order of the film, the vector always has a positive ordinate and can have either a positive or a negative abscissa. The y-axis represents the time of the film that flows from its beginning to its end, and the vector has always a positive ordinate, indeed our expectations are

---

[4] The abscissa and the ordinate of a point are, respectively, the signed measure of its projection on the x-axis and on the y-axis.

Film	Cartesian graphic
$e_1\ e_2\ e_3$	
$e_2\mathbf{e1}\ e_3$	
$e_2\ e_3\mathbf{e1}$	
$e_3\mathbf{e1}\ e_2$	
$e_3\mathbf{e2\ e1}$	
$e_1\underline{e3}\ e_2$	

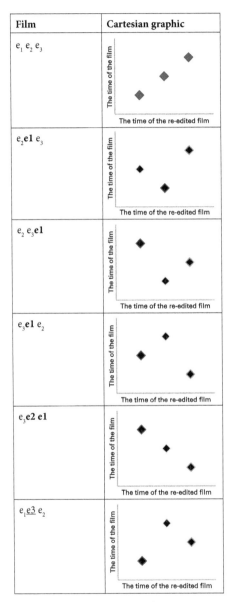

Figure 1.1 Cartesian graphics of a film consisting of three events, $e_1\ e_2\ e_3$, according to the order in which they are presented to the audience.

always oriented towards the end of the film, we are always looking forward to finding out what will be shown. Whereas on the x-axis there is the time of the re-edited film, and the vector can have either a positive or a negative abscissa because, while our expectations are always oriented towards what will be shown, the event that will be presented may pertain either to an episode that will happen in the future or that took place in the past of the diegetic world. When we long to find out what will happen in the diegetic future, we experience suspense, and when we want to see what took place in the diegetic past, we feel curiosity or surprise:

> Our distinction between the two clashing components of suspense, hope and fear, relates to two possible expectations about the future resolution of a conflict; that between curiosity and suspense relates to the chronological direction of the missing and desired information (narrative past versus future); while that between curiosity and surprise relates to the perceptibility of the process of gapping and gap-filling.
>
> Sternberg 1978: 244

The difference between gaps of curiosity and surprise is that, in the case of curiosity, the audience 'is at once alerted to the deformation of antecedents', whereas with surprise: 'the awareness of the gap's very existence and/or relevance and/or true significance is retrospective, being delayed to the point of closure rather than heightened at the point of opening' (244). In the case of a surprise gap, a hypothesis: 'is made to arise immediately upon the hidden opening of the gap – as the automatic, self-explanatory, or at least overwhelmingly probable explanation; so that it may be effectively demolished and replaced by a subsequently sprung explanation, with a superior intrinsic authority of contextual power of accounting for the facts' (245).

Together with suspense, curiosity and surprise, I add another emotion or state of mind: 'strong surprise' which arises when a gap, whose existence we did not know of, is filled in, thus we realize its existence when it is explained. Strong surprise is typical of jumbled plots in films in which the order of scenes and sequences is different from their diegetic chronological succession so that spectators cannot guess if they are going to see a scene that happened in the past or will take place in the future (for a definition of jumbled plot, see Ramírez Berg 2006: 41–4). Whereas in the case of a surprise ellipsis we revise our previous hypothesis and substitute it with another explanation, in that of a strong surprise we realize that we have not perceived a gap or that we have been cheated in thinking that there was no ellipsis when the gap itself is revealed and filled in. For example, in *Pulp Fiction* when we are first shown Vincent and Jules in the boys' apartment retrieving the mysterious briefcase, the scene ends with the slaughter of the boys while Jules recites the famous alleged quote from Ezekiel 25:7 followed by shots of the two protagonists. Almost at the end of the film, three shots of Vincent and Jules in the house are repeated, but rather than being followed by other shots of them, are succeeded by shots of a character hiding in the bathroom while we listen to Jules' voice off that repeats the last part of the alleged quote. When we first see the scene, we neither imagine that a boy is hidden in the bathroom nor are we shown the bathroom. Thus, when this scene is repeated, a gap is unexpectedly revealed and filled in simultaneously. Similarly, the audience, rather than being shown Butch's (Bruce Willis) match, come to know of his victory when he, escaping from the gym, speaks with a taxi driver about it. And the same Butch meets Marcellus Wallace (Ving Rhames) unexpectedly, while driving away from his house after having killed Vincent, thus the spectator comes to know that Vincent was waiting for Butch with Marcellus. As we will see, in Tarantino's films, as in jumbled plots in general, there are lots of strong surprise gaps. Strong surprise is caused by restricted narration because the audience shares only some characters' or a character's point of view. Narration is unrestricted when it is omniscient, that is, when we can see and hear all that each character can hear and see, and we know as much as or more than what each character knows. It is instead restricted when we see and hear only what a character or group of characters, but not all of them, know (Bordwell 2001: 70–3).[5]

It is worth underlining that suspense, curiosity, surprise and strong surprise are effects wrought by the combination of stylistic and narrative features. According to Bordwell, the rhythm of a film is the play of suspense, surprise and curiosity: 'Rhythm in narrative cinema comes down to this: by forcing the spectator to make inferences at a certain rate, the narration governs what and how we infer' (2001: 76). Thus, rhythm is what we experience when we watch a film and are actively involved in the play of fear and hope, of hypotheses about past and future events and we are surprised by twists of narrative and strongly surprised by unexpected revelations. Each film is characterized by a unique rhythm that often shares some features with that of films pertaining to the same genre and/or period of release – e.g. *Armageddon* (Michael Bay, 1998) shares the growing suspense emphasized by numerous countdowns typical of the disaster movie – or of the director's filmography – the majority of Michael Bay's films are based on a progressive growing rhythm of suspense. In some cases, such as in Kubrick's and Tarantino's oeuvres, there seems to be an ongoing progression, almost an obsession, with the creation of a unique rhythm. Moreover, each spectator experiences the rhythm of a film differently depending upon individual taste – somebody may be spellbound by an action movie whereas somebody else may be bored, and among these opposite feelings there are countless shades – while an individual's attitude while watching the film is influenced by his state of mind.

In general, in classical Hollywood cinema, suspense hypotheses appear more often than those pertaining to curiosity, and the latter more frequently than surprise (Bordwell 1986: 30), whereas in jumbled films we experience curiosity and surprise more often than suspense, while in backwards plots we usually make curiosity hypotheses. Indeed, both in jumbled and backwards plots, spectators, trying to guess the causes of the effects that they are shown, focused upon the diegetic past. Moreover, in jumbled plots, they cannot foresee what sequence will be shown, and they are often strongly surprised by the scene that appears, particularly when it regards a cause which

---

[5]   In Chapter 5, at surprise and strong surprise, I will add another emotion or state of mind, 'shock surprise'.

has no apparent connection with the events shown up to that point. Robert Davis and Riccardo de los Rios underline the importance of surprise in contemporary Hollywood and Japanese narrative cinema (2006: 163–4). Similarly, Kiss and Willemsen claim that deceptive unreliable films or twist movies are structured on a surprise gap. In these films, spectators make hypotheses as in a classical Hollywood film until it is revealed that they have been cheated by misleading information; when this twist takes place, and the surprise gap is filled in, they have to revise their previous knowledge, reconsidering what they have been shown in the light of the new disclosure. For example, in *Fight Club* (David Fincher, 1999), there is a twist when it is revealed that the two protagonists are the same schizophrenic character, and in *The Sixth Sense* (M. Night Shyamalan, 1999), when we come to know that the protagonist (Bruce Willis) did not survive the initial aggression and is a ghost. According to Kiss and Willemsen, deceptive unreliable films are not complex puzzle films because the spectator's puzzlement is aroused only when the twist is revealed, prior to and after this they unambiguously make sense of the diegetic world (Kiss and Willemsen 2017: 52–6). Thus, twist movies are structured on a surprise gap, and we feel suspense before and after the twist, while when we watch disorienting but solvable puzzle films, we experience curiosity (52; Table 1.5).[6]

Table 1.5 Differences among surprise, strong surprise, curiosity and suspense.

Emotion	Surprise/ Recognition	Strong surprise	Curiosity/ Retrospection	Suspense/ Prospection
Is it oriented towards the diegetic past or future?	Past	Past	Past	Future
Is it caused by a gap? What type?	Hidden gap	Gap created in the very moment in which it is filled in	Perceived gap	–
Which films are more characterized by it?	Jumbled plots, contemporary Hollywood and Japanese narrative cinema, deceptive, unreliable films	Jumbled plots	Jumbled and backwards plots, disorienting but solvable puzzle films, classical Hollywood cinema	Classical Hollywood cinema, deceptive unreliable films

---

[6] So far, I have adopted two main taxonomies for mainstream films that have been released since the mid-1990s and that present a 'complex' narrative structure: that of Kiss and Willemsen and that of Ramírez Berg. The former distinguish deceptive unreliable films from complex puzzle films and, among the latter, disorienting but solvable puzzle films from impossible puzzle films. As discussed, their distinctions are based on two main criteria. Whereas deceptive unreliable films present one or

Without making distinctions between different films, I claim that, generally, our efforts to understand and reconstruct the diegetic past are more emphasized when we are aware of them, as in curiosity, and less so when we are not, as in strong surprise. Apart from these differences among our expectations about the diegetic past, it is important to underline that a sequence or scene may arouse different emotions. For example, the scene in *Pulp Fiction* discussed above, in which we experience strong surprise when we are shown the boy hidden in the bathroom, also arouses suspense because we wonder what he will do, and what Vincent and Jules do when they find him, while in the whole sequence we also experience curiosity because we come to know that the two protagonists were no longer shown in dark suits, but in shorts and T-shirts because they had accidentally shot the boy in their car, staining their elegant attire.

1.3 The duration of represented and representational time

Henceforth, I will call represented or diegetic time 'the duration of a projected period in the life of the characters', and representational or screen time 'the time that it takes the' spectator, 'by the clock, to peruse that part of the text projecting this fictive period' (Sternberg 1978: 14), i.e. the time that it takes the film to show this diegetic span of time. If we analyse only the screen time, if we consider the length of an entire film or of a segment in seconds divided by the number of shots, we obtain the Average Shot Length (ASL).[7] The Median Shot Length (MSL) can be found by arranging the lengths of the shots from the lowest to the highest value or vice versa and selecting the average. According to some scholars, the MSL is a more efficacious measurement than the ASL because it is not affected by the presence of outliers – i.e.: 'shots that are exceptionally long relative to the rest of the shots in a film' (Tsivian).

Gérard Genette defines the speed of a literary work as the ratio between the duration of diegetic events, measured in seconds, minutes, hours, days, months or years, and their length in words, lines or pages, in the literary text. The zero degree is a literary work that moves at a constant speed, without accelerations or decelerations (Genette 1986: 136–7). Similarly, in films, I define the speed as the ratio between the duration of diegetic events and their length on the screen, usually measured in tenths of a second,

more temporary, surprise gaps, complex puzzle films are based on temporary, curiosity gaps or permanent gaps. And whereas in impossible puzzle films spectators usually strive to find answers in the concreteness of the diegetic world, in art films they have to change their point of view, crossing the boundaries of the diegetic world. Ramírez Berg, on the other hand, discusses fiction films – including Hollywood, independent and art films – that attempt to tell a fairly conventional story using unconventional plotting and excludes: 'experimental cinema (like some of Lynch's work), parametric or wholly style-centered films, as well as mockumentaries' (Ramírez Berg 2006: 13). He focuses on the narrative structure of deceptive unreliable films, disorienting but solvable puzzle films and art films that are not wholly style-centred, whereas Kiss and Willemsen are mainly concerned with impossible puzzle films. These two classifications are complementary.

[7] For analyses, discussions and comparisons of the ASL of films belonging to different genres and released in different periods, see Salt (2006, 2009), Bordwell (2006: 121–4) and Cinemetrics (2016).

seconds or minutes. If I divide a film into segments, according to their different speeds, there are five cases:

1. When the ratio between the screening time (ST) and the diegetic time (DT) is one (ST/DT=1), there is a shot or a scene that does not present any gap.[8]
2. When ST>DT, ST/DT>1 and slow motion or freeze-frame are used.
3. When ST<DT, ST/DT<1 and there is accelerated motion or superimposition, and consequently a dissolve when two or more images blend in superimposition.
4. When ST=0 and DT≠0, there is a gap.
5. When ST≠0 and DT=0, we are shown non-diegetic material such as titles.

Things are more complex if I do not divide a film into segments according to their speed – in this case, I obtain only shots, scenes that maintain a strict spatio-temporal unit and do not include even the smallest temporal gap, long takes or sequence shots (*plan séquence*) – but into sequences that are longer segments that may not obey the spatio-temporal unities and constitute a distinct narrative unit. In this case:

2. If ST>DT, the same diegetic time can be repeated, as when two or more actions occur simultaneously, i.e. during chases in which different characters are alternately shown at the same time but in different spaces, in polyphonic or ensemble, parallel, repeated event, hub-and-spoke and branched plots.
3. If ST<DT, there can also be a scene or a sequence that presents gaps among its shots, or a montage sequence during which we watch a succession of shots whose temporal progression suggests, in a few seconds, a change that occurs in a longer diegetic time – i.e.: 'Brief portion of a process, informative titles [...], stereotyped images [...], newsreel footage, newspaper headlines, and the like, can be swiftly joined by dissolves and music to compress a lengthy series of actions into a few moments' (Bordwell 2001: 277–8).

I can draw a Cartesian graphic with the screening time on the y-axis and the diegetic time on the x-axis, and represent each of my five cases with a different segment. The equation of a straight line is $y=mx+q$, where m is the slope that indicates the ratio between the difference of the ordinates and that of the abscissas of two different points of the straight line. That is, if $(x_0 ; y_0)$ and $(x_1 ; y_1)$ are the coordinates of two points on a straight line, then the slope $m=(y_1-y_0)/(x_1-x_0)$. If, for example, the first narrative segment of a film begins at the beginning of the film and ends after 1 minute, covering

---

[8]   In *Rope* (Alfred Hitchcock, 1948), screening time coincides with diegetic time for the entire duration of the film that is constituted by sequence shots edited without gaps between them. For a close analysis of this film, see Ghislotti (2012: 90–100). See also his close analysis of *High Noon* (Fred Zinnemann, 1952), in which, from the spectator's point of view, screening time seems to coincide with diegetic time, but actually it does not (101–26).

10 minutes of diegetic time, the coordinates of the point that indicates the beginning of the narrative segment are (0 ; 0) and those of the point at the end of the narrative segment are (1 ; 10). Consequently, $m=(1-0)/(10-0)=1/10$ and the equation of the straight line is $y=(1/10)x$. In my analysis, $(y_1-y_0)\geq 0$ because screening time either increases or not, but cannot be negative. On the other hand, $(x_1-x_0)<0$ when a shot is projected backwards and diegetic time flows in reverse, whereas in all the other cases $(x_1-x_0)\geq 0$. Thus $m\geq 0$, whereas $m<0$ if and only if a shot is projected backwards. In the equation $y=mx+q$, q is the vertical or y-intercept, the point where the straight line intersects the y-axis. In my discussion of screening and diegetic time $q=0$, if the beginning of the narrative segment that I want to draw coincides with the beginning of the film. In the example above, if the narrative segment begins 30 minutes after the beginning of the film, lasts 1 minute of screening time and covers 10 minutes of diegetic time – the very first 10 minutes of diegetic time – it can be described by the straight line $y=(1/10)x+30$. I can draw a Cartesian graphic for each of the five cases discussed above hypothesizing, for simplicity, that $m\geq 0$ (Table 1.6):

1. If ST/DT=1, $m=1$ and $y=x+q$.
2. and 3. If ST>DT, $m>1$ and if ST<DT, $0<m<1$, and the narrative segment can be represented by the straight line $y=mx+q$ where $0<m<1$ or $m>1$, respectively.
4. If ST=0 and DT≠0, the equation that describes it is $y=y_1$ where $y_1\geq 0$.
5. If ST≠0 and DT=0, the straight line that describes it is $x=x_1$ where $x_1\geq 0$.

Table 1.6 Straight lines to represent the ratio between screening and diegetic time.

ST, DT and slope	Equation	In which narrative segment it appears	Cartesian graphic
ST/DT=1 m=1	*y=x+q*	Shot or scene that does not present any gap	
ST>DT	*y=mx+q with m>1*	Slow motion or freeze-frame	
ST<DT	*y=mx+q with 0<m<1*	Accelerated motion, superimposition, dissolve, a scene or a sequence that presents gaps among their shots or a montage sequence	

Table 1.6 Continued.

ST, DT and slope	Equation	In which narrative segment it appears	Cartesian graphic
ST=0 and DT≠0	$y=y_1$	Gap	
ST≠0 and DT=0	$x=x_1$	Non-diegetic material	

I have already mentioned that ST>DT also when the same diegetic time is repeated. Indeed, if we are shown the same diegetic time more than once – because the same character or group of characters act in the same time but in different spaces or realities, or because an event is shown from different characters' points of view – represented time is obviously shorter than representational time. In this case, each event that occurs in the same represented time in which the other episodes take place can be described with different equations: $y=m_1x+q_1$, $y=m_2x+q_2$, ..., $y=m_nx+q_n$. If $m_1=m_2=...=m_n$, the straight lines pertain to the same sheaf of parallel lines and the ratio between diegetic and screening time is the same in each narrative segment, otherwise it is not. As discussed, when represented time is repeated, contemporaneous events can be cross-cut or an episode can be shown from the beginning to the end before the next event begins (Figure 1.2).

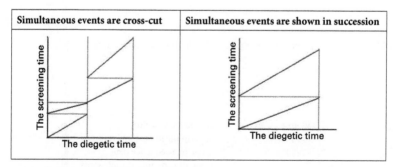

Figure 1.2 Cartesian graphics of simultaneous events that are cross-cut (left) and succeed one another (right).

Genette claims that between possibilities of the repetition of represented episodes and narrative segments there can be three relations:

1. One diegetic event is narrated once, or n represented episodes are narrated n times – 1S/1D or nS/nD (where S is our shown event and D the diegetic episode).
2. An event that occurs once in the diegesis is shown n times in the film, as in the case discussed above – nS/1D.
3. An event that takes place n times in the diegesis is shown only once in the film – 1S/nD. (1986: 166)

The first relation does not present any problem from the point of view of the description of narrative development. The third case is a specific case of a flashback or flashforward because we are shown what usually occurs once, that is to say, what typically occurred in the past or what will normally occur in the future. Unlike in the written medium, where the imperfective aspect is used to describe a habitual and iterative action, in the cinematic medium a montage sequence is usually adopted to show a character or a group of characters that repeat the same actions over a span of time. The second case is complex because it overlaps with simultaneity or flashbacks or flashforwards, or both. Indeed, as discussed, during chases in polyphonic or ensemble and parallel plots different characters are shown, either through parallel editing or in succession, acting in the same time but in different spaces. While there is repetition of diegetic time, there is no repetition of the same action, but simultaneity of different events. In repeated event and hub-and-spoke plots, we see the same action from different characters' points of view. Progressively, our restricted knowledge becomes unrestricted because each narrative segment fills in a gap or some gaps (as in *Jackie Brown* or *The Killing*) or our knowledge is further complicated, leaving us with permanent ellipses (*Rashomon*, Akira Kurosawa, 1950). In branched plots, we are shown two or more parallel realities in which diegetic time follows the same physical rules, but we do not experience the diegetic time of each reality as a repetition because we empathize with characters who are unaware of the existence of another or other worlds. It is as if there were as many diegetic times as parallel realities. While montage can encourage us to compare different realities, they pertain to different worlds. If chases, polyphonic or ensemble and parallel plots, repeated event and hub-and-spoke plots can be represented with Cartesian graphics such as those in Figure 1.2, a branched plot should be visualized through a sheaf of planes that have the axis of screening time in common (Figure 1.3). On the other hand, in cases in which the same shots are repeated more than once during the film, we can speak of flashbacks or flashforwards, either due to a character's recollection or premonition or in accordance with the director's narrative or aesthetic reasons.

The case of repeated action plots and time travel in general should be discussed separately because the concept of personal time, and the idea that diegetic time can change for different characters, must be introduced. So far, I have underlined the differences and similarities between branched and repeated action plots, and I have mentioned time travel narratives more than once. Repeated action plots can be

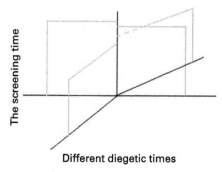

Figure 1.3 Graphic of a branched plot.

considered a subset of time travel narratives in which the traveller enters into his younger or older self's body and does not change the future, as in *Groundhog Day*. Then there are time travel narratives in which the protagonist does not change the future and travels in the past or the future, maintaining his physical appearance and meeting, or not, his doppelgänger – e.g. *The Time Machine* (Simon Wells, 2002) and *Terminator* (James Cameron, 1984). Similarly, there are time travel narratives in which the traveller does change the future and enters into his alter ego's body, e.g. *The Butterfly Effect*; or maintains his body image and meets his doppelgänger, e.g. *Twelve Monkeys* (Terry Gilliam, 1995) and *The Time Traveler's Wife* (Robert Schwentke, 2009), or does not meet his alter ego – e.g. *Back to the Future* (Robert Zemeckis, 1985; Table 1.7). In his taxonomy, Ramírez Berg does not take into account time travel narratives and does not distinguish between *Groundhog Day* and *The Butterfly Effect*, i.e. between films in which the protagonist is imprisoned in a time loop, and does or does not change the future, and characterizes both as repeated action plots. But for my purposes, it is important to distinguish between these two types of film and henceforth I will call repeated action plots only those time travel narratives in which the traveller enters into his alter ego's body and cannot affect the future.

Table 1.7 Differences among various types of time travel narrative.

Time Travel Narratives			
Time traveller changes the future		**Time traveller does not change the future**	
Time traveller maintains his bodily appearance and meets or does not meet his alter ego	Time traveller enters into his younger or older self	Time traveller maintains his bodily appearance and meets or does not meet his alter ego	Time traveller enters into his younger or older self
E.g. *Twelve Monkeys*, *The Time Traveler's Wife* and *Back to the Future*	E.g. *The Butterfly Effect*	E.g. *The Time Machine* and *Terminator*	E.g. repeated action plots, *Groundhog Day*

From the point of view of an analysis of time, there is no difference between repeated action plots and time travels in which the traveller enters into his doppelgänger's body and changes the future, whereas from the point of view of causality there is a huge difference. As discussed, the diegetic time of the protagonists of *Groundhog Day* and *The Butterfly Effect* is different from the diegetic time of all the other characters. Whereas time travellers relive the same diegetic time, giving rise to a different parallel reality whenever they re-enter one of their alter egos' bodies because they preserve memories of past experiences, the other characters relive the same diegetic time as if it were a new experience, each time erasing the past and substituting it with a new present. Thus, whereas the time traveller's diegetic time can be represented through a sheaf of planes that have the axis of screening time in common – as in a branched plot (Figure 1.3) – the other characters' diegetic time can be visualized through straight lines $y=m_1x+q_1$, $y=m_2x+q_2$, ..., $y=m_nx+q_n$. Unlike in branched plots, the different planes influence one another because the time traveller keeps track of previous events, and unlike in simultaneous events shown in succession each straight line is erased as soon as a new straight line is drawn because characters do not remember their past experiences.

David Lewis introduces the distinction between external and personal time: the former is the time lived by us and by characters who are not time travellers, it is the time that develops along a straight line and evenly flows from the past to the future; the latter is the time experienced by a time traveller in which the future can precede the past (1976). Flashbacks and flashforwards in external time become time travel in the past and future, respectively, whereas gaps in external time are no longer ellipses in personal time, but travel in time. For example, if I take once more the three events e_1 e_2 e_3, in which e_2 follows e_1 and e_3 follows e_2 in external time, and if they are shown to us in the order e_1 e_3 e_2, according to external time $\underline{e3}$ is a flashforward and the presence of e_3 before e_2 creates a temporary gap; whereas a time traveller travels from e_1 directly to the future e_3 without creating any gap, and then from e_3 to the past e_2. There is no difference between a time traveller's personal time in repeated action plots and time travel narratives in general, but there is a great difference between the laws of causality that govern their worlds. In *Groundhog Day*, whatever the protagonist does during the day does not change the future, and each morning he and the other characters wake up during Groundhog Day as if nothing had happened after the eve of Groundhog Day. The principle of causality is not contradicted. On the contrary, in *The Butterfly Effect* each time the protagonist travels back in time alters the diegetic world that he inhabits, changing the past, the causes, effectively, he modifies the future, the effects.

The idea that the past can be transformed gives rise to logical paradoxes, such as the grandfather paradox: how is it possible for a time traveller to go back in time and kill his grandfather before he meets his grandmother? In our example above, if e_2 precedes e_3, how is it possible that e_3 causes e_2? In my example, causality is different in external and personal time: in external time e_1 causes e_2 and e_2 causes e_3, while in personal time e_1 causes e_3 and e_3 causes e_2. We can understand the causal logic of personal time if and only if we empathize with the time traveller's personal time and distinguish it from external time. But we cannot solve chronoclasms, unless we hypothesize that the time traveller's actions originate a new parallel world – in which his grandfather dies and he himself was never born – from which he returns to his native reality (Ryan 2006: 658).[9] More complex are time travel narratives in which the traveller meets his alter ego because the episodes in which two doppelgängers meet are lived twice by the time traveller, once by himself as a time traveller and once as his younger or older self, depending upon whether he travels in the past or future. These events are usually shown more than once, each time from a different alter ego's point of view. Leif Frenzel calls these repeated events 'story knots' and claims that in literary works that do not relate time travel narratives when an event that occurs once in diegetic time is recounted more than once, each time it is retold it is from a different character's point of view, whereas in time travel narratives when the same episode is told more than once, each time is narrated from the different alter ego's perspective (2008). Thus, the narrative techniques adopted in repeated event and hub-and-spoke plots are often used in time travel narratives in which the time traveller meets his younger or older self. From the point of view of narration, the doppelgängers are treated as if they were different characters who live the same experience in different ways, and we, as spectators, alternatively share their different perspectives.

Thus, even in time travel narratives, as much as in repeated event and hub-and-spoke plots, when an event that occurs once in diegetic time is shown more than once in the film, I cannot call it a repetition: the different alter egos' points of view are shown in succession and we share the perspective of the time traveller, which is travel in the past or future, and then that of his younger or older self, which is, respectively, a flashback or a flashforward.[10] Similarly, in repeated action plots and time travel narratives in which the time traveller enters into his alter ego's body, we do not experience repetition because we empathize with the protagonist who goes backwards in time, but maintains the memory of past experiences, trying to overcome obstacles to free himself from the loop of time. Thus, summarizing, the idea of repetition seems to be peculiar to the written medium, where it is translated by the imperfective aspect

---

[9] It is interesting to note that Marie-Laure Ryan proposes a taxonomy of multiverse narratives, i.e. based on possible worlds theory, the idea that reality is not constituted of our world alone, but also by other worlds. According to her classification, multiverse narratives comprehend: transworld exploration, alternate or counterfactual history and time travel narrative. In transworld exploration, characters travel from one world to another and the different worlds either belong to the same space-time continuum, e.g. *Star Trek*, *Star Wars*, or to different spaces and times and differ as to what is possible in them, e.g. wormhole narratives such as *The Chronicles of Narnia*. In alternate or counterfactual history, an event or chain of episodes leads to a world that is different from our own and that may substitute it or coexist with it. Unfortunately, I cannot adopt this taxonomy, and I cannot entirely adopt that of Ramírez Berg (2006), because they do not focus on the problem of time and causality. For example, both *Groundhog Day* and *Sliding Doors* should be examples of alternate history, and the only difference between them is that the taxonomy seems to highlight is that in the former there exists only one world at a time, while in the latter there are two parallel worlds. There is no mention of the difference between personal and external time in repeated action plots, a difference that does not exist in branched plots.

[10] I have discussed and compared external and personal time in *Groundhog Day*, *Twelve Monkeys*, *2001: A Space Odyssey* (Pezzotta 2011) and in *The Time Traveler's Wife* (Pezzotta 2016a).

Table 1.8 The presence of simultaneity, flashbacks and flashforwards according to the ratio between how many times an event is presented in the film and how many times it occurs in the diegesis.

1S/1D or nS/nD		
1S/nD	We are shown once what typically occurred in the past or what will normally occur in the future	Flashback or flashforward
nS/1D	Chases, polyphonic or ensemble and parallel plots	Simultaneity of different events
	Repeated event and hub-and-spoke plots	Story knots: Same event from different characters' points of view
	Branched plots	As many diegetic times as parallel realities
	Same shots are repeated more than once	Flashbacks or flashforwards, either due to a character's recollection or premonition or to the director's narrative or aesthetic choices
	Repeated action plots and time travel narratives in which the time traveller enters into his alter ego's body	We empathize with the time traveller's personal time, thus there is an evolution in diegetic time and not a repetition
	Time travel narratives in which the time traveller meets his alter ego	Story knots: Same event from different alter egos' points of view; travel in the past or future for the time traveller is a flashback or flashforward for his alter ego

used to describe habitual and iterative actions, whereas in the cinematic medium it overlaps either with simultaneity or analepsis and prolepsis (Table 1.8).

The problem of overlapping between frequency on the one hand and simultaneity, analepses and prolepses on the other, reappears when I compare simultaneity with internal or mixed flashbacks and flashforwards. A flashback or flashforward is internal when the duration of its represented time is wholly comprehended in the duration of the diegetic time of the film; is external when the duration of its diegetic time precedes or succeeds the duration of the represented time of the film, and is mixed when the beginning of the diegetic time of the film is included in the flashback, or the end of the represented time of the film is included in the flashforward (Genette 1986: 96–9). If I use Cartesian graphics that represent two simultaneous events (Figure 1.2) and those that represent an internal or mixed flashback or flashforward, there is no difference: in both cases, there are segments that have at least one abscissa in common. It is not sufficient to distinguish between consecutive or non-consecutive segments, claiming that if two segments are consecutive, the events that take place during the diegetic time they have in common occur simultaneously, and if the two segments are not consecutive, one represents a flashback or a flashforward. Much like in time travel narratives, I have had to introduce the distinction between personal and external time, in this case I have to use that of deictic centre.

Prior to this, I need to explain embodied simulation theory, a theory of social cognition that explains how we manage to understand the actions, feelings and experiences of another – and empathy, a concept that I have already adopted, but not yet defined. 'The embodied extension of the cognitive approach has become one of the most significant additions of the "second generation" [...] of cognitive sciences. By challenging early computational and disembodied views of first-generation *cognitivism*, the embodied approach acknowledged and scrutinised the human body's and the lived environment's formative role in cognition' (Kiss and Willemsen 2017: 31–2, original italics). Embodied simulation is based on Vittorio Gallese's discovery of mirror neurons – first found in the premotor cortex of the macaque monkey – that are active both when we act and when we observe somebody else acting. Thus, both when we act and when we observe another living creature accomplishing the same action, the same neural mechanism is automatically activated (Gallese and Guerra 2015: 57). Embodied simulation is a functional mechanism of our brain through which we use some of the neural resources that we usually adopt to physically interact with the world, to feel and imagine the other living creature's actions in the world. Thus, embodied simulation becomes a crucial contribution to the theory of intersubjectivity and, consequently, to the reception theory of films. We understand the majority of another's behaviours and experiences thanks to the reuse of the same neural pathways on which our experiences as human beings that act and feel are based: we reuse our mental processes and states attributing them to others – be they living beings in front of us or characters on a screen (24). Empathy – verbatim feeling with somebody else – acquires an important, scientific meaning, because when we watch somebody else acting or feeling, both when we look at him directly, and when we watch his image projected on a screen, our mirror neurons become active as if we ourselves were acting or feeling. Thanks to empathy, we understand what somebody else is doing or feeling without losing the distinction between ourselves and the other (287–8).

To understand time travel narratives, we either have to empathize with external or personal time. From our point of view as spectators, time travel narratives become impossible puzzle films when we have to continuously switch our point of view, empathizing, for example, not only with a time traveller and all the other characters, but also with different alter egos of a time traveller who simultaneously travel in time. For example, in *The Time Traveler's Wife*, we are assisted by the fact that, in the central part of the film, we follow the love affair between the protagonists that mainly takes place in what can be considered the development of the female protagonist's present, who is not a time traveller, in which different doppelgängers of the male protagonist, a time traveller, arrive either from the past or the future. Mainly anchored to the female protagonist's present and focusing upon her love relation, we are able to keep track of the story even if we do not understand all the alter egos' travels (Pezzotta 2016).

Time travel narratives are a special case of film in which we have to continually change our point of view, anchoring it to different characters and doppelgängers. In general, whereas in the written medium verb tenses usually tell us whether we are reading about an episode that took place in the past, is taking place in the present or will take place in the future of a given character, in the cinematic medium we always watch scenes that unfurl before us, independent of the diegetic time in which they occur. But when we empathize with a character, we share his time line, distinguishing between his past, present and future. It is from this relative point of view, from the point of reference of the character with whom we empathize, that we distinguish between simultaneity and flashback or flashforward. When we are shown an episode that, from the point of view of the character with whom we empathize, occurred in the past or will happen in the future, it is, respectively, a flashback or a flashforward that can be a regular or simple flashback/flashforward if it is external or internal or mixed but shows actions that we have not already witnessed or will not witness; or a flashback/flashforward of simultaneity if it is internal or mixed, and reveals actions that happened or will happen simultaneously with other actions that we have already seen or will see (Table 1.9). What I have naively called 'point of view' or 'point of reference' will henceforth be named 'deictic centre':

> In everyday navigation, the deictic centre refers to the embodied ego-reference point from which we navigate space and monitor time (establishing dimensions such as front, back, up, down, or before and after). When extended to narrative, the notion denotes our constructions of 'where we are' in the story, referring to the constructed spatio-temporal coordinates of 'here and now.' [...] This allows viewers to determine 'where they are' in the story, and enables them to determine not only the 'here and now' but also, for instance, what is a flashback to earlier or flash forward to upcoming events.
>
> Kiss and Willemsen 2017: 190

I have argued that in time travel narratives in which there are different alter egos, the spectators' task is to continually alter their deictic centre and, sometimes

Table 1.9 Differences between external, mixed and internal flashbacks and flashforwards, and between simple analepses and prolepses, and flashbacks and flashforwards of simultaneity.

Flashback			Flashforward		
Internal or mixed		**External**	**Internal or mixed**		**External**
Simple flashback: Actions that we have not already witnessed	*Flashback of simultaneity*: Actions that happened simultaneously with other actions that we have already seen	*Simple flashback*	*Simple flashforward*: Actions that we will witness	*Flashforward of simultaneity*: Actions that will happen simultaneously to other actions that we will see	*Simple flashforward*

simultaneously keeping track of more than one deictic centre becomes impossible, at least if they watch the film once without taking notes and sketching graphics or drawings of time. More comprehensively, Kiss and Willemsen claim: 'We hypothesise that impossible puzzle films can disorient viewers by either denying the designation of a clear deictic centre, or by asking them to map the story from multiple deictic centres' (190).

Measuring screen time with certainty is always possible, but it is usually impossible to know for sure how much time passes between two scenes or sequences. Titles, dialogue and *mise-en-scène*, especially the presence of clocks or characters who look at their watches or the intensity of daylight and the length of shadows can help us, but most of the time our hypotheses about what time it is are approximate. Thus, the opportunity to represent an entire film through a Cartesian graphic is infrequent. Moreover, diegetic time can include several years or centuries, but show only a few weeks, so that the attempt to represent diegetic time along an x-axis becomes counterproductive because, being hard to visualize, it becomes useless. On the other hand, in some cases, such as in countdowns, extensively discussed in Chapter 4, Cartesian graphics and other types of graphics that allow us to compare represented and representational time are a valuable instrument for close analysis. Similarly, even if we do not have an accurate measure of diegetic time but only an estimate, we can draw a graphic that visualizes the development of the ratio between represented and representational time in a whole film or in some of its sequences. Furthermore, Cartesian graphics are a helpful instrument in understanding that: frequency in the cinematic medium overlaps either with simultaneity or flashbacks and flashforwards; the necessity of distinguishing between internal and mixed flashbacks and flashforwards on the one hand, and flashbacks and flashforwards of simultaneity on the other, and the need to adopt a deictic centre to discuss a character's or group of characters' diegetic time and, in particular, of distinguishing between external and personal time in time travel narratives.

It is useful to understand whether, when the order or duration of represented time are different from those of representational time, the spectator's experience of diegetic time is similar to that of their real time, the time they experience in their present or that that they recollect or imagine. According to Gregory Currie's 'Claim of Presentness', from a phenomenological perspective, the audience experiences the events that unfold on screen as present, taking place in the moment in which the audience is watching them. Metaphysically, the film grants the feature of presentness to the episodes represented in a film. Thus, cinema cannot show tensed properties, events as being past or future, but only present and linked by tenseless relations such as precedence and simultaneity (Terrone 2017: 332–3). Enrico Terrone advances the hypothesis that, as cinematic experience involves two spaces, that of the screen and that inhabited by the spectator, it can involve two temporal dimensions. He calls this hypothesis 'Wallon-Vuillaume' because he derives it from these two scholars' discussions. The film experience entails two temporal series: the 'egocentric series' and the 'pictorial series'. The former is based on the spectator's proprioception of his own body, at the centre of his egocentric space; the latter on the experience of the episodes that unfurl in the pictorial space.

There can be three different cases: when we watch live television, we experience what occurs on screen as if it is occurring simultaneously with what we experience as present in our egocentric series; when we watch a recording of a real event, we experience it as prior to what we experience as present in our egocentric series; and when we watch fiction, the pictorial and egocentric series are disconnected, parallel and never meet. Thus, episodes in the pictorial series are experienced as present at the perceptual level, but at the cognitive level are lived differently if they are part of a live television show, a recording or a fiction (334). In the case of fiction, the pictorial series allows us to live temporal experiences that are not possible in our lives, such as flashbacks and flashforwards, ellipses, fast and slow motion and freeze-frames (336). As regards analepses and prolepses, as soon as we are shown the past or future episode, respectively, we perceive it again as present. Concerning fast and slow motion and freeze-frames, phenomenologically the audience's temporal experience is shaped, ontologically they are shown the temporal features of the fictional world, and psychologically they experience how characters live their time (335–6). When the pictorial series violates the 'real-time principle' – i.e. when the duration of screen time does not coincide with that of diegetic time – 'the film experience overcomes ordinary perception thereby turning the spectator into a sort of time explorer, who can do in time what he normally can do only in space' (337). In the Cartesian graphic in which the x-axis represents diegetic time and the y-axis screen time, I imagine the spectator moving along the segments that represent the relation between represented and representational time with the same speed as the screen time. His present coincides with the present of the diegetic events, but he has to jump backwards or forwards in represented time as soon as a flashback, a flashforward or an ellipsis appear, not unlike a time traveller. When there is slow motion and the slope $m>1$, he has to walk more quickly; when there is fast motion and the slope $0<m<1$, he has to walk more slowly; and when there is a freeze-frame and $x_0=x_1$, he has to walk even faster than during slow motion. In these latter examples, he experiences a different time from that of his life that flows at the same constant speed, at least in the case of clock time.

1.4 Temporalities

Are the concepts listed in the sections above sufficient to describe how we experience the time of a film, how we live represented time within representational time? Do we always empathize with a character or group of characters and live their temporal experience? Are we always anchored to a deictic centre? The answer to the two last questions is affirmative, at least in films that are not impossible puzzle movies or art cinema, because to understand a narrative structure we need a deictic centre, as we do to empathize with characters – or, better, according to embodied simulation theory, we cannot avoid empathizing with characters because, thankfully or regrettably, our mirror neurons are activated independently of our will. On the other hand, the answer to the first question is negative because each of us experiences the time of a film differently, for countless reasons such as personal taste, mood during viewing, etc.

A more interesting question would be: Are the concepts listed above sufficient to describe how represented time is shaped within representational time? For example, let us take *Pulp Fiction*. If I were to write or tell a summary of this film, I would probably list the bound and dynamic motifs either following the chronology of diegetic events, or that of their succession in the film. The latter possibility is more likely because the fact that *Pulp Fiction* is a jumbled plot is one of its main narrative features. I would probably omit from my summary the fact that Jules recites a passage allegedly taken from the Bible, or that he speaks with Vincent about foot massages, or that Vincent dances with Mia Wallace (Uma Thurman) on a stage, and other similar scenes that, presenting free and static motifs, are useless in the temporal and causal chain of events, in what Tomashevsky calls 'fabula'. But when I think again, alone or with friends, I evoke images and dialogue taken from those very memorable scenes that I would have left out of the fabula. The film, as is discussed in Chapter 5, is a jumbled plot in which suspense prevails, although our responses alternates with curiosity, surprise and strong surprise, but what happens to the spectator's hypotheses, mainly focusing on the diegetic future, and to the overall rhythm of the film during the most unforgettable scenes? The to and fro of bound and dynamic motifs towards the diegetic future and past, our expectations of the development of the film are momentarily frozen, forgotten, in order to enjoy these scenes. The whole rhythm of the film would be drastically modified if we re-edited it, omitting these scenes, although its fabula would not change. A film such as *Eyes Wide Shut* is dominated by suspense about whether Bill will cheat on his wife and the development of their marriage, and unsatisfied curiosity about the identity of the mysterious woman. This permanent gap, which would certainly be mentioned in a summary of the film, is only the tip of the iceberg of permanent ellipses about characters: their slow, nonsensical dialogue full of repetition, and Bill's wandering retard and distort the development of the fabula, bringing to the fore the void of loneliness and incommunicability. Slowness is one of the adjectives that would better describe this film, a feature that would not appear in the outline of its fabula.

Forster, as already discussed, claims that life in time is to story what life by values is to plot. Time in a story is the chronological succession of diegetic events and their duration, and time in life is the temporal development of our experiences measured by clock time. Whereas value is the intensity of diegetic events in the plot, and of our experiences in life (Forster 1927: 48–9). It is well known that the mechanisms of emplotment are very similar to those that we adopt to construct our life review – i.e. a tale of our life that we tell ourselves in the attempt to find meaning and coherence in our past to deal with our future with apparently justified aims (Singer and Bluck 2001; McAdams 2001). For example, if I had written a page for each day of my years spent at university, what I would reread would be the 'story' of that period, in which each day follows the previous one at a constant speed – the 'story' being in quotes because it would be almost impossible to find a diary without a rough outline of cause-and-effect links. But if I rethink those years, I probably remember both the routine common to all students – such as taking classes, organizing notes, supplementing them with further materials and studying to take exams – and my peculiar routine – driving to the university with a friend and endlessly looking for a parking space, but also having lunch with friends – as well as the people I used to stay with and see, and some of their habitual behaviours. Together with memories of habitual actions, which constitute my world in that particular period of my life, there are particular events that I remember as if time had not passed. What is strange is that, if I do not need to review my life for myself or for others, if I free myself of the commitment to find meaning and coherence in my life, the scenes that vividly reappear in my mind are not necessarily linked to a temporal and causal chain that stretches from my past experiences to my future aims. While I vividly remember my graduation day, I do not recall all of my exams but, for example, I remember the day during which I was surprised by heavy rain and I ran with my best friend along flooded streets, or when my bad temper and very low tolerance for authority led me to challenge a professor.

If from the diary of my years at university I select only the bound and dynamic motifs, I obtain a fabula. My life review of that period, whether I recount it following the chronological succession of events or in another order, for example if I begin from graduation day and tell of all the exams in a flashback, is a classical narration. Indeed, a life review usually obeys the rules of canonical narratives: temporal coherence, i.e. the chronological succession of events; thematic coherence, i.e. the transformation of past events in lessons for the future; causal coherence, i.e. the search of causes for effects; and the cultural concept of biography, i.e. the knowledge of which events must or must not be included in our life review (Singer and Bluck 2001: 95).[11] On the other hand, the tale of the scenes that may not be important in my life review, but that I remember exactly, raised up from the backdrop of my habitual actions in that period, may be compared either to an art film or to my memories of a film, such as those described in the cases of *Pulp Fiction* and *Eyes Wide Shut*.

What I will henceforth call the temporalities of a film are the interaction of: its narrative structure – given by the relations between the order and duration of diegetic events, and their order and duration in the film – and its overall style – in particular, montage, camera movements and characters or objects in-frame, *mise-en-scène* and soundtrack – which create the time that characterizes the diegetic world of the film, together with peculiar scenes or sequences during which the overall time of the diegetic world is subverted or frozen. As some events of our lives escape our life review, from the tale in which we would like to coherently comprehend them, some scenes from films rise up from the prison of time that envelops the diegetic world of the film. I have chosen the term 'temporalities' to name the overall idea of time that we experience while watching a film, the time that governs it, as well as that of those scenes that seem to be dominated by a different time, because it seems to convey the idea of different concepts of time that interact among themselves, born both of narrative and stylistic techniques and of our experience of them.

---

[11] Elsewhere, I compare life review to films (Pezzotta 2016b).

The idea that beyond represented and representational time there is a time lived by the audience while watching the film, which is given by the interaction of diegetic and screen time, style and the spectator's experience of them, is not new. Daniel Yacavone calls this time 'expressed time': 'there is a subjective duration which transcends, and from this perspective, determines, each [screening and diegetic time]' (2008: 96–7);

> The objective/subjective duality marking the viewer's experience of a film's world, with respect to the apprehension of its *actual, represented,* and *expressed* time, in some cases mirrors the duality between objective and subjective time *within* its represented or fictional world, that is, time as it is experienced by its characters. [...] the affective relation between them [represented characters and situations] and the viewer is something deeper and broader than a specific identification (emotional or otherwise) with a character's thoughts, feelings, or actions. It is instead a consequence of a shared world-feeling that the film world expresses and which, with respect to representation, may be seen to provide the intuited 'existential' context within which the characters think, feel, and act. In sum, as the result of an affective connection between the viewer and its expressed spatial-temporal structure (including the sense of duration attendant upon its total rhythm) a film conveys a unique world-feeling, recognized by the viewer as such.
>
>   97–8, original italics at 98

Similarly, Stefano Ghislotti claims that within screen time flows the flux of the spectator's impressions, emotions, thoughts and observations evoked by the images and sounds of films; that is to say, the whole iconographic, narrative and cultural richness given by films and mentally elaborated by viewers flows from this. What he calls the spectator's 'psychological time' is the ongoing experience of a continuous fruition during spectating that creates mental representations and constantly keeps the spectator up to date. Thus, viewers judge a duration briefer or longer according to their mental flux, which cannot be measured, at least not by clock time: their attention is more or less focused according to their interests, knowledge, on the possibility that their mental schemas adhere to the elements presented by the film. The duration of screen time and the feeling of duration experienced by spectators are different, and a film, or parts of it, seem briefer or longer according to whether their psychological time is compressed or extended (Ghislotti 2012: 59–60).

The difference between temporalities on the one hand, and Yacavone's expressed time and Ghislotti's psychological time on the other, is that I attribute special importance to those scenes and sequences in which the overall time of the film changes, and seems to be overturned. As discussed, these narrative segments can be compared to those memories of the film we watched, or of our past that vividly come to mind for no apparent reason, without clear placement in the narrative structure of a film or in our life review. Analysis of these temporal segments seems extremely useful to define both their temporalities and, through comparison, that of the whole film, and to understand why in these moments time seems to be frozen, to escape from the rules in which it is imprisoned, avoiding the very awareness of the passage of time. During these scenes and sequences, we are free of the narrative structure of the film and its rhythm, we suspend our hypotheses about what will be shown, and we are able to feel experiences beyond time during which we really live our present as if it were unconnected to the passage of time and joined with timeless experiences. According to Terrone's Wallon-Vuillaume hypothesis, when the time of the pictorial series is equal to that of the egocentric series – i.e. in scenes or real-time sequences – the spectator's experience of diegetic time is very similar to that of lived time in their everyday experiences. The audience 'walks' along a segment described by the equation y=x in which slope m=1. Interestingly, Terrone adds that: 'such an emulation allows films to elicit intense emotions of fear, hope, suspense, disappointment, surprise, exultation' (2017: 337). In the following chapters, I show that, often, when characters experience tragedy, desire, excitement and intense joy, the duration of represented time is equal to that of representational time.

In an experiment conducted at the Università Cattolica del Sacro Cuore in Milan, part of wider research into 'Subjective Experience and Estimation of Moving Image Time' (SEEM_IT) and set 'within the framework of Neurofilmology: through a dialogue between film theory and cognitive science', Ruggero Eugeni and his team found that rapid editing causes an increase in the rate of time's flow and in the observed action rate, as well as an overestimation of the duration of screen time. On the other hand, when there is no montage, there is no decrease in the time flow rate and in the observed action rate, but there is once more an overestimation of the duration of screen time (Eugeni 2018). Thus, in action sequences, when the speed of editing increases, represented time seems to run faster than representational time, but the duration of diegetic time seems longer than that of screen time: we feel the race against time together with an expansion of time itself. This seems to be what I feel when I find myself in a dangerous situation, e.g. when I am going to fall on a hiking trail, or when I am driving very fast and find a unexpected obstacle: the flow of time seems to be inversely proportional to its duration. On the other hand, when I am feeling intense emotions, in the most tragic, amusing or exciting moments of my life, time seems to no longer exist and mark my life; I live in an atemporal dimension. These situations are usually shot in films in real time, as underlined by Terrone.

Up to now, I have introduced embodied simulation theory, and exploited its concept of empathy, but I also claim that during some scenes and sequences it is possible to go beyond empathy with a character or group of characters to live experiences beyond the flow of rhythm that dominates a diegetic world. How is it possible to go beyond empathy with a character? According to Martin Hoffman, empathy can be defined as an affective response that is better suited to another person's condition than to the situation in which the bystander finds himself – i.e. the spectator, the observer of the other person. This definition implies that empathy is: an emotional reaction, not a cognitive understanding; it focuses upon the narrative context in which the observed person finds himself or on his state of mind; and it is based on awareness of the distinction between the observed person and the bystander. Hoffman, moving on from developmental psychology – which studies behavioural evolution from birth to maturity – claims that there are different levels of empathy that can be represented along a continuum that goes from the less to more elaborated forms following the phases of our development, that is, from primitive reactions that surface in the first months of life to complex ones that emerge during teenage years. The first level of the continuum is mimicry, a rapid, unintentional reaction that is isomorphic to that expressed by the person who is observed. Mimicry first implies motor imitation of another person's countenance or posture, and, second, feedback that induces in the observer an emotion that coincides with that expressed by the person observed.

Besides mimicry, there are two other forms of empathy that are elementary and involuntary: the classical influence and the direct association. In the former, the association between an unconditioned stimulus and a bystander's feeling means the stimulus induces the feeling. In the latter, the observed person's status gives rise to similar feelings in his spectator, but based on the bystander's past experiences. Mimicry, influence and direct association are considered forms of empathy for parallel sharing and are still self-centred. On the other hand, in the cases of forms of empathy for participatory sharing, the bystander abdicates his point of view to endorse that of the observed person, creating a representation of his situation through imagination – the cognitive mediator. The spectator achieves fuller awareness of the observed person's experiences and of the distinction between himself and the other. In mediated association, emotional status is expressed through language. In role-taking, the observer steps into the observed person's shoes, either imagining how would he feel if he was in the other's situation or directly imagining how the observed person might feel (Carocci 2018: 103–5).

Spectators of a film may experience different forms of empathy when presented with a character or group of characters. For example, in disaster movies such as *Armageddon*, I do not shed even a tear at the beginning of the film, when meteors kill hundreds of people, but I burst into inconsolable crying when the protagonist (Bruce Willis) sacrifices himself to save his daughter's fiancé and the whole world. Narrative and stylistic techniques guide my feeling: I do not know the extras shown during the natural disaster, and special effects and some amusing gags divert attention from human casualties, whereas by the end of the film I have become fond of father and daughter, of their profound relation, emphasized by the shot-reverse-shot between their close-ups when they speak to each other for the last time. Crying finally exacerbates my empathy for participatory sharing. During both of these sequences, so different from a narrative and stylistic point of view, as well as the empathetic perspective that they give rise to – mimicry in the former scene and role-taking in the latter – there are escapes from the prison of time that envelop the diegetic world. The tight rhythm of suspense, emphasized by countdowns, is frozen when the audience is momentarily released from the ongoing tension either during humorous scenes, laughing or during extremely dramatic sequences, crying and grieving for the hero's losses and miseries. It is not by chance that in these very different scenes the audience passes from an extreme of the continuum of empathetic forms of empathy to another, from mimicry, during which spectators, notwithstanding the forthcoming end of the world, can briefly laugh at or with characters, to empathy for participatory sharing during which the audience experiences the characters' tragedy. As will be discussed in the case studies, it is often possible to escape the prison of time in which a diegetic world is enveloped, and that arises from the diegetic world itself, either when we empathize a little with characters, such as during humorous gags, erotic or particularly violent scenes, or when we strongly empathize with them, as during tragedies. While the audience's emotional reactions are mainly anchored by characters, consequently to the narrative and stylistic techniques through which they are represented, empathy alone does not explain all the departures from the rhythm of the diegetic worlds, especially when these evasions lead to the very contemplation of temporalities.

I do not believe that a more comprehensive study of the difference between identification and engagement, empathy and sympathy or indifference and antipathy will shed more light on my emotional relations with characters; as regards temporalities, empathy, as defined and analysed by Hoffman, is sufficient for my purposes (see Plantinga 1999: 244–7; Carocci 2018: 83–103). A more fruitful approach would be the discussion of moods and their relation to emotions of interest and fascination, which are less linked to characters and more to diegetic worlds in general. According to cognitive philosophy, the main features of the prototypical emotion are: action tendencies – if we are afraid of big dogs, we may avoid approaching them – orientation towards objects – we are afraid of big dogs, not afraid in general – and goal orientation – we may pick up the pace when we encounter a big dog. As Greg M. Smith notes, if a film, as classical Hollywood films often do, concentrates on characters and their actions, and stylistic techniques are mainly adopted to clarify and underline characters' actions and behaviours, it is often sufficient to discuss the emotions that share the characteristics of the prototypical emotion (1999: 104–7). In *Armageddon*, the father's unconditional love for his daughter – orientation towards an object – leads him to choose death and her fiancé's life to enable her to create a new family – in this case, action tendencies and goal orientation coincide. But in other films, that do not follow a classical Hollywood narration and style, such as *Eyes Wide Shut*, we wonder whether the protagonist really loves his wife, if he is more thrilled or jealous or upset about her confession, etc.

Overall, several different emotions seem to simultaneously or subsequently accompany the protagonist during his nightly wanderings, and style and narrative structure emphasize his getting lost in a maze-like diegetic world where memories, dreams and the present intertwine. The protagonist does not express his emotions verbally or through facial expressions; style conveys his mental turmoil to the audience. Neither his action tendencies nor his goal orientation are clear, nor is his orientation towards objects. The film is dominated by other, non-prototypical emotions, mainly conveyed by stylistic features, through which we progressively gain access to the complex diegetic world, without understanding the protagonist's emotions or empathizing with him, but intuiting his loneliness amid his existential crisis. The emotion system not only focuses on characters and their actions, but also guides the audience's attention towards the diegetic world in general and, in particular, towards those clues that recur, eliciting a set of coherent emotions. Moods are orienting emotions and preparatory states, spectators' expectations that peculiar, prototypical emotions are going to arise. Unlike prototypical emotions, moods are low-level, diffuse, long-lasting and inert emotional states because they keep the audience's attention focused on evidence that is likely to confirm and strengthen an ensemble of similar emotions. By contrast, brief bursts of prototypical emotion fan the flames of mood that, otherwise, is extinguished (111–14). For example, in *The Shining* (Stanley Kubrick, 1980), the Steadicam that follows Danny (Danny Lloyd) along the corridors of the Overlook Hotel, evoking an uncanny presence that is chasing the boy, increases our mood – fear – that erupts when the two Grady girls appear in front of Danny – prototypical emotion. Similarly, Nicholson's stare heightens our fear that, sooner or later, he is going to lose his mind and exterminate his family. Smith adds that some brief bursts of emotion are caused by 'emotion markers':

> configurations of highly visible textual cues [… that] signal to an audience traveling down the goal-oriented path of a narrative, cuing them to engage in a brief emotional moment; […] often such moments could be excised from a film with little or no impact on the achievement of narrative goals or the state of story information. However, these markers fulfil an important emotive function in the text.
>
>   118

Emotion markers can be adopted to describe those scenes of our past that, as discussed, we would omit from our life review, but that are useful to summarize and recall the mood of a particular period of our life – the happiness of running with a friend under heavy rain is an indicative example of the freedom and insouciance of that period of my life. Similarly, in *Pulp Fiction*, there are several scenes that would be left out of its fabula, but that are paramount for the creation of the peculiar mood of a film in which nonsense and overstatement are mixed with triviality. As discussed in Chapter 5, many of Tarantino's films adopt emotional markers that convey an absurd, almost unreal atmosphere, in which we are able to laugh about atrocious crimes and violent scenes. My hypothesis is that, often, when emotional markers prevail, characterizing with particular emotions a scene that slows down the rhythm of narration, the audience experiences a different time from that that which prevails in the diegetic world. Tarantino is a borderline case because in some of his films, diegetic worlds are characterized by two different temporalities that are mixed or succeed one another: a pressing narrative rhythm of action scenes versus the almost surreal time of overlapping dialogue.

Much like moods are preparatory and orienting emotion states, which focus audience attention on evidence that appears more often in the diegetic world, eliciting a set of coherent emotions, interest and fascination are emotions whose action tendency respectively focuses the spectator's attention, increasing the urge to keep watching the film. According to Ed S. Tan, there is emotional interest when there is an increase in the audience's will to follow diegetic events, based on the formulation of hypotheses about future developments. Unlike interest, emotional fascination is not focused upon characters' situations, but on narration and spectacle. The audience is not rewarded by the chance to better understand narration or the actions and behaviours of characters, or by an improvement in fate of characters, but by enjoyment of the spectacle. According to Carl Plantinga, fascination, together with suspense, surprise, curiosity, euphoria and expectation, are emotions that derive from the spectator's involvement and interest in the narrative development. Fascination is an 'artifact emotion' because it does not regard the diegetic world, but the film as an art object. Indeed, fascination can accompany a character's discovery; however, it not only comprehends the character's emotions, but also the spectator's hypotheses about future developments. Thus, fascination is a cognitive mechanism that overlaps with interest, regarding interest in the development of narrative events, as well as the pleasure of witnessing a work of art (Carocci 2018: 140–3). To clarify the difference between empathy and fascination, Carocci explains that, whereas empathy refers to objects of perception, and involves emotional and sensory-motor mirroring mechanisms, implying several reactions from mimicry to role-taking, fascination concerns the act of perception and is based on an ensemble of impulses from euphoria to interest and cognitive anticipation (181–2). Whereas empathy and mood are emotions that I believe assist spectators to understand the diegetic time of characters and how they experience it, as well as how the diegetic time of the fictional world is constructed or conversely, how the diegetic world creates time, interest and fascination are emotions that partly explain the audience's concern in complex films, and in films that deal with the abstract concept of time, i.e. those that play with time, both at the pragmatic level of narrative schemas, and at the abstract level of ideas about time.

I have chosen to discuss the oeuvres of four directors rather than selecting films pertaining to different genres or released in different periods of film history. If my ideas about temporalities outlined above have been mainly obtained through a deductive method – as in the case of the Cartesian graphics that enable me to distinguish among simultaneity, internal or mixed flashbacks and flashforwards, and flashbacks and flashforwards of simultaneity – I now look for examples of films to demonstrate and explain my hypotheses. Or better, I would have devoted a chapter to each group of concepts – the order of represented and representational time, their duration, etc. – enriched with various examples. But these ideas derive from close analysis of some films and especially from that of specific filmmakers' oeuvres, from the comparison of different films by the same director, and of different directors, thus using an inductive method. Why should I overturn my inductive method to protect myself from possible charges of adopting *auteurist* directions? Moreover, if I chose films by different directors released around the same time and pertaining to the same genre, on the one hand I would sketch a history of temporalities in different periods or genres of film history, which is beyond the goal of this work, while on the other, unable to analyse all the films, I would be obliged to choose a sample, thereby endangering my pretence of objectivity. My purpose is the discussion of how different temporalities are created through narrative and stylistic techniques and experienced – how spectators are involved in them, in their rhythm, how they adopt a deictic centre or shift between different perspectives, how they empathize with character's diegetic times and, most of all, how they raise themselves beyond the prison of time created by the film to reach a time beyond time itself, as it were. I here invoke Yacavone:

This irreducible world-feeling or expression which could also be described as an atmosphere which permeates and animates represented characters, objects, and situations, is not unique to a film, but also unique to its creator. [...] Yet although the expressed world or world-feeling of a given Lynch film is singular, surely it would not be surprising that it is closer to that of another Lynch film, than to one by von Trier or Kubrick. And in experiencing more films by the same director we may hope to become more attuned to such a general, director-specific feeling or affect, which may in turn also allow us to be more receptive to the differences between a director's films in this expressive respect. [...] the stylistic features of an art work are all the symbolic properties which exemplify it [...] and which are always (potentially) discernible upon close analysis of it. [...] Recognising and appreciating artistic styles necessarily involves comparing and contrasting art works and their worlds [...] Style is therefore viewed as a kind of impersonal machine for making art worlds as symbolic objects. We classify these world objects by attaching an artist's name to them – thus a 'Lynch' world, a 'von Trier' world, etc. – without necessarily making reference to any intentions or expressions on the part of David Lynch or Lars von Trier.

Yacavone 2008: 100–1

As claimed, temporalities are the interaction between style and narrative features and our experience of them, and close analysis is the method that I have found most useful to study them. Moreover, I have inductively looked either for more general concepts to define temporalities, and possibilities of realization of different kinds of temporalities, or for peculiar temporalities or time-feelings – if I wish to evoke Yacavone's definition of world-feeling – and I found them in particular directors' oeuvres.

I have chosen four well-known filmmakers, born either in the United States or Great Britain, who made some films that have acquired cult status. Two of them, Michael Bay and Quentin Tarantino, were born in the 1960s and began making films in the 1990s; whereas Stanley Kubrick and Adrian Lyne were born in the 1920s and 1940s, respectively; the former began his career as a filmmaker in the 1950s and the latter in the 1980s. I believe that being famous directors who have made cult films may be a clue to the peculiarity of the temporalities of their films, or conversely, the temporalities of their bodies of work may be one of the reasons for their success. I have chosen these directors rather than other well-known filmmakers because almost all the films they made are characterized by different rhythms. Lyne's films are mainly organized on the succession of events and dominated by suspense; Bay's on simultaneity, while suspense and curiosity are alternated; Kubrick's first seven films are characterized by very different temporalities that progressively overturn classical Hollywood style, indeed, in his last six films, permanent gaps and unsatisfied curiosity prevail; and Tarantino is a master in the manipulation of simple flashbacks and flashforwards, analepses and prolepses of simultaneity and, consequently, of temporary ellipses, and curiosity, surprise and strong surprise prevail.

Moreover, I looked for directors who, more or less explicitly, play with time so that time itself, and our experience of time, is emphasized, while these directors' films remain mainly anchored in a simple or complex narration that spectators are able to reconstruct and understand. I analyse how these directors create temporalities, and play with them, focusing on the development of the fabula, although they sometimes manage to overturn and hinder our expectations. The choice of these four directors has also been dictated by the different ways in which it is possible, while watching their films, to briefly escape from their dominant times: through comedy or tragedy or eroticism or violence. These directors are masters of creating different diegetic worlds and temporalities, and in suspending clock time. My hypothesis is that, thanks to their peculiar narrative and stylistic techniques, in Bay's, Lyne's, Tarantino's and the first Kubrick films, in humorous, erotic, violent and tragic sequences we experience different temporalities, beyond the overall rhythm of narration, whereas in Tarantino's and the last six Kubrick films, interest and fascination begin to predominate over empathy, bringing to the fore the very concept of temporalities. The films closely analysed here offer a wide and interesting range of temporalities, although spectators almost always empathize with a character or group of characters living their temporal experiences, anchored to a deictic centre, experiencing prototypical emotions – empathy and mood, and not interest and fascination, and do not have to advance poetical, lyrical and allegorical meanings. Aside from mentioning the last six Kubrick films, I have chosen not to analyse either art cinema directors such as Andrei Tarkovsky or Ingmar Bergman, or impossible puzzle films, such as David Cronenberg's or Lynch's, because spectators are disoriented by permanent gaps, and are suspended in a cognitive hesitation, unable to decide whether to adopt a narrative or poetic and aesthetic mode of meaning-making (Kiss and Willemsen 2017: 139, 190). These directors will be the core of future work.

2

Stanley Kubrick's temporal revolution

We spend our life running down fingers along the lists of directories looking for our real names, our permanent addresses. No man is an island? Perhaps that was true a long time ago, before the Ice Age. The glaciers have melted away and now we're all islands. Part of a world made of islands only.

Fear and Desire (Stanley Kubrick, 1953)

If we analyse Stanley Kubrick's oeuvre from the perspective of time, we can trace a fascinating history of how he created, through narrative and stylistic techniques, peculiar temporalities for each of his films. He began his career as a photographer. In a photograph time seems frozen. He first experimented with temporalities in photo-essays, three shorts, and in his first feature *Fear and Desire* (1953), in which he explicitly denied the existence of time. Then he focused on the order of represented and representational time in his films noirs – *Killer's Kiss* (1955) and *The Killing* (1956) – on the diegetic time of different characters and narrative situations in *Paths of Glory* (1957) and *Spartacus* (1960). He disrupted, mainly through satirical gags, the represented time of characters and events in *Lolita* (1962) and *Dr. Strangelove or: How I Learned to Stop Worrying and Love the Bomb* (1964), and implicitly represented the concept of time in his last six films – *2001: A Space Odyssey* (1968), *A Clockwork Orange* (1971), *Barry Lyndon* (1975), *The Shining* (1980), *Full Metal Jacket* (1987) and *Eyes Wide Shut* (1999) – in which characters, as well as spectators, remain trapped in temporalities characterized either by slowness or by a particular rhythm that encompasses the diegetic, as well as the extra-diegetic world, a feat he had already attempted to achieve in *Fear and Desire*, but did not fulfil this aim until later.

2.1 The emergence of rhythm in photographs and photo-essays

Since the beginning of his career, first as a photojournalist at *Look* magazine from 1945 to 1949 then as a film director, Kubrick aimed to reach an international mass audience. When he joined *Look*, the editorial philosophy of the journal was to 'surprise, enthral, delight, and inform the reader' (Mather 2013: 28) as *Look* at the time sought to reach at least 17 million readers in order to make a profit (96); useful training for Kubrick's future goal of making: 'well-researched and entertaining movies' (28). As a filmmaker, 'Kubrick's career was a balancing act between maintain control over his films and securing both financing and substantial returns on investment for what he envisioned to be projects with sufficient audience appeal' (Krämer 2015: 51). Kubrick aimed to release his films through the major studios, thus conform to their narrative and stylistic tastes, as much as he tried to remain independent of big-studio supervision. His first two shorts, *Day of the Fight* (1951) and *Flying Padre* (1951), were both sold to RKO, whereas his first feature, *Fear and Desire*, was released by Joseph Burstyn, an arthouse distributor, after having been rejected by the majors. Kubrick's last short, *The Seafarers* (1953), was commissioned and presented by the Seafarers International Union (SIU). Subsequent films, *Killer's Kiss*, *The Killing* and *Paths of Glory*, were sold to United Artists, and *Spartacus* to Universal.

> One way to understand Kubrick's early career, then, is to say that, having aimed, from the outset, at making movies to be released by the major studios to a mass audience and having currently failed to do so with *Fear and Desire*, from 1955 to 1960 he moved even closer – in terms of both genre and budget – to the commercial heart of Hollywood: starting with low-budget crime films and a medium-budget military movie (all released by United Artists) and ending with a megabudget historical epic (for Universal).
>
> Krämer 2017: 257

After the Second World War, classical Hollywood style remained the most adopted way to shoot narrative films, although some changes were introduced, such as subjective narration, more complex narrative structures, a new realism in lighting and narration, long takes and deep-focus composition. The subjective, complex narrative structure of *Citizen Kane* (Orson Welles, 1941) builds on different characters' flashbacks to recall the same event from various points of view, bringing the story back and forth, and introducing the possibility of playing with the relation between the progression of the fabula and the film without disrupting the link between causality and temporality, and motivating narrational choice with the conventions of mystery films in which questions about past secrets are answered through an intrusion into the past. This structure is used in *The Killing*, which is also an example of a semi-documentary – a fiction set in real places – a trend which responded to the mounting cost of constructing sets during the Second World War. *Citizen Kane* also enhanced the use of long takes and deep-focus compositions, which were increasingly used at the end of the 1940s and at the beginning of the 1950s when, thanks to the new dolly crab, which allowed smooth camera movements, it became possible to shoot sequence shots. These stylistic devices were significantly adopted in films noirs, such as *Killer's Kiss* and *The Killing*, and are one of the features of Kubrick's style. If the complex narrative of *The Killing* deals more explicitly and, paradoxically, more superficially with rhythm, alternating suspense and curiosity, deep-focus and long takes play with the very construction of space and movement, creating new relations between in- and out-of-frame, camera movements and characters, building tension and rhythm within one shot. After the Second World War, together with westerns, melodramas and musicals, the epic was enjoying increased success (Bordwell and Thompson 1998: 48–56). The commercial success of *Spartacus* assured Kubrick a leading role in the industry, allowing him growing control over his films, increasing his freedom in shaping their narrational and stylistic construction (Krämer 2015: 59).

Discussing still photographs, Roland Barthes distinguishes the 'spectrum' – the referent, the object captured in the image (2003: 11) – from 'studium' – an interest in the photograph without significant intensity – and 'punctum' – a certain poignancy that stings, hurts, grasps us, a slight out-of-frame sensation (27–8, 60). Whereas the spectrum is something that 'was', the punctum no longer regards a shape, but an intensity, it is time itself, the emphasis on the *noema* 'was', the very representation of that 'was' that we experience when we look at some photographs (95). Discussing photomontage, Clive Scott claims that this technique, which substitutes the past associated with a single photograph, its progress suggested by the overlapping of two or more photographs, introduces a narration. Similarly, Philippe Mather argues that some compositions in depth create a dialogue among different planes (Mather 2013: 164). Indeed, some of the features of Kubrick's photographs, such as sharp focus and deep space, characters looking at the camera and frames within frames – i.e. windows and doors, mirrors and inset photographs – (Mather 2015: 35, 42–3, 46) – invite us to make hypotheses about the relations among the referents, between them and us –why do the people look at us? – and between the photographer and us – why did he take that particular picture? Against photography's long-established cultural links with the past, stasis and death, I propose to discuss its possible associations with life. In 1766, G. E. Lessing claimed that some paintings may represent a 'pregnant moment' that, transcending its diegetic present and evoking both past and future, offers a narration (cited in Mather 2013: 163–4). Shifting the issue from time in general to rhythm, while it might sound paradoxical to discuss rhythm in still photographs where there is no movement, in some pictures we experience 'rhythm' – a play of our hypotheses growing from the relations among the objects represented and between them and us – we can wonder or remember what took place before, or what will occur after. Causes and effects may not be explicit, since there is only one picture, but evoked through clues that suggest the existence of a past or future beyond the diegetic present of a photograph.

In photo-essays, several photographs, accompanied by titles, subtitles, captions or longer texts, are usually published on a two or more page spreads. The succession of images, at which the viewer has to look sequentially from left to right, aims at establishing causal links among them that are often reinforced by the written medium. Comparing photo-essays and films, Roger Odin claims that, whereas the latter medium does not highlight temporal succession, the former, through its spatial layout, manifests its enunciative function, prioritizing discourse over story (cited in Mather 2013: 172). What of comic strips that share a similar layout to photo-essays? And what of Conceptual Metaphor Theory, according to which time is a metaphor of space, consequently spatial relations evoke temporal links? Wilson Hicks, *Life* magazine editor, claims that joining photographs and words leads to the expansion of the narrative and descriptive content of a story, thus photo-essays: 'take on something of a motion picture's fullness and fluidity' (cited in Mather 2013: 172). As in the case of photography, if I focus on rhythm, I suggest that, while in a film there is an illusion of movement and shots succeed and substitute for one another temporally, in a photo-essay photographs are ordered one after the other spatially, while in both media the sequence of images can create suspense, curiosity and surprise, triggering the spectator's hypotheses and involving them in the development of narration. Mather claims that the photo-essay: 'has the virtue of highlighting formal similarities and differences spatially rather than temporally, in contrast with the film medium' (42). While, as Mather notes, in a photo-essay the comparison between successive photographs is foregrounded, one of the features of Kubrick's oeuvre are cross-references between shots and scenes that enrich and slow the suspense towards the end via a web of stylistic and thematic echoes. This characteristic of the rhythm of Kubrick's films may be a feature derived from the photo-essay.

Moreover, the two media share some techniques such as: 'serial photography and cropping successive images to create a zoom-in effect, as well as printing frames from specially modified motion picture cameras' (Mather 2015: 27); or beginning a photo-story *in medias res* and proceeding with a flashback (38), or creating a kind of photograph album to capture some significant moments of an event mimicking montage sequences (41). For Mather: 'the seeds of Kubrick's transition from photojournalism to film were already present in the unique photographic genre he was practising at *Look* magazine' (27). Indeed, the steps required in the production of a photo-essay are similar to those of a film[1] and, above all, the marketing aim of the review was to reach and entertain a mass audience (43), introducing innovations in compliance with the conventions of the medium (46).

2.2 Experimenting with narrative schemas and style in shorts

It is revealing that both *Day of the Fight* and *Flying Padre* are not only adaptations of two photo-essays published on *Look* – respectively Kubrick's 'Prizefighter', published in January 1949, and 'Flying Priest', photographed by George Heyer and published in October 1946 – but are also, more generally, adaptations of popular post-war photographic genres: the goal-centred and character-centred plots that depict a particular day in the life of a character (Mather 2013: 190–1, 247). Both 'Prizefighter' and *Day of the Fight* present the story of a day in the life of Walter Cartier, before and during his boxing match. The narrative schema, in both media, is dominated by growing suspense surrounding the match, which constitutes the climax of the narration, and is delayed, in the short, by repetitions, as if the director wanted us to note correspondences among shots. Moreover, in *Day of the Fight*, the increase of tension begins during the long prologue – lasting about a quarter of the length of the short – in which the voice-over (Douglas Edwards) poses questions about the existence and success of such a violent sport. When a succession of shots of boxers fighting appears, alternating with shots of fans and journalists, the voice-over comments: 'What is the fascination? What

---

[1] Maher wrote: 'finding story ideas, conducting background research, developing a shooting script with the photographer, going on location with the writer, selecting pictures for the layout, and writing headlines, text and picture captions' (2015: 23).

does the fan look for? Competitive sports? Scientific skill? Partly, but mostly he seeks action, toe to toe body contact, physical violence, the triumph of force over force, the primitive precocious visceral thrill of seeing one animal overcome the other.'

These hypotheses appear even more sardonic when compared with a series of shots of boxers shown performing their daily working activities and exercising for the matches, while the voice-over claims that they fight to earn a living: the metaphor between animals and men is stated visually and orally. Whereas when we see other shots of them fighting, the voice-over adds that they fight for the 'American dream', to gain prestige and to experience thrills. At the end of the prologue, when a journalist appears in-frame before a typewriter and begins to flip through a record book, the voice-over adds that boxers fight for immortality, to see their names: 'forever inscribed in the record book along with the all-time greats'. At this point, the protagonist Walter Cartier is first introduced – 'Let's take one name out of a book, a trend. Say Walter Cartier. What would his story be like? This then is the story of a fight and of a fighter' – and the suspense surrounding the success of his match is already loaded with the efforts and dreams that link Walter with all the other fighters.

Aside from its prologue, the narrative schema of *Day of the Fight* is the source-path-goal schema that begins when Walter wakes up on the day of the match, continues throughout the endless day with activities and duties carried out in preparation for the evening event and ends with the fight. The ASL of the short decreases slightly towards the end but, surprisingly, that of the match (5.5 seconds) is not so different from that of the entire short (6.7 seconds; Figure 2.1).

The greater tension we experience during the fight is due to the quantity and speed of the movements of characters and camera, the alternation between low and high-angles,

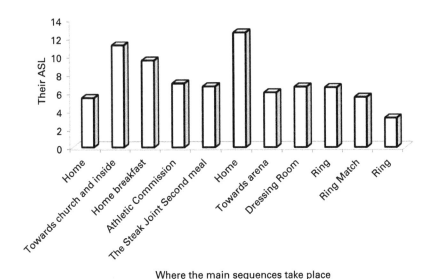

Where the main sequences take place

Figure 2.1 Histogram of the ASL of the sequences of *Day of the Fight*.

shots of the boxers, interrupted by shots of the spectators and to the emphasis on the passage of time of the previous sequences. Alternation between high-angle establishing shots of the ring and low-angle shots of the fight, present in the prologue, too – due to the fact that a closer view of boxers can only be obtained by framing them from under the ropes – is a feature of photo-essays about boxing matches (Mather 2013: 126). Similarly, these photo-essays often alternate photographs of the boxers with shots of their audience (248).

In 'Prizefighter', when the boxer is waiting for the fight, the text underlines: 'time drags heavily'. Throughout *Day of the Fight*, the voice-over places emphasis on waiting: when Walter wakes up – 'the toughest part of being a boxer, the waiting' – when he is at the Athletic Commission – 'what bothers him is the all day waiting of which this is a part' – when he is back home before leaving for the arena – 'for Walter, the bad part is the waiting. Soon it's coming [. . .] the time draws near' – and finally, when he is in the changing room before the match – 'Time is a strange thing. When you have a little of it, and you want it to last, it scatters away in all directions and you never know where it's gone. [. . .] It's only when you want the hours to go like now, the time has a way of staring you in the face as it barely moves along'. This personification of time becomes a menacing presence, a dense fog that does not allow Walter to reach the time of the fight. The voice-over continually stresses the moment of the day when the activities that are shown take place. Beginning when the match will take place – 'Tonight at 10 o'clock' – the voice-over continues to specify what time it is – 'At 6 o'clock in the morning'; 'Now through the quiet morning streets'; 'At noon'; 'And now at 4 o'clock it will be six hours before he enters the ring'; 'At 8 o'clock' – and then he begins the countdown in which he passes from hours to minutes to moments – 'the last two hours of preparation'; 'is going to fight in one hour'; 'in fifteen minutes'; 'few moments are left'.

The rhythm also slows less explicitly thanks to details that often show what the voice-over has already explained or is saying: the poster of the match; the signs where Walter is or is going to, e.g. the 'State of New Jersey Athletic Commission', 'The Steak Joint' and 'Boxing'. The run-up to the fight is further delayed by the presence of Walter's twin brother Vincent, who is present in 'Prizefighter', too, and the voice-over's efforts to distinguish between them. They are first shown in a double bed and the voice-over explains that, 'Walter is at the right of Vincent, his identical twin', thus Walter is on the left of the frame and Vincent on the right. Why not distinguish between them from Vincent's point of view, rendering the distinction less complex for the audience (Figure 2.2)? This ploy of confusing the twins continues in the next shot, when Vincent is in-frame while the voice-over speaks of Walter, and in the next sequence when they walk side by side and the voice-over mixes information regarding the twins' childhoods. *Mise-en-scène*, camera movement and racking focus seem to merge the two brothers: when they are home before leaving for the arena, from a plan américain of Vincent, the camera pans right to a plan américain of Walter, both framed within a window; and when they are waiting in the changing room, there is a rack focus from a detail of Walter's fist in the foreground to Vincent in the background, as if the hand belonged to both twins (Figure 2.3). To further multiply Walter's identity, there is a medium close-

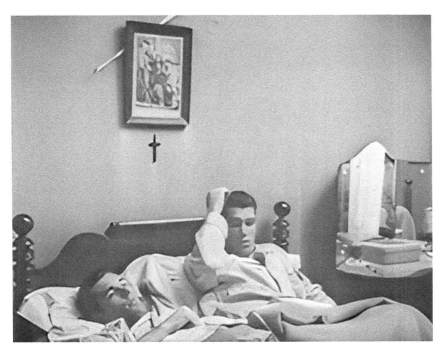

Figure 2.2 *Day of the Fight* (Stanley Kubrick, 1951). Vincent (Vincent Cartier) and Walter (Walter Cartier) in bed.

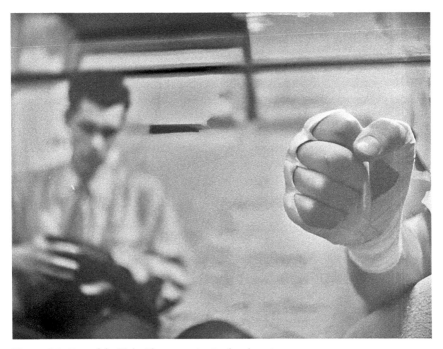

Figure 2.3 *Day of the Fight.* The two twins in the changing room.

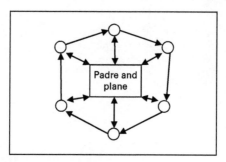

Figure 2.4 Narrative schema of *Flying Padre*.

up of his image reflected in the mirror when he presses his nose and a close-up of his face on a poster of the match.[2]

Unlike *Day of the Fight*, *Flying Padre* and *The Seafarers* are part-whole schemas. In *Flying Padre*, the whole consists of two days in the life of the protagonist, Padre Fred Stadtmueller who is able to reach all the parishioners of his large New Mexico parish by plane, and the parts are his daily activities alternating with chance events. An introduction about the priest's normal activity is followed by a funeral – random event – a mess – normal event – the solution of a minor conflict between two children – random – the Padre's hobbies – normal – and his race with time to rescue a sick child – random (Figure 2.4).

The events that occur by chance are introduced by surprise, and their succession follows a progression from the less to the more suspenseful occurrence. Similarly, in Arthur Rothstein's photo-essay 'Flying Doctor', published in *Look* in November 1947, the climax of the doctor's activities is introduced at the end of the essay by surprise: a waitress in a diner informs him that an important phone call is waiting for him, and in the next photograph the doctor is shown at a farm where a man, as the text explains, would have died if the doctor had not arrived in time. The ASL of the short decreases gradually towards the end, foregrounding the rhythm of increasing tension (Figure 2.5).

Camera movements – mainly panning right and left, and aerial footage when the camera is on the plane – adopted for the most part during the introduction, the funeral and the last sequence, foreground the absence of a unique trajectory in the priest's movements and, by implication, the significance of the haphazard in his life.

Among the themes that recur throughout Kubrick's filmography, *Day of the Fight* presents those of the fight and the double, while *Flying Padre* emphasizes chance and the relation between mankind and technology. Indeed, the element that links all the parts of *Flying Padre*, making all the Padre's activities possible, is his plane. This relation is emphasized by details of the plane and the priest's hands touching its instruments and spinner, and before he takes off with the sick child and his mother there are three flashbacks of simultaneity that increase suspense: a long shot of the plane followed by a close-up of

---

[2] Similarly, at the beginning of *Killer's Kiss*, there are shots of posters of the protagonist's boxing match and, before the fight, he is shown in his apartment pressing his nose in front of a mirror.

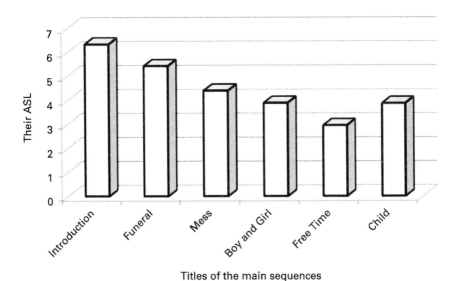

Figure 2.5 Histogram of the ASL of the sequences of *Flying Padre*.

the Padre and a detail of his fingers switching on the throttle. The priest seems to fuse with his plane, and air, more than earth, seems to be his element – e.g. raising birds is one of his hobbies, and there are numerous low-angles of the protagonist. These latter shots emphasize his role as a priest, as well as his more general association with the sky. He can deal with his daily duties and contingencies because he is a man-machine.[3]

Whereas *Day of the Fight* and *Flying Padre* are defined as '"straight" documentaries', *The Seafarers* is an 'industrial or promotional film' that, according to Mather, avoids 'narrative form and "personal journalism"' (Mather 2013: 247), but if we analyse it, we find its narrative schema supporting the story of members of the Seafarers International Union. *The Seafarers* is a part-whole schema enclosed in a container schema. Unlike in *Flying Padre*, all the parts examine the advantages of being a member of the SIU, and are permeated by a peaceful rhythm, the same rhythm that characterizes the sailors' lives. Indeed, every sequence shows seafarers looking for and finding the job they desire, receiving money, bed and board, health care and pension provision and enjoying their free time. They are never shown working – except for once on board a ship for a few seconds – and we see them landing or walking along a street before reaching the SIU headquarters or already there. Similarly, ships are never shown on the open sea but always in a port; a detail of a model of a ship and a world map ward off any suggestion of the possible dangers that may be culturally associated with a seafarer's career.

---

[3] For a discussion of the protagonists of *Dr. Strangelove*, *A Clockwork Orange* and *Full Metal Jacket* as machines, see Prévost-Balga (2017).

Camera movements, long takes, the alternation of voice-over and characters' voices and details create a peaceful rhythm. The camera slowly pans, tilts and tracks to keep in-frame seafarers moving or to show them grouped together or to show ships in a harbour. Long takes are adopted to show seafarers when they listen for which jobs are available, have lunch in a cafeteria, play billiards, receive money from an SIU clerk, as cash benefits and wage increases are shown through graphics and posters, and when a seafarers' representative speaks to them the camera lingers on the advantages of being a member of the SIU. Similarly, the voice-over (Don Hollenbeck) remains silent only once: when characters' words confirm what the images show and the voice-over has already explained. There are details of machines at the service of seafarers: 'Big, modern, efficient and safeguarding the rights and interests of those who go to sea, but never forgetting that the machines and the files or the figures are there to serve the seafarers and not the other way around.' As in *Flying Padre*, machines are commanded by men, and technology is a useful instrument to improve mankind's abilities, yet far from getting out of hand as in *Dr. Strangelove* and *2001: A Space Odyssey*.

The slow rhythm is also created by the circular structure of the container schema and evoked by the very parts of the part-whole schema. The documentary opens and closes with shots of Don Hollenbeck addressing directly the audience as he introduces the SIU (Figure 2.6).

Similarly, a seafarer's life begins when he goes to the SIU to find his first job and ends when the Union gives him money for his retirement or sickness; his working terms alternate with free time, during which he looks for a new job and has fun. This circularity seems to evoke the very structure of the SIU in which all the members are equal, having the same rights and duties. Curiously, the ongoing thrust of the part-whole schema is affected by Don Hollenbeck, who quotes Joseph Conrad, defines the documentary as a story and opens and closes a book at the beginning and end of the short. Hollenbeck intones: 'Joseph Conrad wrote a lot of things about the sea [. . .] The picture you're going to see now is the story of men who are banded together

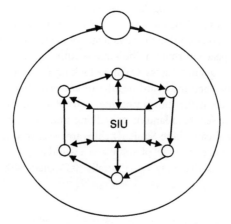

Figure 2.6 Narrative schema of *The Seafarers*.

through one essential common purpose. This is a vital story in their daily lives and their achievements. It's a proud story [. . .] It's the story of the SIU.' At the end, he claims: 'You've seen a story about how the seafarers, conscious of their rights and their responsibilities, are together for their common objectives [. . .] This is the story of the SIU.' Hollenbeck addresses us, looking directly into the camera, but in a long take he stands up behind his desk, walks in front of it and sits down on it in front of a window, framed within a frame. Self-referentiality comes to the fore.

2.3 Staging time: *Fear and Desire* (1953)

Kubrick judged *Fear and Desire* (1953) to be 'juvenilia', not so much for the technical mistakes in the *mise-en-scène* and montage, but because it is so blatantly a reflection about time.

The film is a source-path-goal schema: after a crash landing, four soldiers, Mac (Frank Silvera), Sidney (Paul Mazursky), Fletcher (Stephen Coit) and Lt. Corby (Kenneth Harp), find themselves behind enemy lines. Of time and place, the voice-over (David Allen) explains:

> There's war in this forest, not a war that has been fought or one that will be, but any war. And the enemies who struggle here do not exist unless we call them into being. This forest then and all that happens now is outside history. Only the unchanging shapes of fear, and doubt, and death are from our world.

Addressing us, he adds, 'These soldiers that you see keep our language and our time, but have no other country but the mind', the film space-time can be read as a metaphor of the minds in which the soldiers remain entrapped. To reach their comrades, the four soldiers decide to build a raft and sail along a river under the cover of night. Their plan is complicated by the encounter with a young woman (Virginia Leith) who does not speak their language. While the other three soldiers organize their escape, Sidney is left alone with her, and entertains her with the story of Shakespeare's *The Tempest*, implicitly identifying her with Miranda: the girl first appears in the river with two other young women and they are the only three women in the film, as the heroine of the play is one of only three female characters mentioned. Miranda, having lived in exile on an island since she was a baby, does not know the evil in the world, just as the girl in Kubrick's film seems unaware of the war around her and of her attractiveness for Sidney. The latter, on the brink of insanity after having killed three enemy soldiers with his comrades, and obsessively attracted to the young woman, kills her and, when Mac reaches him, tells him that the magician Prospero is the murderer, before running away alone in the forest. The encounter between Mac and an enemy general is equally meaningful: the killing of the general becomes the purpose of Mac's life. While Mac creates a diversion, Lt. Corby and Fletcher enter the general's dugout and kill him and his captain only to discover that the two dead enemies are themselves – indeed, Harp plays the role of Lt. Corby and the general, and Coit Fletcher and the captain. Following this revelation, the words pronounced by Lt. Corby – cited at the beginning of this chapter – after the murder of the first three enemy soldiers acquire a new meaning, becoming a metaphor for men's loneliness. The men's will to be unique human beings, their desire to conquer a peculiar identity, has led them to voluntary exile and their inability to recognize themselves in the others leads to them murdering themselves. The legerdemain of using the same actor to play different roles will also be adopted in *Dr. Strangelove* – Capt. Lionel Mandrake, President Merkin Muffley and Dr. Strangelove are played by Peter Sellers – to stress how incommunicability impedes men from recognizing themselves. On the other hand, in *Eyes Wide Shut*, Abigail Good plays the role of the mysterious woman at the orgy, whereas her corpse at the morgue is that of Mandy (Julienne Davis), the woman who overdoses during the Christmas party: the mystery of the identity of the masked woman is never revealed. Is it possible to have one specific identity? After having stolen a plane, Lt. Corby and Fletcher manage to reach their camp, but they go back into the forest to look for Mac and Sidney only to find that the former is dead and the latter has gone insane.

The suspense of the source-path-goal schema increases by simultaneity, rendered through several cross-cuts, such as that between Lt. Corby, Fletcher and Mac who build a raft by the river bank and Sidney who watches the girl in a clearing. The last cross-cut, when Lt. Corby and Fletcher are back in the forest looking for Sidney and Mac, remains open: we are shown the lieutenant speaking with Fletcher and then, in the mist, Sidney, singing on the raft with Mac's corpse, but Corby and Fletcher leave. Do they see Sidney? Will they take him away from the forest or will they go back to their camp without him? This openness seems to stress the unreality of the diegesis given by repetition, camera movements, details and, paradoxically, mistakes – spatial and eyeline matches are often not respected, nor is the 180° rule. These mistakes may be due to the fact that Kubrick was a self-educated director and this film was his first feature. Nevertheless, seeing a character in a different position, or moving and looking in another direction in comparison to the previous shot, strikes us as inauthentic. Moreover, when the four soldiers walk in the forest, they often advance towards the camera that either remains still or slowly pans with them, and after a cut or a fade in and out, we are again shown the soldiers approaching the camera, as if they had not advanced and their progress was endless. When Sidney is left alone with 'Miranda', shots of him are superimposed with enacted flashbacks of simultaneity of the four soldiers walking in the forest and killing the enemy soldiers. This mix of images heralding Sidney's madness is preceded by a superimposition of the soldiers' voices-over while they walk into the forest. These repetitions, the stories recounted by Sidney and his insanity, the third person's and the soldiers' voices-over transform the forest into a metaphor of the soldiers' interiority, and the open end seems to stress the impossibility of finding a way out. Loneliness and the struggle against oneself and others to find an identity are themes that Kubrick will explore throughout his career, as well as the creation of metaphorical spaces, although in subsequent films he progressively did not assign the task of explicitly explaining the meaning of voices-over and dialogue, and instead assigned meaning to temporalities that implicitly suggest possible interpretations.

2.4 Between classical and art cinema narration

2.4.1 The order of represented and representational time: *Killer's Kiss* (1955) and *The Killing* (1956)

In *Killer's Kiss* (1955), the rhythm of the narrative schema already mirrors that of style and vice versa. The source-path-goal schema dominated by suspense is embedded in a container schema that introduces curiosity about the source-path-goal schema. As mentioned at the beginning of the Introduction, the film opens and closes with the protagonist Davey Gordon (Jamie Smith) waiting for his train at the station, and this frame appears twice during the course of the film, always accompanied by the protagonist's voice-over. The source-path-goal schema consists of two main parts that succeed one another: the former about Davey's boxing match, and the latter about the love triangle between Davey, his neighbour Gloria Price (Irene Kane), a taxi dancer, and her boss and lover Vinnie Rapallo (Frank Silvera). The first source-path-goal schema reaches its climax in the match that Davey loses. The second schema has two climaxes: one when Albert (Jerry Jarrett), the protagonist's manager, is mistaken for him, and murdered by Vinnie's gangsters, and the second when Vinnie and Davey fight in a mannequin factory. To complicate the source-path-goal schema, itself an enacted internal flashback, there are other three internal and one external flashbacks. Among the internal flashbacks, two regard Davey and Gloria's relationship and are recounted by the protagonist's voice-over, and one enacts Vinnie's unexpected visit to Gloria's and his outburst there. The external flashback is rather an enacted recounted analepsis, during which we are shown Gloria's sister Iris (Ruth Sobotka) dancing on a stage, while Gloria's voice-over tells us of her youthfulness: her sister, an up-and-coming classical dancer, had to give up on her career, and marry a man she did not love to assure her father medical care and when he died, she committed suicide (Table 2.1).

As when during Iris' dance bright spot lights focusing on her prevent us from seeing what is beyond the stage, giving us the feeling that Iris is trapped on the stage, Gloria and Davey seem imprisoned in the *mise-en-scène*, owing to their movements and those of the camera, to details and frame within frame.

For example, when the protagonist is shown at the station, he is trapped in a narrow space because there is no establishing shot, and either the camera remains still while he walks to and fro inside the frame, or tracks right and left with him, keeping him in the centre of the frame. Similarly, the camera pans and tracks with Gloria, Davey and Vinnie when they are inside Gloria's or Davey's apartment or Vinnie's office, avoiding an establishing shot. At the end of Gloria's enacted internal flashback, when Vinnie attacks her and she faints, the camera rotates twice rapidly, mimicking her feeling of being trapped by Vinnie's will. The ring and the mannequin factory become equally claustrophobic spaces. During the former climax, there is cross-cutting between the ring and Vinnie's office where he watches the match with Gloria. As Davey is trapped in the ring, often framed within the frame of Vinnie's television, Gloria is imprisoned in Vinnie's arms that hold her while she bends backwards as if to free herself from his embrace (Figure 2.7).

Table 2.1 Narrative schema of *Killer's Kiss*. On the first two lines (bold) when the episodes take place and in subsequent lines (bold) where they occur. F indicates a flashback.

	Years before	The boxing match, Friday, 25 October; 6:50 p.m. before Albert's call		Saturday, 26 October					Sunday, 27 October
			An hour before	Early morning	Breakfast	Lunch	Sunset	8:15 p.m.	
Train station									
Apartment blocks	x								x, v.o.
Subway coach	x, Uncle George's v.o.								
Gym and dancehall		x							
Gloria along a street		x							
Apartment		x							
Apartment			x						

Apartment	x, F within F					
Apartment		x				
Apartment			x			
Apartment	x, v.o., F within F					
Apartment				x		
Stage	x, Gloria's v.o.					
Apartment					x	
Train station						x, v.o.
Apartment						

(continued)

Table 2.1 Continued.

Years before	The boxing match, Friday, 25 October, 6:50 p.m. before Albert's call	Saturday, 26 October					Sunday, 27 October
	An hour before	Early morning	Breakfast	Lunch	Sunset	8:15 p.m.	
City				x			
Vinnie's office					x, v.o.		
Apartment and gym					x		
Dancehall and streets nearby						x	
Train station						x	
Apartment blocks							x, v.o.
Streets, warehouse, streets, mannequin factory						x	x
Train station							x, v.o.

Figure 2.7 *Killer's Kiss* (Stanley Kubrick, 1955). Vinnie (Frank Silvera) embraces Gloria (Irene Kane) in his office, leaving her no escape.

Moreover, during the fight, low-angle shots of the boxers[4] quickly succeed one another in an escalation of violence that leaves Davey no escape. Similarly, during the latter climax, a montage of shots of Davey and Vincent, during which the camera moves quickly, encloses them among uncanny mannequins, whose spare parts are used as weapons together with Davey's spear and Vinnie's axe – an axe will be used by Jack (Jack Nicholson) in *The Shining*.

Every interior space becomes a prison: when Gloria, Vinnie or his gangsters are in the dance hall, we are shown only one side of the room and the camera either tracks or pans right when they walk towards Vinnie's office, or tracks or pans in the opposite direction when they leave the ballroom. A steep, cramped stair, on which we read 'Watch your step' – the same title that accompanies a photograph in Kubrick's photo-essay 'Fun at an Amusement Park' published in *Look* in June 1947 (Mather 2013: 80), and the same writing that appears along the stairs of the Sonata Café in *Eyes Wide Shut* – connects the street with the entrance of the dance hall. Similar, narrow stairs, lit so that the shadow of the bannisters is projected on the walls, are present in the neighbouring buildings where Gloria and Davey live. As indoor spaces become prisons, outdoor spaces become claustrophobic. For example, Davey's dream is a rapid montage, filmed in negative, of long shots of deserted streets, during which the camera tracks forward quickly. Owing to the speed of the camera that advances along straight, narrow

---

4   As discussed, low-angle shots of boxers are typical of photographs and photo-essays of fighters. Moreover, in both *Day of the Fight* and *Killer's Kiss*, there is a shot of a boxer in the corner of the ring framed between the legs of his adversary.

streets, we almost seem to reach the vanishing point: an open outdoor space, the perspective pointing potentially to infinity, becomes finite. Similarly, long shots of deserted alleys and roofs, characterized by low or high-angles, lit low-key, during which the camera either remains still or moves slowly, are adopted to shoot the sequences of Albert's and Davey's respective chases, trapping them in dark dead ends. The city becomes a maze – a metaphor adopted to describe several spaces in Kubrick's oeuvre, and that finds its full realization in *The Shining* – when the two men in fezzes walk back and forth in front of Davey who is waiting for Gloria outside the dance hall. As in *Fear and Desire*, mistakes in spatial and eyeline matches, together with the absence of an establishing shot, do not enable us to understand exactly where the characters are in relation to their environment.

Likewise, details that pertain either to the characters' public or private spheres foreground their confinement in their social role and past life. After the very first sequence shot at the station, there is a montage sequence of posters of Davey's match in different locations in the city, followed by another montage sequence of photographs of his uncle and aunt and their farm pinned to the mirror in which Davey is looking at himself. Similarly, when he first visits Gloria's apartment, details of photographs of her sister and father, a musical box and an old doll are edited with details of her make-up and sexy lingerie: her role of femme fatale fuses with her tormented persona in the effort to earn a living.[5] The duplicity of the characters, their attempts to find identities, which often culminate in physical fights, are not explicitly staged through their voices-over and encounters with their alter egos as in *Fear and Desire*, but through details and frames within frames. Both Davey's and Gloria's images are often reflected in mirrors or in windows, and they look at each other through windows because their apartments face one another and their images are double-framed by the windows. There are even more complex shots, such as when we see Gloria's image behind the two windows reflected in Davey's mirror, or when we see her behind the two windows and in front of her door or mirror.

Just as the source-path-goal schema is embedded in the container schema, the protagonists are imprisoned in their past and social roles: from the point of view of the editing that presents flashbacks that oblige them to return to a past time; from that of the fabula because Davey is condemned to fight, and Gloria to pretend to love a man as her sister did; and from that of stylistics that traps them in the *mise-en-scène*. *Killer's Kiss* shares many of the stylistic features of film noir such as: low-key lighting to conceal 'faces, rooms, urban landscapes – and by extension, motivations and true character';[6] '*mise-en-scène* "designed to unsettle, jar, and disorient the viewer in correlation with the disorientation felt by the noir heroes"'; and '"claustrophobic framing devices" which separate characters from each other, unbalanced composition with shutters and banisters casting oblique shadows or placing grids over faces and furniture' (Cook and

---

[5] According to Mather, discrepancies between private and public are already ambiguously suggested in Kubrick's photo-essay 'America's Man Godfrey' published in *Look* in February 1949 (2013: 69).

[6] Film noir influenced the photography, and harsh lighting was adopted to increase the realism of some situations such as boxing matches and crimes. Kubrick, during his career at *Look*, used such lighting for some staged photographs (Mather 2013: 87–8).

Bernink 1999: 185). As in film noir, the temporalities of *Killer's Kiss* encompass its narrative schema as well as particular sequences, scenes and shots, but unlike other films, Kubrick's noir foregrounds not only the fight for glory and for a woman's love (appropriately named Gloria; 'glory' in Italian), but also the subtler search for an identity.

The Killing (1956) was adapted from Lionel White's caper novel *Clean Break* (1955), and thenceforth all of Kubrick's films were adapted from novels. It was released at the end of the period of American film noir, which, according to several scholars, began in 1941 with *The Maltese Falcon* (John Huston) and ended in 1958 with *Touch of Evil* (Orson Welles; Curti 2007: 46). Many critics, among them Jean-Luc Godard, compared it to *The Asphalt Jungle* (John Huston, 1950), claiming that Huston's heist film was a masterpiece in comparison with Kubrick's (74). The films' narratives are similar, but their respective narrative structure and style could not be more different. In an interview in 1965, Orson Welles claimed that: 'The problem of imitation leaves me indifferent, above all if the imitator succeeds in surpassing the model . . . What I see [in Kubrick] is a talent not possessed by the great directors of the generation immediately preceding his . . . Perhaps this is because his temperament comes closer to mine' (Hughes 2000: 46–7). Kubrick himself claimed that he liked *Clean Break* not so much for its fabula as for its narrative structure: 'Jim Harris and I were the only ones at the time who weren't worried about fragmenting time, overlapping and repeating action that had already been seen, showing things again from another character's point of view. [. . .] It was the handling of time that may have made this more than just a good crime film' (Walker, Taylor and Ruchti 1999: 17).

The stories of *Clean Break* and *The Killing* can be divided into three main parts, as in all heist films: the planning, execution and aftermath of a theft. The film opens by presenting the characters and the reasons they take part in the robbery. Johnny Clay (Sterling Hayden), fresh out of prison after years of planning an armed robbery during the seventh horse race to redeem himself from the mistakes of his criminal career, meets his fiancée Fay (Coleen Gray), who is looking forward to flying away with him after the hold-up. Randy (Ted de Corsia), a policeman, does not know how to pay his gambling debts to the loan shark Leo (Jay Adler). Marvin (Jay C. Flippen), who hosts Johnny and seems to be in love with him, at the racetrack hands the barman Mike (Joe Sawyer) and the cashier George (Elisha Cook Jr.) a note with the time and place of the first meeting, during which they will receive instructions about the robbery. Mike needs money to treat his bedridden wife. George would like to become rich to satisfy his wife Sherry's (Marie Windsor) expensive tastes, hoping in vain to win her heart. When she tells her lover Val (Vince Edwards) that her husband is involved in a theft, he persuades her to spy on the gang during their first meeting, but she is found out. Johnny decides to get the job done anyway, and succeeds in stealing 2 million dollars with the help of the other three men who are in the dark about the hold-up and the gang members' identities. They are: Maurice (Kola Kwariani), who will keep the police busy while Johnny enters the employees' changing room; Nikki (Timothy Carey), who has to shoot at Red Lightning, the favourite during the Landsdowne Stakes, and who is finally shot to death; and Joe Piano (Tito Vuolo), who rents Johnny a room to first hide the gun used during the robbery and then the loot. When the gang members meet after the robbery and are waiting for Johnny, they are surprised by Val and one of his accomplices; George shoots first and the meeting ends up in slaughter. The sole survivor, George, reaches home and kills Sherry. At the airport, the suitcase in which Johnny put the loot accidentally falls from a baggage truck and all the money flies away. The film ends with two policemen in plainclothes approaching Johnny.

The story plays out over three days: Saturday, when the gang meets for the first time (Table 2.2); Tuesday, when Johnny meets Maurice, Nikki and Joe Piano; and the following Saturday, the day of the hold-up (Table 2.3). Both the first and the last day are mainly narrated through enacted internal flashbacks, usually of simultaneity – the only exception being the external analepsis, during which Randy meets Leo.

The order is further complicated by recounted flashbacks and characters' hypotheses about the future that are introduced through dialogue and the third-person voice-over (Art Gilmore). During both Saturdays, whereas enacted and recounted flashbacks increase curiosity, characters' assumptions about their futures build tension (Table 2.2 and 2.3). This play between curiosity and suspense at the macro level of the narrative mirrors that at the stylistic micro level of the back-and-forth movements of the camera and characters.

When Harris and Kubrick held a preview of the film, many spectators complained about the film's non-linearity and Bill Schifrin, Hayden's agent, claimed that the cut-up format made nonsense of the star's performance. Harris and Kubrick, afraid of a lawsuit, recut the film in a linear format, but unsatisfied with the re-editing they delivered the film to United Artists the way they had played it at the preview (Hughes 2000: 39; LoBrutto 1997: 123). The non-linearity was unusual at that time, having been previously used by only a few directors – e.g. Orson Welles in *Citizen Kane* and Akira Kurosawa in *Rashomon* (1950). Kubrick had to choose between fragmenting and repeating either the time or the space. American film pioneer Edwin Stanton Porter helped to develop classical continuity editing, and in his *Life of an American Fireman* (1903) first repeated the time without fragmenting the space, then recut the short not to repeat the time but to fragment the space.[7] Kubrick's choice of fragmenting and repeating the time must have seemed at the time an anachronistic option compared with the convention in classical editing, whereas since the release of Quentin Tarantino's *Pulp Fiction* (1994), it can be considered a regular practice. According to Stephen Mamber, an important consequence of the temporal strategy of *The Killing* is: 'spatial isolation, although we could as well reverse the equation – the sequences of isolation lead to the temporal overlap. In other words, temporal isolation enforces spatial separation. Also, the spaces are used as isolated fragments.' If time had not been repeated, space would have been more fragmented because the narrative structure should have been constituted by cross-cutting between actions occurring in the same time but in different spaces. Kubrick's choice underlines each character's role and goal rather than cooperation among them for the achievement of a common purpose.

---

[7]   For a discussion of this film, see *The Story of Film*, Disc I (Mark Cousin, 2011).

Table 2.2 The narrative schema of the first Saturday of *The Killing* – the day of the first meeting. When the episodes take place (bold, first line), the characters involved in the sequences (subsequent lines in capital letters), and a brief title of the episodes (subsequent lines in bold).

The last Saturday of September	2.45 p.m.	3.45	6.30	7	7.15		8		
MARVIN, MIKE, GEORGE – **Hand-written note**									
		x							
RANDY, LEO – **Randy and Leo**									
	x								
JOHNNY, FAY, MARVIN – **Fay and Johnny**									
				x					
MIKE, HIS WIFE – **Mike and his wife**									
			x						
GEORGE, SHERRY – **George and Sherry**									
					x				
VAL, SHERRY –**Val and Sherry**									
						x	x		
JOHNNY, MARVIN, MIKE, RANDY, GEORGE, SHERRY – **First meeting**									
							x		
RANDY, MIKE, GEORGE, MARVIN, VAL, VAL'S FRIEND – **First meeting**									
								x	
SHERRY, JOHNNY – **First meeting**									
								x	
SHERRY, GEORGE – **George and Sherry**									
									x

Camera movement, *mise-en-scène* and repetition highlight either different characters' sources and paths or their common goal, the loop. When the camera pans or tracks in one direction, it underlines their movements from one point to another, evoking each character's source and path and their common goal; whereas repetition, on the one hand, helps us to link each character's actions in a coherent whole, or on the other, it underlines the different ways in which they seek to achieve their purpose.

Many scholars have discussed this film's tracking shots because Kubrick used open walls in several interiors to follow a character from room to room without interrupting a camera movement, and this technique has influenced many directors (LoBrutto 1997: 118). Roberto Curti claims that the numerous tracks right with the characters

Table 2.3 The narrative schema of the second Saturday of *The Killing* – the day of the hold-up. When the episodes take place (bold, first line), the characters involved in the sequences (subsequent lines in capital letters), and a brief title of the episodes (subsequent lines in bold).

Saturday	5 a.m.	7	7.30	8.15	8.45	9.20	11.15	11.29	11.40	12.10 p.m.	12.30	Between races	2.15	2.30	3.32	Beginning of the 7th race	During the 7th race	4.23	4.24	6.25	7	7.15	7.29	7.39	Before 9
GEORGE, SHERRY – George and Sherry			x																						
RED LIGHTNING – Red Lightning			x																						
JOHNNY, MARVIN – Marvin's declaration of love				x																					
JOHNNY, JOE PIANO – Johnny at the airport and with the gun				x	x	x																			
MIKE – Mike's role							x	x	x																
MARVIN – Marvin at the track										x	x														
RANDY – Randy's role												x													
MAURICE – Maurice's role														x	x	x									
NIKKI – Nikki's role									x		x			x	x	x	x	x	x						

Scene										
JOHNNY – Johnny and the bag		x								
JOHNNY – The robbery			x	x	x	x	x x			
RANDY, MARVIN, GEORGE, MIKE – The final meeting							x			
RANDY – Flashback										
RANDY, MARVIN, GEORGE, MIKE, VAL, ANOTHER MAN – The slaughter							x x	x		
JOHNNY – Johnny at Joe Piano's							x			
JOHNNY – George and Johnny								x		
JOHNNY – Johnny and the suitcase									x	
GEORGE, SHERRY – George and Sherry									x	
JOHNNY, FAY – At the airport										x

enclose them in a two-dimensional space and, thanks to their direction, which follows the western way of writing, they underline coordination and rationality (2007: 87–8). Similarly, Thomas Allen Nelson claims that at the beginning the camera moves from left to right, whereas after the robbery it tracks in the opposite direction: 'indicating that escape out of the closed structure of the plan and its inevitable consequences will take a right-to-left course' (2000: 36–7). Panning and tracking right and left are the most frequently used camera movements in the film,[8] but movements to right and left are equally distributed throughout. For example, when Mike enters the employees' changing room, he walks from right to left and the camera tracks with him, and when George exits he walks from left to right and the camera accompanies him. Later, when Johnny enters the same room he walks to the left and the camera tracks with him, and when he leaves he walks to the right and the camera accompanies him. It is often the panning or tracking right followed by panning or tracking left, or vice versa, that encloses characters in an indoor space, and, thanks to deep-focus and characters who occupy different planes, places do not seem two-dimensional – e.g. gang members are on different planes during the first meeting at Marvin's.

Chaos is paradoxically first introduced by the repetition of tracking or pans left and right. Significantly, these movements are first adopted after Sherry interrupts the gang members' meeting: outside Marvin's, the camera pans left until Mike, George and Randy leave by car, then it quickly pans right until Marvin is in-frame and tracks right with him until Val and his friend appear in their car. At George's apartment, after Sherry has been found eavesdropping outside Marvin's, the camera first tracks left with George, but then when he walks left the camera tracks right and vice versa, emphasizing his bewilderment and growing jealousy.

Another interesting feature of the narration is that the first day is a *mise-en-abîme* of the last – not unlike the Christmas party and the orgy in *Eyes Wide Shut*: spaces and characters are the same. Moreover, the two days are narrated through the same techniques, although during the robbery at the racetrack, the narration is complicated by the co-presence of more than one character in the same space-time. The first day seems to accustom the audience to the complexity of the narration of the last day. These symmetries are echoed by repetitions among scenes and shots, and will dominate the narrative structure of other Kubrick films – *A Clockwork Orange*, *Barry Lyndon* and *Eyes Wide Shut* (Pezzotta 2013: 56–71).

To understand the complexity of the narration, spectators are assisted by the third-person voice-over, characters' dialogue and repetitions – the latter are another of Kubrick's stylistic trademarks that often create a play of cross-references among scenes and shots, paradoxically introducing chaos (Pezzotta 2013: 71–84). Shots set at the racetrack that show horses before or during a race first appear during the title sequence, and are repeated throughout the robbery sequence, highlighting once more the

---

[8] Of camera movements, 20 per cent pan left, 22 per cent pan right, 13 per cent track left, 14 per cent track right, 14 per cent track out or backward to precede, 8 per cent track in or forward to follow, 5 per cent tilt up and 5 per cent tilt down.

similarities between the first and last day of the story. During the hold-up, these shots and comments hailing from loudspeakers are edited before or after a gang member is shown or there is cross-cutting. The other repetitions, mainly of movements of the camera and characters, help spectators to link different actions that occur in the same place but at different times. For example, Johnny goes three times to Joe Piano's. During the first visit, the camera tracks backward to precede Johnny and Joe, and Johnny alone the second time, while the third time, before the track, the protagonist is shown trying to open the wrong door, introducing a chaotic element, a variation in the repeated pattern. In all the other cases, during which the movements of the camera and characters are repeated, actions are performed by different characters, underlining the extent to which perfect coordination of their actions is essential for the success of the robbery. When Johnny enters the bus station, the camera tracks backward to precede him until the locker where he puts the flower box with the gun away, then it tracks forward to follow him when he leaves. The same camera movements are repeated when Mike goes into the bus station to take the box from the cabinet and exits (cf. Curti 2007: 85–6).[9]

The disruption of the time schedule subtly surfaces in these scenes in the bus station: the big clock above the main entrance has neither hands nor numbers (Figure 2.8).

The gang members try in vain to manipulate time to their advantage, but the clock is ticking for Sherry and Val, too, and the unscheduled rhythm of chance is ready to overwhelm their plans. Moreover, the narrator cunningly makes two mistakes. Before Marvin's declaration of love, the voice-over claims, 'At seven o'clock that morning

Figure 2.8 *The Killing* (Stanley Kubrick, 1956). In the bus station, the big clock has neither hands nor numbers.

---

[9]   See Curti (2007: 93) for other examples.

Johnny Clay began what might be the last day of his life,' and when Marvin asks Johnny what time it is, he replies: 'It's early yet. Only seven.' But in the subsequent scene, the narrator claims: 'It was exactly 7 a.m. when he got to the airport.' When the gang members wait for Johnny at Marvin's, George, referring to the protagonist, claims: 'He's supposed to be here at seven.' Whereas when the leader draws up outside Marvin's building, the narrator explains: 'Johnny arrived at the meeting place at 7.29, still 15 minutes late.' The detachment of this disembodied narrator, echoing *The March of Time* technique (Walker, Taylor and Ruchti 1999: 54), on the one hand, assures the spectators of his authority and the indisputability of his statements, and on the other, through clear mistakes, introduces chaos. 'A central theme of *The Killing* and Kubrick's work as a whole is the fallibility of the individual' (Falsetto 2001: 5); 'By endowing this narrator with human fallibility, the film acknowledges the limits of human knowledge' (97).

2.4.2 Different diegetic times: *Paths of Glory* (1957) and a virtuoso style, *Spartacus* (1960) and massive configurations

The narrative schema of *Paths of Glory*, adapted from Humphrey Cobb's 1935 novel of the same name, is, like those of all the director's subsequent films, simple and it resembles that of *Killer's Kiss* without the container schema. Indeed, it presents two source-path-goal schemas that succeed one another, and ends with a climax preceded and announced by a less suspenseful climax. During the First World War, French General George Broulard (Adolphe Menjou) persuades General Paul Mireau (George Macready) to command his division to attack a well-defended German position called the 'Anthill', offering him a promotion in return. Colonel Dax (Kirk Douglas), who is in charge of the 701st Regiment, tries in vain to protest against the suicidal mission, but is forced to organize it. Lt. Roget (Wayne Morris), Cpl. Philippe Paris (Ralph Meeker) and Pvt. Lejeune (Kem Dibbs) are sent on a scouting mission during the night: Roget, drunk and afraid, throws a grenade, killing Lejeune. Paris accuses him, but Roget, being a higher-ranking officer, feels safe. At dawn, the attack begins and ends in slaughter: one of the three companies does not even succeed in leaving the trenches because the enemy fire is too heavy, and Mireau, supervising the mission from a safe dugout, orders his artillery to open fire on them to force them to advance, but the artillery commander refuses to obey. Mireau decides to court martial a great quantity of the survivors for cowardice, but Broulard contests his decision, and they agree to prosecute one soldier from each of the three companies. The commanding officers of the companies are asked to choose a man: Paris is cowardly chosen by Roget who wants to get rid of him; Pvt. Maurice Ferol (Timothy Carey) is selected because he is considered a 'social undesirable'; and Pvt. Pierre Arnaud (Joe Turkel) is picked at random. The process, during which Dax unsuccessfully tries to defend his soldiers, is a farce and the men are executed.

Each of the two main climaxes – the attack against the 'Anthill' in the first schema and the execution in the second, is preceded by a less suspenseful climax – the scouting mission and the court martial, respectively. These four climaxes are characterized by temporalities that seem endlessly prolonged as if to freeze suspense, trapping characters in the spaces they inhabit and in their wretched destinies. Climaxes are accompanied by sequences, during which rhythm is almost cancelled in timeless and directionless spaces, appearing as a stylistic evolution of the forest of *Fear and Desire*. These scenes alternate with suspenseful dialogue sequences shot in interior spaces, during which either decisions are made or power is used to determine the soldiers' fate. During these scenes, the shot-reverse-shot technique alternates with long takes either enriched with convoluted, complex movements of the camera and characters when power is used, or dominated by tracks right and left and characters who move along the same plane when a choice is made.

For example, three sequences take place in the same lavish room of a French château: when Broulard persuades Mireau to send his regiment in a suicidal attack; when they call Dax to bargain for how many soldiers will be court martialled; and when Mireau is accused of having ordered his artillery to open fire against his regiment and, when he leaves the room, Broulard offers his job to an outraged Dax who refuses. During the first sequence, the camera pans right with Mireau who approaches the door to welcome Broulard, and in the next shot the camera pans left with them until they sit down, then slowly tracks backward. There follows a shot-reverse-shot between them and, when they stand up, in a long take the camera tracks and pans to accompany them. Another shot-reverse-shot is followed by the last two shots, during which the movements of characters and camera become more and more complicated – from simple pans and tracks right and left to a camera that follows or precedes characters who walk around tables, chairs and a sofa – mimicking the way in which Mireau's flattery and corruption find fertile ground.[10] In the next sequence, set in the same room, Dax joins Broulard and Mireau. Their discussion closes with a shot in which Dax is in background centre, and Mireau and Broulard in foreground left and right respectively. This composition is repeated when Dax leaves the room: a long take in deep-focus ends when Mireau and Broulard are in foreground right and left, respectively, and Dax, who is speaking with another soldier on a staircase, is in the middle background. The choice to not frame him alone seems to announce his future behaviour: he will be the defence attorney, doing his best to fight the system and its madness from within, following its rules; he will not be a hero like Spartacus, who understands that fighting against the system means overturning it, together with its rulers and rules. After the execution, in the last sequence shot in this room, when Dax and Broulard remain alone, and the latter tries in vain to corrupt the former, the characters walk and the camera follows them, mainly via pans and tracks right and left, through less virtuoso movements than those that had previously followed the two generals: Broulard's manoeuvring does not succeed in circumventing Dax's loyalty. These sequences are dominated by a rhythm of suspense created by characters' dialogue, and increased by complex camera movements that hunt down characters in their ceaseless promenade around the room of power.

[10] Cf. Coëgnarts (2017: 66–7) for another interpretation of this scene.

On the other hand, in other scenes the growing tension is staged through a dispute, as it were, between camera movement and *mise-en-scène*. For example, when Mireau visits the trenches, he twice enters Dax's dugout, and shot-reverse-shot between them alternate with long takes, during which they move around the room, and the camera strives to keep both of them in-frame: their difference does not allow them to share the same frame, even if they find themselves in a cramped, underground dugout. Similarly, after the scouting mission, when Paris joins Roget who is writing the report in his dugout the scene consists of two long takes. While they are in the frame together, there is always a pole or lamp between them and, when Dax enters, he is in-frame among them.

The rhythm freezes during the climaxes as if to endlessly extend the agony. When the three men sentenced to death walk towards the poles to which they will be tied for the execution, tracks backward to precede them alternate with point of view shots of the other soldiers, who are aligned along two opposing rows, while the camera tracks forward. This alternation of forward and backward movements, together with the decision to show us the place of the execution almost at the end of the men's walk, prolongs this moment as if to make us feel their experience of time. During the process, Ferol, Arnaud and Paris are interrogated separately by Maj. Saint-Auban (Richard Anderson) and Dax, but the *mise-en-scène* and the pressing pace of the prosecutor's questions and sentences are the same: shots of the accused, the defence counsel, the president of the court martial and the prosecutor alternate, and the camera almost exclusively moves when the latter is in-frame, panning right and left with him, highlighting the extent to which he is in control of the situation. Suspense is frozen by repetitions that foreshadow the obvious outcome of the process. During the closing statement, both Dax and Saint-Auban move back and forth and the camera accompanies them, but whereas the former is framed behind the court and in front of the accused, the latter is in front of the court: once more, Dax is the link between the soldiers of his regiment and the generals, but remains trapped between them, unable to free himself from the constraints of power (Figures 2.9 and 2.10).

The approach to the 'Anthill' is also endless. At the beginning of the scouting mission, the camera remains still or tracks or pans left with Roget, Paris and Lejeune. These shots are divided by fades in and out, and alternate with point of view shots of the 'Anthill'. The enemy position always appears far away, no matter how the characters strive to advance. This sequence is a *mise-en-abîme* of the attack in which there are high-angle shots of the soldiers in which the camera either remains still or pans left with them, alternating with level shots of Dax, during which the handheld camera tracks to precede or follow him, or tracks or pans left with him, and with level shots of corpses or dying soldiers. The camera acts at moments like a soldier among soldiers, marching, as it were, side by side with Dax – not unlike in *Full Metal Jacket* when American soldiers advance in the enemy territory – or like a powerless spectator of the massacre, while Dax appears once more as a naive optimist encouraging his men.

Unlike the place of the execution and the 'Anthill', the trenches are a tortuous, underground maze of which we are never granted a high-angle or an establishing shot, and in which both the camera and characters can only move back and forth. The first

Figure 2.9 *Paths of Glory* (Stanley Kubrick, 1957). Saint-Auban (Richard Anderson) in front of the court martial.

Figure 2.10 Dax (Kirk Douglas) behind the court.

time we see the characters is during Mireau's visit: in a long take the camera tracks backward to precede him, and stops three times when he repeats the same question to three different soldiers – 'Hello there, soldier. Ready to kill more Germans?', adding: 'Working over your rifle, I see. That's the way. It's a soldier's best friend. You be good to it, and it'll always be good to you.' Similar sentences are pronounced by Sgt. Hartman (R. Lee Ermey) in *Full Metal Jacket*. In *Paths of Glory*, the third soldier smiles and absent-mindedly looks nowhere while his companion speaks about 'shell-shock' – anticipating Pyle's (Vincent D'Onofrio) madness in the Vietnam War film, and evoking Sidney's insanity in *Fear and Desire*. Mireau repeats the same nonsense sentence, thereby fuelling the insanity.

Paths of Glory does not end with the suspenseful sequence, during which Broulard asks Dax to substitute for Mireau, closing the narration where it had begun, in the room in the château, but in a bare room where soldiers listen to a weeping German girl (Christiane Kubrick) who is obliged to sing in front of them. Shots of soldiers alternate with those of the young woman, and the distance between them and the camera is progressively reduced from long shots to medium close-ups. French and German, executioners and victims, are all equal when the rhythm of events and rules is suspended. This last scene was added when shooting had already begun. According to the original screenplay, the film should have ended with the soldiers' execution (Daniels 2015: 96), a bitter epilogue in which Dax's efforts would have appeared completely worthless, whereas in the film his men share compassion towards humankind, a sour victory that mitigates his defeat.

Spartacus features a protagonist who, unlike Dax, does not fight the system from within, but rebels against it. We are certain of his integrity and heroism from the first moment he appears in-frame and the third-person voice-over introduces him:

> In the last century before the birth of a new faith called Christianity [...] the Republic lay fatally stricken with a disease called human slavery [...] A proud, rebellious son who was sold to living death in the mines of Libya before his thirteenth birthday. There, under whip and chain and sun, he lived out his youth and his young manhood dreaming the death of slavery two-thousand years before it finally would die.

He is the only revolutionary in Kubrick's oeuvre who does not negotiate with the system. Kubrick did not choose a story through which he would have reneged on one of the main themes of his *corpus*. Kirk Douglas, star and executive producer, asked him to substitute the filmmaker Anthony Mann after shooting for less than three weeks (LoBrutto 1997: 171–2), and in his memoir of the film, Douglas emphasizes that Kubrick used to omit *Spartacus* from his curriculum, stating that the film lacked a good story (Douglas 2013: 207). Moreover, Kubrick lacked the control he had with previous films because he had to deal with international stars such as Douglas, Charles Laughton, Lawrence Olivier and Peter Ustinov (Radford 2015: 100–1). But Kubrick's lack of control over *Spartacus* was mainly due to the peculiar sociopolitical period of its production and release, and to its subject. The production and post-production of the film was controversial, as well as the various interpretations of Spartacus that succeeded and countered each other since the first century BCE.

Spartacus led the Third Servile War which took place in Italy and almost overthrew the Roman Republic – 73–71 BCE, following the first two Servile Wars which took place in Sicily in 135–2 BCE and 102–98 BCE, respectively. There are several sources concerning the Gladiator War dating from the first century BCE to the fifth century CE – the end of the Roman Empire – which can be divided roughly into two groups. On the one hand, some authors express a positive judgement of Spartacus regarding his bravery and military acumen – e.g. Varro Reatinus, Sallust, Diodorus Siculus, Pliny the Elder and Plutarch (often admitted by the negative criticism, too), as well as his virtue and worthiness – while on the other, the great majority of writers saw the gladiator as a deserter, an outlaw. Following this latter judgement, during the Civil Wars – from the first century BCE to the fourth century CE – Spartacus became the embodiment of the menace and, finally, subversion of the oligarchic ideology of the Roman Republic and during the Roman Empire, through the emphasis placed on his barbarian origins and slave status, he became the symbol of all the civil wars and those against enemy populations that had characterized the final era of the Roman Republic. Meanwhile, the ancient myth of Spartacus developed from positive criticism of his rebellion, interpreted as an insurrection against the moral unfairness with which slaves were treated, and continued to animate historiography and literature (Dogliani 1997: 10–14). In the second half of the nineteenth century, the socialist movement transformed the ancient myth of Spartacus into a new, 'strong ideological myth', according to which the gladiator became the embodiment of the proletarian revolt. In particular, Marx's enthusiastic judgement was expressed before the American Civil War (1861–5), when the American crisis surrounding slavery was exacerbated (32–4).[11] During the same period, Mommsen, in his *History of Rome* (three volumes published, respectively, in 1854, 1855 and 1856), addressed the theme of slavery in the Roman Republic, both breaking with the indifference towards and removal of traditional historiography, and directly referring to American slavery, creating a new, 'weak myth' of Spartacus (41). According to both, the 'strong ideological' and the 'weak' myth, the brave gladiator became the symbol of the release and redemption of all those who are exploited.

Thanks to Kubrick's film, Spartacus became the emblem of freedom and self-determination. The film was adapted from Howard Fast's *Spartacus* (1951), a novel in which the protagonist is physically and mentally strong, brave and resolute, and places the other slaves' life, dignity and value above his own life, and Dalton Trumbo's script adapted these heroic features. Both Fast and Trumbo were blacklisted during the McCarthy era and denied employment because they were accused of being communist or communist sympathizers. The former had to self-publish the novel in the United States, after serving his sentence, because he refused to name those who contributed to a fund for a home for orphans of American veterans of the Spanish Civil War. The latter,

---

[11] In 1918, Lenin underlined the link between the slaves' rebellion and the socioeconomic structure of a Roman Republic built on slavery. Whereas in 1933, Stalin went as far as to suggest that the slaves' revolt had been crucial to the end of the ancient productive system based mainly on slavery in agriculture (Dogliani 1997: 33–4).

one of the 'Hollywood Ten' who refused to answer questions before the House Un-American Activities Committee about their alleged involvement with the Communist Party, had to work secretly and adopt a pseudonym while writing the screenplay. During shooting, Kubrick read other sources about the slaves' revolt: he cited Sallust and Plutarch in an interview and Arthur Koestler's *The Gladiators* (1949; Radford 2015: 105). In Koestler's novel, Spartacus is a man of many facets who cannot be called a hero: he is not a great speaker and is often passive, waiting for others' suggestions or for events to unfold, and he shares his leading role with another slave, Crixus, with whom he is often in disagreement. When the first rough cut of *Spartacus* was screened in August 1959, Trumbo wrote a detailed analysis of it, the 'Report on Spartacus', in which he identified a 'small' and a 'large' protagonist: basically, the former, introduced by Kubrick, was mainly adapted from Koestler's novel; whereas the latter was adapted by Trumbo from Fast's book. According to Trumbo, for the sake of the film's coherence, these two interpretations of Spartacus could not coexist, and the writer was recalled to work on the screenplay in June–July 1959 (105–6). It could be hypothesized that Trumbo fought for a 'large' Spartacus not only for narrative reasons, but also to evoke the myth of a man who challenged the establishment in the name of freedom. With Douglas' and Kubrick's support, other battle scenes were shot that should have emphasized the greatness of Spartacus' military talent and his attempt to overthrow Rome (Douglas 2013: 170). But after the first press screening in July 1960, the distribution company, Universal, entitled to decide the final edit, and had accepted Trumbo's name in the titles, was concerned about the film's political message, and made 42 cuts without Douglas' or Kubrick's approval. The censors were not only concerned with sex, violence and language, but above all with the 'large' Spartacus, and the suggestion that his uprising almost overthrew the Roman Republic (191–3). While on screen the final Spartacus was not as 'large' as he should have been, in the sociopolitical context in which the film was adapted, he became once more the symbol of freedom because Trumbo received public screen credit, while the Hollywood blacklist began to lose influence.[12]

Spartacus is a source-path-goal schema in which three main themes are intertwined: slavery, love and the political warfare inside the Roman Senate for the conquest of power. The slave Spartacus (Kirk Douglas) is sold to Batiatus (Peter Ustinov), who owns a gladiatorial school in Capua. There he falls in love with the slave Varinia (Jean Simmons). When Crassus (Lawrence Olivier), his wife Helena (Nina Foch), his sister Claudia (Joanna Barnes) and her fiancé Glabrus (John Dall) visit the school, they pay to see two fights to the death. Whereas the first ends with the death of one of the two gladiators, during the second fight Draba (Woody Strode), rather than killing a disarmed Spartacus, throws his trident against the spectators and, as Draba hangs on the guests' stage, he is beaten to death. Moved by the inhumanity with which slaves are treated and, in particular, by his friend's sacrifice and the sight of Varinia who, sold to Crassus, leaves the school, Spartacus first kills the gladiators' trainer Marcellus (Charles McGrow) and then escapes from Batiatus' mansion with all the other slaves. They free

[12] Before *Spartacus*, but also in 1960, Trumbo was given screen credit for *Exodus* (Otto Preminger).

more and more slaves who join them. Meanwhile, Varinia and Antoninus (Tony Curtis), a singer who has run away from Crassus' mansion and becomes Spartacus' right-hand man, join them, too, and an army is formed whose aim is to march to Brundusium where, using the Cilician pirates' ships, they will reach their country. The Roman Senate first undervalues the slave army, and the senator Gracchus (Charles Laughton) sends Glabrus against them with a few legions but he is defeated. However, Gracchus' manoeuvre has another purpose. During Glabrus' absence (he is Crassus' brother-in-law), his political role is undertaken by Gracchus' protégé Caesar (John Gavin). This strategy proves to be self-defeating because Gracchus does not take into account Caesar's loyalty to Rome and its nobility and when he tells him that he paid the pirates to provide the salves with their ships, Caesar takes Crassus' side. Crassus, determined to overcome the slaves' army to defend Rome's invincibility, and secretly moved by his fear and jealousy of the legend of Spartacus and his turbid desire for Varinia and Antoninus, reaches an agreement with the pirates and asks the armies of Lucullus and Pompey to join Roman forces to encircle the enemy. The surviving slaves are crucified, with the exception of Spartacus and Antoninus who have to fight to the death. The winner, Spartacus, is crucified but, before dying, he sees Varinia with their baby.

Both Antoninus and Varinia are Crassus' slaves, but Crassus is not satisfied with merely possessing them, and thinks he is loved by them. He does not use his power and strength to abuse them, but waits in vain for them to be seduced by him. There is a long take that lasts more than two minutes, during which the camera remains still to frame Antoninus in long shot as he is asked by Crassus to wash him in a huge bathtub. The master ambiguously sustains that it is not immoral to eat oysters and snails, although eating snails is unusual whereas eating oysters is customary. The stillness of the camera, on the one hand, coldly frames Crassus' play of seduction without emphasizing it, but on the other, it makes us conscious of being voyeurs, titillating us without satisfying our curiosity. Similarly, the scene during which Varinia, after the defeat of the slaves' army, is in Crassus' mansion, consists of two long takes followed by a shot-reverse-shot between the two of them. During these shots, the camera is involved in a more conventional flirtation, during which, to win Varinia's love, Crassus first offers her wealth and then threatens her baby. Crassus' behaviour departs from the conventionally overt cruelty of the classical Hollywood villain and bears some of the ambiguity of art film.

Each of the main themes is shot in a different style – not unlike in *Dr. Strangelove* where style changes depending upon the location of the action: long takes dominate during love scenes; tracking and panning right and left or tilting up and down, and characters arranged along horizontal lines prevail when there are slaves in-frame and characters in a circle appear when there are hand-to-hand or political conflicts. For example, at the beginning of the film, slaves are shown along the ridge of a mountain in Libya, gathering and carrying rocks. When a slave falls under the weight of the rocks on his shoulders, Spartacus breaks ranks to help him, and when Batiatus arrives to buy slaves, the only character who is not aligned is Spartacus, tied to a rock. Lines not only cross the frame from right to left or from foreground to background or vice versa, but also from up to down and vice versa. In these cases, shots are always set inside the school, and the camera tracks or tilts up or down from underground to ground floor or vice versa. Ranks are broken first by Spartacus, then by Draba and, finally, by all the gladiators who begin their revolt. During the fight to the death, the Romans are on a stage and the gladiators in the arena below. Draba, jumping on the stage, breaks both the circular border of the arena and the up/down dynamic respectively defined by the stage and the arena.[13] This scene seems to announce the sequence during which gladiators begin their revolt inside the school: when they break down all the fences and walk on them, high and level angles alternate to foreground how every border between inside and outside and up and down has been dismantled. The sequence closes with a long take, during which the camera, using a high-angle, long shot and a pan left, shows the freed slaves running up the hill outside the school. At the end of the film, after the defeat of their army, slaves appear crucified in two rows that fringe the Appian Way: lines and borders are re-established.

On the other hand, Romans are shown in rows only twice: when Crassus speaks to them before leaving to fight against the slave army and in the final battle sequence. The first sequence cross-cuts between Crassus' and Spartacus' discourse. In Rome, characters are gathered in three groups: Crassus and some Roman soldiers are on steps; other Roman soldiers are aligned in the square underneath; and Gracchus and other senators are on the steps outside the Senate. The three groups appear in-frame together when the camera is behind Crassus or behind the senators or in front of all, framing the senators on the left, Romans soldiers in the middle and Crassus on the right (Figure 2.11). In some shots, the camera is also placed between senators and Roman soldiers or between the latter and Crassus. The three groups are spatially divided, and the camera positions emphasize this split, except when it is in front of all of them, and the buildings and hills in background seem to enclose them, reinforcing Crassus' idea of a Rome that fights to maintain its territory and glory. On the other hand, when Spartacus speaks to his comrades he is on a hill, but in front of him there are men as far as the eye can see, delimited by the sea on the left and a hill on the right. The camera is either behind Spartacus (Figure 2.12), or between him and his comrades who are often framed in medium shots or medium close-ups. Whereas the camera's distance seems to underline both their individuality and their common dream of freedom, its position seems to foreground that they do not feel connected to Rome, but to the possibilities suggested by the sea.

Before the battle, the armies are in place on two opposing hills. Spartacus' men are divided into two groups: one on horses and the other on foot, and they are framed both in long shots and in plans américains or medium shots. On the other hand, the Roman army is never in-frame alone, and depending on the position of the camera, it appears with the slaves in the background or foreground, unmistakably leading us to share the slaves' point of view. The Romans are divided between Crassus and a few soldiers on horseback, and an impressive deployment of legions in testudo formations. Their synchronized movements increase suspense, and foreshadow the inevitable defeat of the slaves' army. This effect is emphasized by montage and the soldiers' movements that follow the rhythm of the extra-diegetic music, the first time that Kubrick adopts this technique to transform a prelude before violence into an uncanny spectacle.

---

[13] Cf. Coëgnarts (2017: 58) for a discussion of this sequence.

Figure 2.11 *Spartacus* (Stanley Kubrick, 1960). The senators on the left, Roman soldiers in the middle and Crassus (Lawrence Olivier) on the right.

Figure 2.12 The camera is behind Spartacus (Kirk Douglas).

Whereas slaves mainly appear in exterior spaces, Romans are usually framed indoors in their sumptuous mansions, in the thermae or in the Senate. The latter is a semicircle, in which stands the senator who gives a speech or is questioned by the other members, and around which there are benches where the other senators sit. In this political arena, senators fight each other, while in Batiatus' arena gladiators combat hand-to-hand, and inside a circle of Roman soldiers Spartacus and Antoninus have to fight to the death. The circle is used by Romans to construct real and symbolic places where they trap their prey and, as in the case of horizontal and vertical lines, it is broken by slaves only. The circle that the slaves form around Glabrus is broken when he leaves, and they cluster around Spartacus until they raise him up in triumph, and when the gladiators go back to Batiatus' school they oblige two Romans to fight in the arena, while slaves sit on the fence around it, unifying internal and external space. Suspense increases both when lines and circles are broken, but also when circles are formed.

During the main climax, the final battle, the slaves' army is surrounded by Crassus' forces, Lucullus' and Pompey's armies, and paradoxically by the sea that represents their dream of returning to their country.

2.4.3 Interruptions in diegetic time: *Lolita* (1962) and *Dr. Strangelove or: How I Learned to Stop Worrying and Love the Bomb* (1964)

The protagonist of *Lolita* (1962), the middle-aged European Professor of French Literature Humbert Humbert (James Mason), is an anti-hero who seduces, or worse, rapes, the teenager Lolita (Sue Lyon) and, consumed and tortured by his passion, becomes a killer, shooting to death the man, Clare Quilty (Peter Sellers), whom he held responsible for the loss of his lover. The film opens and closes with this murder, Humbert's final revenge. When he enters Quilty's mansion and asks him, 'Are you Quilty?' the former answers, 'No, I'm Spartacus. Have you come to free the slaves or something?' and suggests: 'Let's have a game, a little lovely game of Roman ping-pong like two civilized senators.' This line seems to state the contrast between Spartacus and Humbert, besides subtly implying Kubrick's ironizing the 'large' Spartacus. *Lolita* remains suspended, from the very beginning, between the tragedy and the comedy of a devouring desire: our empathy for Humbert and his passion is intertwined with our cynical view of pathetic behaviour that prevents him from understanding what is happening around him – he himself will admit: 'Queer how I misinterpreted the designation of doom.' Our ambivalent, complex view of Humbert and his knowledge of the events is multiplied by similarly conflicting feelings for Quilty, Lolita, and her mother Charlotte Haze (Shelley Winters). This play between what we and the characters know, especially what we know that the characters cannot or do not want to understand, creates the peculiar temporalities of this tragicomic narration that swings between, on the one hand, the unsatisfied curiosity of knowing unfathomable characters and witnessing an inevitable tragedy and, on the other hand, mockery of the gravitas with which characters interpret their story.

Lolita is a source-path-goal schema embedded in a container schema, the frame that opens and closes the film introducing curiosity. As in *Killer's Kiss*, the protagonist's voice-over shares some information using the past perfect, but whereas in the film noir the frame in which Davey is at the train station is reused at the end of the film when Gloria reaches and leaves with him, in *Lolita* the frame does not suggest that the protagonist's destiny, in which he remains trapped from the very beginning, can be changed. Moreover, as in *Killer's Kiss*, the source-path-goal schema can be roughly divided into two parts and is dominated by love triangles. During the first part, Humbert, moving from Europe, decides to spend the summer at Ramsdale, New Hampshire, where he finds a room for rent at a house belonging to Charlotte Haze. She falls in love with him, whereas he becomes besotted with her daughter Lolita. He agrees to marry the mother so as to have the chance of living with her daughter. The jealous Charlotte finds and reads his secret diary where he confesses his disdain for her and passion for Lolita. Out of her mind, she runs outside, is hit by a car and dies. The love triangle Charlotte–Humbert–Lolita dominates this first part, although the character of Quilty appears or is evoked in several scenes where he seems to titillate both mother and daughter. During the second part, when Humbert and Lolita wander by car and then settle near Beardsley College, Quilty constitutes one of the vortexes of the love triangle Humbert–Lolita–Quilty, although the Professor, unlike the audience, is unable to identify the new Lolita's lover until the end of the film. The apparent simplicity of the narrative structure is complicated by the fact that, as is frequently the case in art cinema, the reasons for the actions of the characters can only be hypothesized – subjective verisimilitude. Moreover, when one character makes fun of another, we laugh with him, sharing his wanton malice, as much as we empathize with Humbert's immoral passion.

The film was adapted from Vladimir Nabokov's novel *Lolita* (1955). The writer was asked by Kubrick to write the screenplay – published with the title *Lolita: A Screenplay* in 1974 – which the director himself subsequently rewrote. It is unclear how far the differences between the novel and film are due to Kubrick's personal interpretation and adaptation, or to the censor. One of the main differences between the two media is the incipit. In the novel, the protagonist is writing his memoirs in prison and relates his life from his birth, dwelling on his first love adventure as a boy, tragically ended with the death of his beloved Annabel Leigh, thus comparing Annabel with Lolita, and cunningly suggesting an extenuating circumstance for his attraction to nymphets: 'Between the age limits of nine and fourteen there occur maidens who, to certain bewitched travellers, twice or many times older than they, reveal their true nature which is not human, but nymphic (that is, demoniac); and these chosen creatures I propose to designate as "nymphets"' (Nakokov 2000: 16). In the film, Lolita is older: a teenager of about 16 years old who, aware of her beauty, seems to exploit her power over Humbert. 'Kubrick re-shaped him as a character consumed by his current love and passion for Lolita, rather than as a character consumed by deviant lusts, emerging from the effects of his past life on his psychological development' (Stuckey 2015: 124). According to Kubrick: 'The mood of the book must be preserved. The surface of gaiety and humour, the … wit of Humbert, the bon mot … [with] flippantly dispatched [dialogue] and the tempo and vitality of comedy' (121). Whether omitting Humbert's past and beginning with Quilty's murder – transforming the story from an erotic confession to a murder mystery (Stam 2005: 230) – raising the age of Lolita and privileging comedy over sexuality were stylistic choices or strategic decisions to meet the Production Code's requirements,[14] rendering the film a tragicomedy. The complexity and subtlety of temporalities is achieved through style, especially through the alternation of long takes and takes in deep-focus shot with a still camera or virtuoso camera movements and shot-reverse-shots.

The last sequence of the film is a cut version of the first, accompanied by extra-diegetic music rather than diegetic dialogue and noise, and the differently positioned edit changes its rhythm: from suspense, curiosity and comedy, to inevitable tragedy. At the beginning of the film, the sequence opens with a long shot of Humbert's car driving in the fog, the camera following it, mimicking a presence that haunts him (not unlike

---

[14] Karyn Stuckey states that the director: 'raised Lolita's age for the reasons having to do with his aesthetic choices regarding the film's genre, narrative structure, and character development, and not to satisfy the censors, as some critics have claimed' (2015: 134). By contrast, Daniel Biltereyst writes: 'Next to choices of casting, most eminently raising the age of the Lolita character […], one strategic decision was to de-emphasise sexuality and to highlight comedy' (2015: 141).

the opening of *The Shining*). In a play of cross-reference, the track forward to follow seems to announce the unknown presence – however, known to other characters and the audience – that pursues Humbert when he decides to travel by car with Lolita. Similarly, when Humbert enters Quilty's mansion for the first time, on his right is visible a painting of a lady with a white wide-brimmed hat (Figure 2.13), the same painting that is present on the first floor (Figure 2.14), behind which Quilty tries to hide before Humbert shoots him. There are three shots in which the camera frames Quilty near the painting until he drags himself behind it, and when Humbert shoots him, he repeatedly shoots at the painting while a zoom-in closes the sequence with a close-up of the lady's face. In the next sequence, when Humbert and the audience are first shown Lolita, she wears a white wide-brimmed hat: the painting becomes a prelude of the love triangle Humbert–Lolita–Quilty. In the first sequence of the film, our lack of certainty regarding Quilty's destiny and our curiosity about his relation to Humbert alternate with comedy, courtesy of Quilty's acting and his nonsense gags that ridicule Humbert's gravitas. On the other hand, at the end of the film it is Humbert's tragedy that dominates: we might feel guilty for having laughed at Humbert with Quilty.

In the second sequence, when Humbert visits Charlotte's to rent a room, it is the Professor who makes fun of the widow and we laugh with him. The sequence consists of long takes, during which the camera accompanies Humbert and Charlotte, passing through walls as in *The Killing*. The camera also remains near the protagonists, never leaving them out of frame. Charlotte keeps speaking and Humbert never interrupts her, but adds sarcastic comments. He also appears trapped in her house thanks to her figure that is often in front of him, blocking his path. When in the widow's bedroom, the Professor seeks to leave, the camera tracks with them towards the door, but Charlotte stands on the threshold in front of him speaking. In-frame with a photograph of her husband, she begins to speak about him, while Humbert nervously touches a little statue with a phallic form, Charlotte commenting, 'These are his ashes', giving rise to the Professor's and our mixture of bewilderment and mockery. When Humbert finally succeeds in exiting the room, he is obliged to walk backwards, stumbling over a painted *separé*. He seems to avoid her body, to be almost disgusted by it. At the dance at Ramsdale High School, when John Farlow (Jerry Stovin), a friend of Charlotte's, asks her to dance with him, she leaves her half-eaten hot dog with Humbert who, repelled, puts it on a table and tries to clean his hands with a napkin. When a car runs over her, and Humbert reaches the place of the accident, her corpse, covered with a cloth, lays on the street near the sidewalk. Humbert neither lifts the sheet to see her corpse, nor stops in front of it while awaiting the ambulance, but with a long step coldly bypasses it. At this moment, we might feel guilty about having empathized and laughed with such an unsympathetic man.

Suspense engendered by the love triangle Lolita–Humbert–Charlotte gives way to eroticism twice, when Humbert and Lolita remain alone and close to each other, although in both cases Charlotte summons Lolita, interrupting their intimacy. The first scene takes place in Humbert's bedroom. Lolita brings him a tray with his breakfast and walks near him as he sits at his desk. He reads her some lines of *Ulalume* by Edgar Allan Poe. The neologism 'ulalume' – from the Latin *ululare*, meaning to howl but also to wail, and *lumen*, light – on the one hand, through its meaning, evokes Humbert's

Figure 2.13 *Lolita* (Stanley Kubrick, 1962). The painting of the woman with the white-brimmed hat.

Figure 2.14 The same painting of Figure 2.13 is upstairs. Both paintings appear in the first sequence of the film.

desire for Lolita that secretly materializes in the words that he writes in his diary, enclosed in the darkness of his drawer, but that would like to be howled in daylight with animal violence and directness; while on the other, there is alliteration between 'ulalume', Lolita and love. It is interesting to note that the letter 'L' frequently occurs in the names of Poe's female characters, such as Annabel Lee, Eulalie, Ligeia and Lenore, and in Nabokov's novel Humbert's first love, who tragically died of typhus, is called Annabel. Following Humbert's reading of these romantic lines, the temptress Lolita takes an egg fried sunny-side up in her fingers to feed the famished Humbert, who eagerly grasps her arm and eats the egg. A cut to Charlotte in the kitchen prevents us from knowing whether the man manages to touch the girl's fingers with his lips, but our attention during these shots focuses on the diegetic present, suspended in this erotic moment. The same occurs, although less poignantly, when Lolita has to leave for summer camp. A long shot of the girl running inside the house is followed by another shot, during which the camera quickly accompanies her upstairs until she embraces Humbert. When the suspense reaches its climax and Lolita exclaims, 'Don't forget me!' temporalities seem to be frozen in erotic suggestions.

During the dance at Ramsdale High School, the love triangle Lolita–Humbert–Charlotte is complicated by the presence of Quilty and a mysterious woman, Vivian Darkbloom (Marianne Stone), who accompanies him, about whom we know nothing and who does not say a single word during the whole film. When Quilty and Vivian dance, Charlotte enters in-frame left, taking Vivian's place, again physically imposing her presence with her body. After having recognized Charlotte, Quilty asks, 'Listen, didn't you have a daughter, didn't you have a daughter with a lovely name? Yeah, what was it now? A lovely, lyrical, lilting name like . . .' – and in describing 'Lolita', he plays with the alliteration of the letter 'l' as Poe's poem *Ulalume* does. In the subsequent sequence, back home mother and daughter begin to speak of Quilty. The triangles Lolita–Humbert–Charlotte, Lolita–Quilty–Charlotte and Humbert–Lolita–Quilty follow and complicate one another.

Before Quilty's murder, Humbert meets Lolita in her new house. Now married and pregnant, Lolita explains that she did not leave him for her actual husband, Richard Shiller (Gary Cockrell), but for Quilty, the only man she has ever loved, and with whom she made a fool of Humbert. As Charlotte, before her death, understands that Humbert never loved her, the Professor during this meeting rereads his past, finding out his true role in Lolita's life, a pawn that she moved as she saw fit to reach her goal. In this scene, suspense ends in tragedy, in a suspension of temporalities in which, much as in classical tragedy, Humbert's passion for Lolita becomes love and sorrow par excellence. In this tragic sequence, I see – together with the incipit of the film that orients our hypothesis to the protagonist's reactions – one of the most powerful arguments against the censor's decision.

At Lolita's house, shot-reverse-shots between her and Humbert often alternate with deep-focus compositions, during which Lolita, Richard and Humbert are in-frame together. In a long take, the camera accompanies Lolita and her stepfather until she is in middle-ground left, Humbert in foreground centre and in background right there is Richard, in the garden and visible through the window. Humbert asks, 'Is that him?' believing Lolita left him for Richard. Whereas when Humbert asks Lolita for the identity of the man he is looking for, there are shot-reverse-shots between her, in-frame alone, and Humbert in-frame in foreground right with Richard in background left. This style underlines, on the one hand, the differing knowledge between Humbert and Lolita and, on the other, links Humbert and Richard and their ignorance about her feelings and past. During this dialogue, Lolita helps Humbert to reinterpret the past, giving us a summary of all the scenes during which Quilty appeared:

Lolita   Do you remember Dr. Zempf? [...] Do you remember the car that used to follow us around? [...] Do you remember mother's old flame at the school dance? [...] Do you remember the guy you talked to at the motel on the way back from camp? He pretended he was part of that police convention. [...] Do you remember the guy who called you at the motel? [...] And yet you still haven't guessed? [...] He was Clare Quilty.

Humbert   Who was Clare Quilty?

Lolita   All of them, of course.

Then she abruptly comments: 'I don't suppose it ever occurred to you that when you moved into our house my whole world didn't revolve around you. I had a crush on him ever since the times that he used to come and visit mother. He wasn't like you and me. He wasn't a normal person. He was a genius.' When she speaks, she is once more framed in a deep-focus composition with Humbert and Richard, linked by their unrequited love for her. Finally, in close-up she makes one of the most pitiful statements about Humbert: 'I guess he was the only guy I was ever really crazy about.' Before the end of this sequence, there is a long take that lasts about a minute and a half, during which Humbert tries in vain to persuade Lolita to run away with him. This is the long climax of his tragedy that, together with the camera's proximity to the protagonists, suspends temporalities in the timeless agony of loneliness.

There are two other scenes during which we empathize with the characters' distrait, which play out in the timeless interior space in which human passions become all-consuming. The day after Humbert and Lolita spend the night at the Enchanted Hunters Hotel, he tells her that her mother died. During the night, we see Humbert lying on a bed in the motel while the camera slowly tracks towards him; we hear Lolita's desperate and inconsolable off-screen crying. In the next long take, we see her through Humbert's eyes; she is alone on the bed, the camera tracks away, preceding her until she lies down on Humbert's bed close to him.

Humbert   Try to stop crying. Everything is going to be all right.

Lolita   Nothing will ever be all right.

Humbert   I'm sure that we're going to be very happy, you and I.

Lolita   But everything has changed all of a sudden. Everything was so, I don't know, normal. [...] there is no place to go back to.

Humbert seems not to understand Lolita's grief, implying that he will be able to substitute for her mother and, repeating 'we' and 'you and I' in the same sentence, he underlines that only the two of them remain, a selfish notion to emphasize at this peculiar moment. Similarly, when the Professor drives to the hospital in the middle of the night and learns that Lolita was discharged in the evening, he loses his temper. This sequence ends with a long shot of the hospital staff who help Humbert to stand up and reach the exit. The camera tracks forward to follow them but then stops, and Humbert and the nurses advance into the background, projecting long dark shadows onto the floor. Humbert's exhausted, dangling body becomes as ephemeral as a shadow, embodying the tragedy of loss.

In the second part of the film, suspense is usually triggered by the possible outcomes either of the love triangle Humbert–Lolita–Quilty or of the intimate relationship between Humbert and Lolita. In the first case, suspense alternates with comedy, as in the love triangle Lolita–Humbert–Charlotte, whereas in the latter it often ends in eroticism, as in the first part of the film. When Humbert and Lolita arrive at the Enchanted Hunters, the hotel hosts the Ohio Police Convention, and when the couple enter into the hall, Vivian and Quilty are among the guests. Suspense engendered by the love triangle Humbert–Lolita–Quilty and the presence of police officers is mixed with suspense around the first night that Humbert and Lolita spend together in the same room. The Professor leaves the room to let Lolita prepare for the night and, having asked at reception whether a cot is available, he exits onto the patio. There he meets Quilty who, pretending to be a policeman, faking another accent and hiding his face, asks Humbert about Lolita and his wife, making fun of him but in a subtly menacing way. When Humbert returns to his room, the suspense entailed by being denounced as a paedophile by a policeman, and the excitement of spending the night alone with Lolita is counterbalanced by a gag, during which an old bellboy, with the Professor's help, attempts to open the camp bed. Whereas Humbert is anxious not to wake Lolita, the bellboy makes a lot of noise, falling on the bed, then on the floor, until Humbert throws himself on the bed to open it. In the next scene, when Humbert has to lie on the cot, it collapses under his weight. Comedy prevails over suspense, and we almost overlook the thrill of Humbert and Lolita's first night alone. In the morning, when Lolita wakes Humbert, in a long take of them, during which their gestures and dialogue are emphasized by the stationary camera, our suspense progressively gives way to eroticism. While they play with their hands, and Lolita caresses Humbert's unshaven face, they discuss what to do:

Lolita   Why don't we play a game?

Humbert   A game, come on. No, you get on to room service at once.

Lolita   No, really. I learned some real good games in camp. One in particular was fun.

Humbert   Well, why don't you describe this particularly good game?

Lolita   Well, I played it with Charlie.

Humbert   Charlie, who's he?

Lolita   Charlie? He's that guy that you met in the office.

Humbert   You mean that boy? You and he?

Lolita   Yeah. You sure you can't guess what game I'm talking about?

Humbert   I'm not a very good guesser.

Lolita then whispers in Humbert's ear, Humbert replies, 'I don't know what game you played,' and Lolita whispers something else, adding aloud, 'You mean you never played that game when you were a kid?' A close-up of Lolita who moves in front of Humbert and a fade to black close the sequence. This scene does not seem as erotic as those previous when she fed Humbert an egg or jumped upstairs to embrace him, because she is already acting, pretending to be the innocent girl that she no longer is, leading the game, but not so that it leads to passion.

This sequence at the Enchanted Hunters announces what will occur, and the following scenes evoke it in a typically Kubrickian play of cross reference. Quilty, Lolita and Humbert will be again in-frame together, and the former will play other parts, such as Dr. Zempf, the school psychologist. When the latter meets the Professor, there is comedy: from the juxtaposition of simple sentences, some important to the girl's education, others completely useless, but always uttered with the same serious tone, and from Quilty who mimics a German accent:

> She is defiant and rude. Sighs a good deal in the class. [...] Chews gum vehemently. [...] Handles books gracefully. [...] Her voice is pleasant. Giggles rather often and is excitable. [...] A little dreamy. Concentration is poor. [...] Has private jokes of her own. Which no one understands. So they can't enjoy them with her. She either has exceptional control or she has no control at all. We cannot decide which.

Dr. Zempf adds: 'She is suffering from acute repression of the libido, of the natural instincts. We Americans, we are progressively modern. We believe that it is equally important to prepare the pupils for the mutually satisfactory mating and for the successful child rearing.' Dr. Zempf contradicts exactly what we have been shown up until now.

The narrative structure of *Lolita* is simple, but complicated by subjective verisimilitude and evolving temporalities. The behaviour of characters is often contradictory. On the one hand, Humbert is obsessed with Lolita, is jealous about her boyfriends, but is unable to see Quilty; on the other, he is afraid of being accused of being a paedophile, but he does not evince any moral doubts about his relations with his stepdaughter. He shows disdain for Charlotte's body, and coldly climbs over her corpse, although when he marries her, his voice-over confesses that he feels, 'some faint tenderness', even 'a pattern of remorse'. When Charlotte falls in love with Humbert, she decides to remove her daughter from the house, and when she finds out that Humbert is in love with Lolita, she accuses and blames her daughter more than her husband.

Why, at the end, does the cunning Lolita decide to remain with the anonymous, penniless and not particularly handsome or witty Richard, with whom she is not in love? Why does Quilty, a famous playwright, accompanied by the mysterious Vivian and adored by all women, chase Lolita? And who is Vivian? Suspense and curiosity, either arousing from subjective verisimilitude or from the development of intertwined love relations, the differences between the characters and our knowledge of events, alternate for the first time in a Kubrick film, with comedy, sometimes resulting in tragedy or eroticism. Whereas when there is comedy, we often empathize with a character who makes fun of another, when there is tragedy, we empathize with the character who suffers a loss. Not unlike tragedy, eroticism often emerges from suspense about the relationship between Humbert and Lolita. As discussed, Quilty's murder at the beginning of the film, Humbert's voice-over that narrates events using the past perfect, and the long pauses between a fade out and the subsequent fade in that divide the sequences, trap the protagonist in the episodes that have fostered Humbert's devouring passion (Pezzotta 2015).

Dr. Strangelove (1964) is a source-path-goal schema in which different characters' aims do not coincide, much as in *The Killing*. The source is General Jack D. Ripper's (Sterling Hayden) madness that leads him to believe that Russian people, through the fluoridation of water and other liquids and foods, are slowly poisoning and weakening the American people. This obsessive belief, together with his insane hatred for the Russians – uncanny metaphors for the Cold War – result in his criminal decision to order a nuclear attack against the USSR. His aim to destroy the Soviet Union, and Major 'King' Kong's (Slim Pickens) determination to drop a nuclear bomb on a Russian target, at the cost of him and his crew's lives, contrast with the will to avoid a nuclear holocaust shared by the US President Merkin Muffley (Peter Sellers), his staff in the War Room, the Russian Ambassador Alexi de Sadesky (Peter Bull) and Russian Premier Kissoff. The explosion of the bomb dropped by Kong's B-52 automatically triggers, independent of human will, the Doomsday Machine, a web of nuclear bombs buried underground with the power to annihilate all living organisms. Apart from the Russian Premier, nobody is aware of this device, the main purpose of which is to deter an enemy nuclear attack, and whose existence should have been announced in the next few days. When all attempts to avoid the end of the world fail, those present in the War Room agree with and support Dr. Strangelove's (Peter Sellers) plan to save a 'part' of the population in order to repopulate the planet. Ignorance, the lack and difficulty of communication between individuals who cannot or refuse to come out of isolation, together with the narrative schema, the irrevocable countdowns, the relation between diegetic and screening time, create the mix of suspense and humour that characterizes the film.

The narrative schema can be compared to that of *The Killing* because in both films scenes and sequences often occur at the same time but in different places, thus diegetic time roves back and forth in a play of flashbacks of simultaneity. Whereas in *The Killing* the locations that are seen via analepses are often the same or contiguous spaces in which several characters, usually alone, perform distinct tasks, in *Dr. Strangelove* there are only three places that are geographically far and occupied by different groups of characters. In the latter film, spectators no longer have to reorder the scenes in a chronological chain so as to understand the development of the fabula, but follow their succession as it is presented through editing. There is continuous cross-cutting between: the War Room inside the Pentagon where the President, Gen. 'Jack' Turgidson (George C. Scott), Dr. Strangelove, the Russian Ambassador and other American politicians are gathered; Burpelson Air Force Base where there are Ripper, Group Capt. Lionel Mandrake (Peter Sellers) and where two regiments fight, which is a fictional place that houses the Strategic Air Command's 843rd Bomb Wing whose B-52 bombers, armed with hydrogen bombs, are two hours' away from their targets inside the USSR; and Kong's B-52 which flies to its target.[15]

From Figure 2.15, we can draw a couple of conclusions. From the point of view of screening time, none of the three main locations described above is privileged over another: the scenes shot at Burpelson Air Force Base occupy 29 per cent of screening time; those that take place inside or around the B-52, 31 per cent and those shot inside the War Room, 33 per cent. The first location to be introduced is Burpelson Air Force Base, which is also the first to disappear from the cross-cutting, as soon as Mandrake manages to deduce and communicate the recall code; the second is the B-52, which recurs throughout the whole film; and the last is the War Room, which closes the film. These observations partially explain why the sequences shot at Burpelson Air Force Base occupy less representational time than those that take place in the War Room or inside the B-52 (Figure 2.15).

A comparison between diegetic and screening time demonstrates that the former expands to increase suspense, as often happens in action movies, discussed in Chapter 4. Represented time is prolonged a little in the film overall because, whereas the first hour of diegetic time lasts about 19 minutes of screening time, the second hour takes

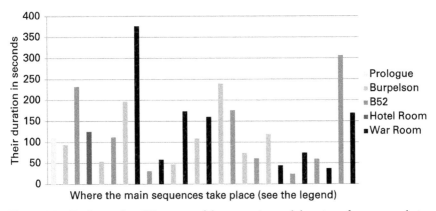

Figure 2.15 *Dr. Strangelove*. Histogram of the succession and duration of sequences shot in different places.

---

[15] Cf. Broderick (2017) for cross-cutting, suspense and cut scenes.

up around 26 minutes of representational time.[16] Similarly, during the first countdown in which politicians predict the number of minutes before the B-52s will be inside Russian radar, diegetic time is expanded: the first 7 minutes of represented time last 1 minute and 46 seconds of representational time, whereas the last 3 minutes take 2 minutes and 15 seconds of screening time.[17] Along with the first countdown, measured in minutes, there are two other countdowns measured in miles, both ending in an explosion: the first advises the audience and Kong's crew how far the Russian missile is that will strike them, the second how far they are from their target. These countdowns are humorously anticipated at the beginning of the film, when Turgidson is in a hotel room with his secretary and fiancée Miss Scott (Tracy Reed), and before leaving claims: 'You just start your countdown, and old Buckie will be back before you can say "blast-off".'

Suspense also arises from the isolation of the three main spaces in which the action takes place, and by the increasing difficulty in communicating by phone or by other means. The first phone conversation takes place inside Burpelson Base between Ripper, who is in his office, and Mandrake, who is in another office. There is cross-cutting between them that allows us to see who is speaking. In the sequence inside the hotel room, Miss Scott talks on the phone with Col. Puntridge, whom she calls Freddy, without making herself heard by Turgidson. We can neither see Freddy nor can we hear him, but Miss Scott first repeats what he says to Turgidson, then repeats to Freddy what Turgidson tells her, softening and polishing the latter's brief and coarse sentences. When Turgidson comes to the phone to speak with Col. Puntridge himself, we see and listen only to the former. Similarly, during all the subsequent phone conversations we see and listen to only one of the two interlocutors. Moreover, when the Russian Ambassador speaks with his Premier, we cannot understand him because he speaks in Russian and there are no English subtitles. And after Ripper's suicide, Mandrake believes he has found the recall call to avoid a nuclear war, but has difficulties getting in touch with the President because all the phones are out of order and he does not have enough coins to use the only functioning public phone. Thus, communications progressively become monologues rather than dialogues, as they occur as verbal exchanges rather than phone conversations. When inside the B-52, the communication code changes, the crew consults the *Top Secret Aircraft Communications Codes* to find out that the new code stands for a nuclear attack against the USSR. After they receive confirmation of the code from Burpelson, all communications are cut off and, when the Russian missile hits them, the autodestruct mechanism does not allow them to receive any further communication.

---

[16] Kong and his aircrew receive confirmation of the message Wing Attack Plan R after 6 minutes and 40 seconds from the beginning of the film, and they are two hours from their targets. During the first phone call with Kissoff – after 25 minutes and 40 seconds of screen time – the President claims that the B-52 bombers will reach their targets in about one hour. Kong's B-52 reaches its target 51 minutes and 35 seconds after the beginning of the film.

[17] B-52 bombers are 25 minutes from detection by Russian radar at 16 minutes and 11 seconds from the beginning of the film; at 18 minutes after 17 minutes and 57 seconds, and are at 15 minutes after 20 minutes and 12 seconds.

Similarly, from his office Ripper gives commands to his soldiers outside Burpelson Base through loudspeakers. While there is cross-cutting between Ripper and his soldiers, only the former is heard, whereas the latter cannot ask questions. When the Base is conquered by another regiment, neither Col. 'Bat' Guano (Keenan Wynn) nor his soldiers are aware of the goal of their mission or of what is going on. Not only is establishing a line of communication difficult, but achieving successful and productive communication is impossible, and the attempts give rise to gags: Ripper is deranged, and Mandrake's attempts to reason with him are completely useless; Turgidson and Alexei are so obsessed with the Cold War that, in a childish play of skirmishes and puns that end in physical fights, they are unable to understand the gravity of the situation, and the Russian Premier, when first called by the President, is playing loud music in the background and is drunk, and the President speaks with him as if he were a child.

The differences between and isolation of the three main settings is also emphasized by the different styles used to shoot the differently located sequences. Among the eight sequences shot at Burpelson Air Force Base, five are shot entirely inside the base, and in the other three there is a cross-cutting between exteriors and interiors. Overall, shot-reverse-shots between Ripper and Mandrake or Mandrake and Guano prevail over shots in which both characters are framed together. These shots echo the cross-cutting that dominates sequences that link the interior with the exterior of the base. First we see Ripper who gives his speech to the soldiers outside from his office. Shots shot inside alternate with cross-cutting between long shots of 'enemy' soldiers and their vehicles approaching the base, and plans américains and medium shots of soldiers watching them through a spyglass, and then shooting at them; finally, cross-cutting alternates Ripper's office with the soldiers fighting outside, but this time using a handheld camera that pans right or left, like a soldier among soldiers, sharing the point of view of the 'enemy' soldiers. Suspense increases not only through cross-cutting between inside and outside, and between the two regiments, and through the increasing rhythm of editing and use of a handheld camera, but also through the growing incommunicability that ends in violence and chaos. American soldiers kill each other, and a deranged Ripper commits suicide: he is shot in a low-angle close-up, with a blank look on his face, heralding the well-known Kubrickian stare, before shooting himself in the bathroom, as Pvt. Pyle (Vincent D'Onofrio) will do in *Full Metal Jacket*. The posters outside the base and in Mandrake's office, 'Peace is our profession', and in the corridor outside Ripper's office, 'Civil defence is your business. See dad! Thanks for thinking of us!', satirize the escalation of violence. It is tempting to jump in the future Kubrick's filmography till Joker's (Matthew Modine) helmet with the written 'Born to kill' and the peace sign.

When the action takes place in the B-52 there is also cross-cutting between the exterior and the interior. Shots inside the bomber alternate with aerial footage, but, in this case, the cross-cutting seems to emphasize how the plane is a completely rogue unit, far from everything – except when a Russian missile hits it. Moreover, unlike at the base, Kong and his crew constitute a compact group working for a common goal. Scenes inside the B-52 mainly consist of an alternation of close-ups and medium shots of the characters, during which they and the camera move little, with details of the instruments often emphasized through zooms. When they receive confirmation of the nuclear attack, Kong gives a speech, during which his voice-off accompanies a montage of shots of his crew, not unlike when Ripper speaks to his soldiers. The same strategy is used when he gives instructions about the target: he reads the content of the survival kit; a crew member explains that they do not have enough fuel to land in a safety zone; and when Kong gives instructions to open the damaged doors to throw the hydrogen bomb. During these sequences, suspense is not only increased through countdowns but also through style. Before and during the collision with the Russian missile, the editing is more rapid and, immediately after the bomber is hit, a handheld camera is adopted to mimic confusion and the stress of crashing. During the last sequence shot inside the bomber, when Kong goes down into the cargo hold to unblock the doors, there is cross-cutting between outside the plane and the lower and upper parts of the B-52. It is only when Kong reaches the hold and straddles one of the bombs that he is no longer able to communicate with his men. He does not make it in time to dismount the bomb, and we finally see him riding it and waving his cowboy hat, enthusiastically sacrificing himself to reach his target, not unlike Ripper who commits suicide for fear of not being able to withstand being tortured to divulge the recall code.

When the action takes place inside the War Room, we are never shown what is outside, nor are we allowed to see from which entrance the Russian Ambassador uses; he simply appears inside the room. We are shown an aerial shot of the Pentagon only at the beginning of the first scene in the War Room. Long shots of the room, in which men sit down around a table, lit by the circle of lights hanging from the ceiling and the semicircle of the three maxi screens leaning along one of the walls, alternate with shot-reverse-shots mainly between the President and Turgidson that appear in-frame alone or with other figures. This rhythm of alternation between long shots and shot-reverse-shots and the placement of characters in a circle is disturbed when Alexei arrives, announcing and explaining what the Doomsday machine is, and Dr. Strangelove takes the floor, and then when the recall code is acknowledged but Turgidson's prayer is interrupted by a phone call from the Russian Premier. Here, discussions between the warmongering Turgidson, motivated by anti-Russian and anti-communist obsessions, and the apparently more balanced American President, are interrupted by news of vital importance, or by the Russian Alexei or the German Strangelove – interestingly both non-Native Americans. The latter is first called into question when the President asks him whether the Americans have a plan like the Doomsday machine: a medium shot of Strangelove, during which the camera quickly tracks backward while he advances on his wheelchair, is followed by a low-angle, long shot as he approaches centre-frame, while in foreground right and left are, respectively, the President and Alexei, representatives of the right and the left wing. Moreover, while Strangelove is approaching the camera, Alexei lowers his right arm, and his right hand is foregrounded and, suddenly the German tries in vain to take his cigarette with his right hand. In this shot, the character who, in the end, reconciles the Russian Ambassador with the American President, is framed between them, and a detail that comes in-frame apparently at random appears to foretell a series of gags based on Strangelove's inability to control his right hand (Figure 2.16).

Figure 2.16 *Dr. Strangelove* (Stanley Kubrick, 1964). Dr. Strangelove (Peter Sellers) is in centre-frame, while in foreground right and left are, respectively, the president (Peter Sellers) and Alexei (Peter Bull), representatives of the right and the left wing.

In the last scenes shot in the War Room, the order shown at the beginning and symbolized by men sat around a round table, is partially restored by men who arise, constituting first two semi-circles around the President and Turgidson, respectively, and then one semi-circle around Strangelove: discussions between Turgidson and the President are restarted only to be silenced by Strangelove's proposal. In this film, recalling *Spartacus* and the orgy scene in *Eyes Wide Shut*, a composition that privileges circularity is mainly used to symbolize power.

When we watch *Dr. Strangelove*, we are subjected to a crescendo of suspense, making hypotheses about future developments, but we often pause to laugh, apparently unconcerned about the destinies of the diegetic humanity. Aristotle claims that what makes us laugh seems to be useful during debates because it overwhelms the opponents' seriousness. Similarly, in *Dr. Strangelove* the gravity of the subject is almost constantly undermined by amusing gags. In his *Poetics*, the Greek philosopher argues that laughing can arise either from language or facts. In the former case, it can originate from homonymy, synonymy, repetition, terms of endearment, distortions created with the voice and other figures of speech. In the latter case, laughing can derive from what is impossible or from what is possible, but unlikely, or from the decision to drop important issues to choose unimportant ones, or from a discourse that does not logically succeed what precedes it, etc.

To discuss what makes us laugh in Kubrick's black comedy, apart from distinguishing between language and facts, I would like to propose a distinction between which narrative and stylistic techniques create and sustain a humorous mood and which give rise to satirical gags that make us laugh. According to Luigi Pirandello, there is humour when we feel or ponder a discrepancy between our real and ideal life, or between our ambitions and desires, and our miseries and weaknesses. This contradiction causes bewilderment between crying and laughing because we would like to laugh, but our laughing is troubled and frustrated. Recalling Aristotle's distinction between what is possible, but improbable, and what is impossible, when we watch *Dr. Strangelove* we can judge the facts impossible or possible, but unlikely or, better, our perspective continually fluctuates between these two hypotheses. When we regard the facts to be impossible, we are more willing to laugh, otherwise, if we judge them possible, however improbable, we are more inclined to cry.

I claim that the sociohistorical context in which we watch the film can influence our view of it. When it was first released, during the Cold War between the USA and the Soviet Union, as well as during the more recent crisis of North Korea and the nuclear menaces of Kim Jong-Un or the war between Russia and Ukraine, spectators may be more inclined to cry because they may regard the diegetic facts as possible, however unlikely. In Kubrick's film, the humorous mood is given more by narrative than by stylistic choices that find us oscillating between different judgements of the diegetic facts. For example, is it possible that a man alone – Ripper – can command a nuclear attack? That the US Army can provide only a handful of soldiers to reach Burpelson Base in time? That these soldiers are completely in the dark about their mission? That the Russian army is unable to find and shoot down Kong's B-52? On the other hand, satirical gags, which make us burst into laughter, forgetting either the forward movement of narration and the increasing suspense, are due to narrative and stylistic techniques. Evoking again Aristotle's classification, in *Dr. Strangelove* we laugh when important outcomes do not prevail, when a discourse does not logically follow from the context from which it arises or when certain figures of speech are adopted. The very cause of the American nuclear attack is laughable: Ripper believes that Russians are poisoning Americans through the fluoridation of water and other substances, he realizes this: 'during the physical act of love. A profound sense of fatigue. A feeling of emptiness. [. . .] A loss of essence.' Illogical conclusions are drawn from unimportant facts and the consequences are crucial for humanity.

Similarly, in the War Room, both Turgidson and Alexei seem less concerned about the imminent nuclear war than about sarcastic anti-Russian and anti-American jokes: the Russian Ambassador refuses a Jamaican cigar so as not to 'support the work of imperialist stooges'; Turgidson accuses the Russian Premier of being a 'degenerate atheist' because of the difficulty of reaching him by phone because he is having fun with a woman, but Turgidson himself does not want to answer the phone when he is with Miss Scott, and answers her when she calls him directly in the War Room; Turgidson accuses Alexei of possessing a camera, the latter blames the former of having planted it on him, and their quarrel ends up in a fight; while Turgidson is so excited and confident about Kong's claim that he can pilot the B-52 so low as to fry 'chickens in a barnyard', without realizing the consequences of his success. And the American President and the Russian Premier quarrel about who is sorrier about what is happening. On board the B-52, Kong, during his brief speech, assures his men that they will receive 'promotions and citations when this is over', 'regardless of your race, colour and creed' – similar words will be pronounced by Sgt. Hartman (R. Lee Ermey) in *Full Metal Jacket*. As soon as the crew is ordered to attack Russia, Kong opens the safe to change his helmet for a stetson, as if he was about to take part in a rodeo rather than a nuclear war, and in the end he rides the bomb waving his hat.

Also laughable are those moments in which Strangelove is unable to control his right hand, which seems to have a life of its own or, better, cannot avoid betraying his Nazi background. In all of these cases, the humorous mood is enriched with satirical gags that, on the one hand, reinforce the mood, but on the other make us laugh, momentarily forgetting the forward drive of the dreadful narrative. When Strangelove's right hand independently rises in a Nazi salute and he attempts to forestall it with his left hand, we no longer feel the passage of time, we simply laugh at the timeless prospect of remembered hubris. As discussed in Chapter 1, emotion markers provoke brief bursts of prototypical emotion that fuel mood. While they are not necessary for the development of narration, they have an essential emotive role in the film. In *Dr. Strangelove*, emotion markers are often stylistic techniques that exaggerate vices, creating what Pirandello calls 'satirical' gags. When in a dialogue or monologue unimportant things prevail over essential issues, or when illogical statements are seriously pronounced, or when a character's defect is magnified, satirical gags interrupt the flow of humour, during which spectators hesitate between laughing and crying and burst into laughter.

2.5 Art cinema narration: Beyond classical diegetic time

As mentioned in Chapter 1, I only briefly come across temporalities in the last six Kubrick films because in art films, temporalities are often foregrounded, and the spectator speculates over whether to adopt a narrative or poetic and aesthetic mode of meaning-making to fill in permanent ellipses, a discussion that I would like to develop in another work.

In his first feature, *Fear and Desire*, Kubrick explicitly stages time, but it is only with *2001: A Space Odyssey* that he succeeds, within the representational time of the film, going beyond diegetic time, suggesting a time 'outside history' that becomes, in the spectator's mind, a reflection on time itself.

The director's last six films are characterized by relatively simple narration. In *A Clockwork Orange*, *Barry Lyndon* and *Eyes Wide Shut*, the narrative structure is symmetrical and the end recalls the beginning, and in all six of Kubrick's last films, narration is divided and ordered into parts, often underlined by title cards or a voice-over – e.g. *2001*, *Barry Lyndon*, *The Shining* and *Full Metal Jacket*. These narrative structures consist of *tableaux vivants* and sequences often separated by explicit, undetermined ellipses, usually strongly marked through cuts. These gaps, which are also due to cinematic techniques other than editing, cannot be adequately filled in by cause-and-effect chains. Moreover, thanks to the style, scenes and shots often evoke one another. This play of cross-reference, on the one hand, reinforces the macro divisions of narration, and on the other, leads spectators along a tortuous, complex path, beyond the requirements of classical rhythm and diegetic time. This apparent confusion, that exposes the inadequacy of causal logic, is symbolized by the image of the maze, the use of a handheld camera or a Steadicam and the sinuous movements of the camera when it moves around characters, enveloping them. The rhythm of suspense that hails the future, the curiosity and surprise that fill in past gaps to facilitate a thorough understanding of the story, is replaced by the complex, multidimensional rhythm of life in which the borders between past, present and future, as well as among different films, no longer exist. Similarly, protagonists no longer walk in a straight line, triumphantly overcoming obstacles to reach their desired goals; in art films, they lack motive and purpose, are lost in a society in which they cannot find their place, and remain alienated, alone, unable to communicate with other characters. Kubrick's protagonists are passive wanderers, at sea in a dreamy atmosphere haunted by an incomprehensible past that they cannot forget, and an obscure future that neither they can nor want to mould. Newtonian time cannot explain the construction of narration and characters that become the core of the audience's hypotheses.

Thanks to these techniques, Kubrick's last six films share the three schemata of art cinema narration – objective and subjective verisimilitude and over narrational commentary. As discussed in Chapter 1, the narration of classical Hollywood films is based on an ontological merger between the temporal and logical succession of events. Art cinema abandons this logic both at the objective level of story development and at the subjective level of character construction. While art cinema enjoyed a heyday in the late 1950s and 1960s, shaped the 'New Hollywood' films of the 1970s (Kubrick's last six films were released between 1968 and 1999), the director can be considered a Hollywood Renaissance figure who, like Robert Altman, Francis Ford Coppola and Martin Scorsese, among others, merged the genre film with art cinema.[18] According to Ruggero Eugeni, Kubrick is one of the greatest modernists of the twentieth century, its 'embodiment and self-conscious epitome: his cinema wants to adopt and summarize the whole modernist project' (2017: 217–23, my translation). 'New Hollywood' directors often 'mixed and shifted stylistic and generic directions' (Jaffe 2008, 13), promoting what Ira Jaffe calls 'hybrid films', i.e. 'odd mixtures', 'inherently subversive, since in mingling genres and styles [they] choose heterogeneity over homogeneity, contamination over purity'. As these films 'embrace incongruity and incidents [...] they verge on disorder and chaos' (6), although they are characterized by a 'surprising unity' (7). Kubrick's films: 'inhabit and deconstruct genres rather than exemplify them' (Hunter 2015: 277). His last six films are hybrids, in which one or more genres are mixed with the features of either 'slow cinema' or musicals, apart from *The Shining*.

---

18 For the schemata, see Bordwell (2001: 205–33). For an analysis of the last six Kubrick films, see Pezzotta (2013).

2.5.1 Slowness

2001, *Barry Lyndon* and *Eyes Wide Shut* share some features of what has been called 'slow cinema'. In slow cinema, for example, Jim Jarmusch's *Stranger than Paradise* (1984) and *Dead Man* (1995), Gus Van Sant's *Elephant* (2003), Béla Tarr's *Werckmeister Harmonies* (2000) and *The Turin Horse* (2011), characters and camera either remain still or move slowly, long takes prevail, during which diegetic time is endlessly prolonged, and long shots prevent spectators from interpreting characters' feelings and reactions, which often cannot even be guessed from dialogue and actions due to their paucity (Jaffe 2014: 3). Together with time, style comes to the fore: 'the formal artistry of slow movies belies their indication of human incapacity, of nothing happening, of time as empty or dead' (14).

In *2001*, the evolution from ape to astronaut to Star-Child is conveyed through a stylistic journey through several techniques of representing diegetic time and, consequently, through various audience expectations. When in long takes either the camera or the characters and objects in-frame do not move or move slowly, or when we do not know whether the camera or the characters and objects in-frame are moving, or when the camera tracks or pans with a ping-pong effect, temporalities are foregrounded, extending and prolonging our experience. During the Star-Gate sequence, and in the sequence shot in the eighteenth-century room, we seem to experience a time beyond time in which the borders between past, present and future merge in the timelessness of the mysteries of the universe. In *Barry Lyndon*, the protagonist remains trapped in an immobile world where the dream of escaping from the rules of time is staged through the illusion of a three-dimensionality given by deep-focus and light effects, tracking with other characters, and destroyed by the zoom, static long takes and a freeze-frame: 'the mobile dialectic, that the film establishes between stillness and motion, interiority and exteriority, decorum and indecency, and [...] portrait and landscape [...] contributes to an understanding of the characters' entrapment within their social milieu and within the aesthetic forms they inhabit' (Pramaggiore 2015: 146). The last time we see Lyndon is in a long shot, during which he enters into a carriage. The shot ends with a freeze-frame that emphasizes the end of his time: 'he becomes a virtual photograph, signifying the immobility of death' (149). Similarly, *The Shining* closes with a photograph in which Jack appears at a 1921 party at the Overlook Hotel that symbolizes the stillness of past and, more generally, history. But this film cannot be defined as 'slow' because it does not share the style of slow cinema, and its rhythm of suspense increases to the end, although it slows down in comparison with more classical examples of the horror genre, owing to the spectator's hesitation between a natural and a supernatural explanation of events. In *The Shining*, the horror genre is mixed with features of the fantastic-marvellous tale and the uncanny (Pezzotta 2013: 128–41). The pre-production notes mention Freud, Bettelheim and Hess, signs that Kubrick: 'was interested in horror on the condition that he could coldly intellectualise it' (Mee 2017: 59). In long takes in *Eyes Wide Shut*, during which the camera remains still, tracks or swirls around the protagonist, he is imprisoned and confused in a world where past, present and future, as well as fantasy and dream become indistinguishable.

In these films, the diegetic present is one step in the forward movement of narrative, as well as a mirror of the temporalities that characterize the diegetic world as a whole. The infinity of spaces and times in *2001*, entrapment in the sociohistorical moment in *Barry Lyndon*, and in a supernatural past that tries to envelop a futureless present in *The Shining*, the impossibility of escaping from fantasy and dream, and that of distinguishing them from reality in *Eyes Wide Shut*. *2001*, *Barry Lyndon* and *Eyes Wide Shut* adheres to the tradition of slow cinema inspired by early de-dramatized European art cinema, which developed the themes of alienation, isolation and ennui.[19]

2.5.2 Musical moments

In Kubrick's last six films, the rhythm of music often conducts narration and style and vice versa, substituting the superstructure of classical Newtonian time with new, more complex rhythms. Montage, but also movements of the camera and characters follow the rhythm of music, and dialogue and voice-over are used more for their aural nature and musicality than for their meanings. Furthermore, music often itself moves the story forward,[20] becoming the 'reason' for the characters' actions – e.g. Alex's visions materialize when he listens to Beethoven's *Ninth Symphony*, and he is inspired to attack his droogs when he hears Rossini's *The Thieving Magpie* coming from an open window. These features prevail in *2001*, *A Clockwork Orange* and *Full Metal Jacket*; however, they were first adopted in the final battle in *Spartacus*. Whereas in *2001*, the rhythm of music, montage and movement is slow, in *A Clockwork Orange* and *Full Metal Jacket* the rhythm is faster and syncopated, linking the action in an increasing rhythm of suspense towards the climax.

A *Clockwork Orange* and *Full Metal Jacket* are hybrid films in which, respectively, the dystopian science fiction and the Vietnam War genres are mixed with the musical genre. In the 1960s non-musical films were released in which 'a staged musical performance', used 'to underline meanings about characters and plot', was 'integrated into the narrative' – for example, Audrey Hepburn's rendition of 'Moon River' in *Breakfast at Tiffany's* (Blake Edwards, 1961), or the Yardbirds' cameo in *Blow-Up* (Michelangelo Antonioni, 1966; Conrich and Tinchnell 2006: 5). In *A Clockwork Orange*, when Alex and his droogs perform violent actions in front of the camera, their dancing follows the rhythm of the music, when the recruits sing and march following the rhythm of their refrains in *Full Metal Jacket*, the narrative and rhythm of suspense is not suspended but continues and increases. Thanks to musical choices – the liveliness of Beethoven's *Ninth Symphony*, Rossini's *The Thieving Magpie* and 'Surfin' Bird' – temporalities are accelerated. In the 'new musicals' of the late 1970s and 1980s, music and dance are 'demarcated from the main narrative, even while realistically arising from it', and represent the possibility of temporarily escaping a diegetic world characterized by difficulties and frustrations – e.g. *Saturday Night Fever* (John Badham,

---

[19] See Ciment (2003) and Pezzotta (2017).
[20] Cf. the use of music in *Barry Lyndon* (Lash 2017)

1977), *Flashdance* (Adrian Lyne, 1983) and *Dirty Dancing* (Emile Ardolino, 1985; Telotte 2006: 49). If the new musicals suggest utopian answers to the sociohistorical contradictions of the diegetic worlds, and performances are confined in places that remain isolated from the rest of the diegetic world (53), in *A Clockwork Orange* and *Full Metal Jacket* staged musical performances become dystopian spectacles that emphasize and increase the diegetic conflicts as well as encompass the entire diegetic worlds. Alex and his droogs enter Mr. Alexander and the Cat Lady's house, and Marines march into Parris Island and in Vietnam, their performances dragging, as it were, the seemingly controlled atmosphere of their societies into chaos and violence.

2.6 Conclusion

Conforming resolutely to the conventions of classical Hollywood style, Kubrick ended up overturning its rules. His silent, stealthy revolution began at the beginning of his career, and can be traced in how he progressively imbued his works with peculiar temporalities which, encompassing narrative structures as well as style, attract the audience's interest in an almost hypnotic way.

Some features of Kubrick's photography paradoxically introduce a play of suspense and curiosity. This rhythm is developed in his photo-essays, foreseeing what will become a Kubrick trademark: the subtle cross-references that encourage hypotheses about a boundless web of stylistic, thematic and narrative echoes. In his first feature, *Fear and Desire*, Kubrick explicitly stages the concept of time, rather than creating a rhythm that implicitly suggests it. From then on, Kubrick always 'trusted' his spectators and, creating encompassing temporalities that embrace narrative and style, rewarded their efforts with a complex physical and cultural experience.

Killer's Kiss, The Killing, Paths of Glory and *Spartacus* are source-path-goal schema works, in which characters remain imprisoned: the rhythm of the narrative schema mirrors that of the *mise-en-scène*, cinematography and editing and vice versa. It is worth noting that András Bálint Kovács regards film noir as a bridge: 'between classical and modern art cinema narration: "it breaks up classical narrative logic while maintaining classical narrative structures"' (Kiss and Willemsen 2017: 46). Whereas art cinema, through objective and subjective verisimilitude, challenges causal and temporal logic to foreground the psychological and philosophical implications of the succession of shots, film noir, overcomplicating the dictum *post hoc ergo propter hoc*, problematizes it (ibid.). Thus, the very genre of film noir offered Kubrick the opportunity to move beyond the classical rhythm enshrined in Hollywood style.

In *Paths of Glory* and *Spartacus*, each space envelops characters in peculiar temporalities. The virtuoso style of the former is substituted in the latter by massive configurations, and Roman might is best seen when its army is deployed in testudo formations whose movements, together with the editing, follow a musical rhythm. This is the first time that Kubrick adopted music to conduct narration, editing, *mise-en-scène* and cinematography, creating a visual and auditory spectacle that became one of the trademarks of his temporalities.

In *Lolita* and *Dr. Strangelove* the director disrupted the represented time of characters and events, momentary halting the suspense and curiosity in moments in which comedy, tragedy and eroticism prevail in the former case, and comic gags come to the fore in the latter, fostering its humorous mood. If in *Lolita* the difference between what the audience and the characters know or cannot know, or what the characters choose not to understand emphasize subjective verisimilitude, in his last six films Kubrick can be fully considered a Hollywood Renaissance director. In particular, creating hybrid films through the mélange of different genres either with slowness or with musical moments, he gave rise to temporalities in which characters and spectators, remain encapsulated either in an expanded time or in a rapid, immersive rhythm of suspense.

3

The play of suspense and eroticism in Adrian Lyne

Connie *We can spend the rest of our lives on that beach, and when we die we can just push out to sea. What do you think?*

Edward *Perfect, sounds perfect.*

Unfaithful (Adrian Lyne, 2002)

Adrian Lyne began his career in the 1970s with two shorts, *The Table* (1973) and *Mr. Smith* (1976). He shot his first two feature films, *Foxes* (1980) and *Flashdance* (1983), followed by two video shorts, *Irene Cara: Flashdance . . . What a Feeling* (1983) and *Michel Sembello: Maniac* (1983), and six feature films, *Nine ½ Weeks* (1986), *Fatal Attraction* (1987), *Jacob's Ladder* (1990), *Indecent Proposal* (1993), *Lolita* (1997) and *Unfaithful* (2002). He worked mainly in the 1980s and 1990s, realizing films about love and passion, often about a character's irresistible desire towards another, almost a hunger that he/she is unable to master, destroying the balance of his/her life, and his/her relations with others and him/herself. His last film, *Unfaithful*, opens with an evocative visual metaphor: a strong wind that drags all along its path. In a montage sequence accompanied by melancholic extra-diegetic music, there is a long shot of the protagonists' countryside villa around which the treetops sway, a boat idles in the lake in front of the house, a pinwheel swirls and a bicycle falls on the moist grass. Fades to black divide these shots, as if the wind was ceaseless. In the next sequence, the protagonist Connie (Diane Lane) is shown in SoHo, New York, unable to walk with her shopping bags against the strength of the wind: she falls against a young bookseller who is carrying a pile of books. Their meeting is unavoidable and violent, as much as the fiery passion that immediately hits them. In an interview enclosed in the DVD, Lane says: 'We go back to the metaphors that Adrian is so good at [. . .] The wind blew over the bicycle [. . .] Oh, wherever you are, you never know when the wind is going to blow over your bicycle because there was no justification built into the plot for her infidelity.' This is what happens in the majority of Lyne's films, in which passion sometimes grows into obsession, rising unexpectedly, inexplicably, and is mainly shown visually, not verbally explained. Rereading Lacan, Massimo Recalcati claims that:

> every love meeting suspends the natural and ordinary flow of time, it digs a hole, a vacuum space, it creates a gap, a discontinuity that we couldn't have predicted [. . .]

Every love is like a party if the party is where the routine is disrupted by the explosion of a forbidden joy.

Recalcati 2019: 26

The charm of a love meeting always implies a mystery. Why him, why her? What does this X-factor, that has lighted my desire, preserve? [...] It looks like fate, but is always the son of chance.

27

[Eroticism] is like a spring wind, a summer rain, an anarchic vital force that is not guided by the compass of impulse. It brings in its wake a luxury that does not know rules. In this context Lacan speaks about an editing of drives that he compares to surrealists' puzzles underlining how much sexual drive is far from the schematic linearity of impulse.

42, my translation

The suspense that precedes and accompanies the birth of this feeling, becomes or alternates with eroticism, and often ends up in the suspense that guides the characters' unavoidable destruction. The play of suspense and eroticism, of temporalities that respectively lead spectators to make hypotheses about the future, and slows down the rhythm of the film to contemplate passionate outbursts, is one of the main features of Lyne's work. His protagonists are imprisoned in their untameable passion, and in the relentless rhythm of their diegetic worlds.

In the following sections, roughly respecting the chronological succession of Lyne's films, I analyse his first two feature films, then all of his other films, with the exception of *Jacob's Ladder* and *Lolita* which I discuss separately – the former being characterized by peculiar temporalities, different from those experienced in the rest of his oeuvre, the latter being the second adaptation to the big screen of Nabokov's *Lolita* which I would like to compare to Kubrick's adaptation.

3.1 *Foxes* (1980) and *Flashdance* (1983)

Foxes (1980) explores the lives of four 16-year-old friends – Jeanie (Jodie Foster), Annie (Cherie Currie), Madge (Marilyn Kagan) and Deirdre (Kandice Stroh) – who are growing up in a depressed outskirt of Los Angeles in the San Fernando Valley. They have to come to terms with their formative years, and with their parents who either do not care about them, being absent or violent, or seek support from them.

The first time we see Jeanie's mother is when the girl sneaks into her room to take the car keys to go to school with her girlfriends: her mother is sleeping with a new lover. Later, the mother, who is studying for a high school degree, confesses to Jeanie that she continually looks for men because she is scared of remaining alone: during the night, they read Plato together and sleep in the same bed. It is the mother who complains about her own situation, without understanding the complexities of her daughter's teen years, while Jeanie sympathizes with her mother. After a party at the house of Madge's boyfriend ends badly, with alcohol and drug abuse, a fight, the destruction of the apartment and the arrest of the participants – Jeanie and her mother quarrel as if they were two young girls. Later, the mother leaves her daughter alone for a man, to come back disappointed after some days. Jeanie's father is shown only once, during a concert when they meet by chance. He promises to spend their Christmas holiday together on a ranch, and she asks him for money to rent an apartment with her girlfriends. The father seems economically secure and we never see him again. He has a new life and does not care for his former family that he abandoned and forgot. In spite of her difficult family life and environment, at the end of the film Jeanie manages to escape in search of a better life by leaving for college.

Annie's destiny is dramatic. From the beginning of the film, she seems the most roguish of her set. She oversleeps because she stayed up too late drinking and was sick. She disappears from the house and school for a whole week and, after the arrest after the party, her father locks her up in a psychiatric hospital, but she escapes. With her school friend Brad's (Scott Baio) help, Jeanie finds her, drunken and drugged, but she runs away, jumping into a car driven by a drunken couple and dies in a car accident. Annie is the more indomitable, but also the unluckiest of the group. Her father is a violent policeman and her mother is metally ill.

The entire film is dominated by a classical Hollywood style, mainly shot-reverse-shots during the frequent dialogue scenes. A fast montage sequence, together with rapid movements of characters and a handheld camera are adopted only when Annie's father finds her at Jeanie's house at the beginning of the film, and when Annie and Jeanie quarrel and fight because the former does not want to go back home for fear of being locked up once more in a psychiatric hospital. This style, which is used only when Annie is the protagonist of the scene, increasing suspense, conveying a feeling of uncertainty and brutality, heralds her violent death. To increase suspense, simultaneity through alternated montage is used only once, when Jeanie and Brad look for Annie while Annie attempts to call Jeanie in a phone booth.

After her disgrace, at the end of the film, Jeanie, before leaving for college, parks in front of Annie's grave. From a plan américain of Jeanie, sitting at the grave, the camera zooms in to a close-up of her while her voice-over recalls what they used to say about death. The film ends with a sad freeze-frame which seems to encapsulate the impossibility, for Annie, of escaping her tragic fate, the stillness of her life and death.

The source-path-goal schema does not accurately describe the film. Jeanie, Annie, Madge and Deirdre's only aim seems to be to leave their parents. Only Jeanie attempts to improve her life, leaving for college, whereas Madge settles for marrying her boyfriend and Deirdre for continually changing boyfriends. Similarly, Jeanie's mother and Annie's parents never speak of their future goals. Character actions and behaviours are determined by a chaotic flow of events, and are often unclear and unexplained, in keeping with the subjective verisimilitude associated with art cinema. Do Jeanie's parents care for their daughter? Why the threatening behaviour of Annie's father? Madness or warped love? In Lyne's oeuvre, subjective verisimilitude is often restated when erotic passion overwhelms characters, but is usually accompanied and sustained by suspense alternating with the frozen temporalities of eroticism. In *Foxes*, surprise and suspense dictate the pace of narration.

There are two scenes in which the director adopts a style that characterizes the majority of his films. First, although there are no erotic scenes, when Madge is going to lose her virginity with her boyfriend, there is a fade to black. The film opens when the four girlfriends are sleeping together in Jeanie's bedroom, but before an establishing shot, there are details of the girls' bodies alternating with details of their belongings and close-ups, during which the camera either tracks slowly or remains still. These shots are divided by fades in and out, and accompanied by extra-diegetic music. These montage sequences of bodily details and close-ups or medium close-ups that succeed one another, sometimes punctuated by brief gaps and accompanied by music, characterize the erotic scenes of Lyne's oeuvre. Second, there is a sequence that links *Foxes* with the director's second feature film, *Flashdance*. When the girlfriends are at a concert, low-angle shots of the band – Angel, whose musicians play themselves – alternate with shots of the girls and other spectators, as often happens when the showgirls dance in *Flashdance* and we share the diegetic audience's point of view.

Unlike *Foxes*, in *Flashdance* there is no subjective verisimilitude. Characters' aims are clearly explained through their actions and dialogue. Rich entrepreneur Nick (Michael Nouri), one evening at Mawby's Bar, is entranced by a young girl's dance and falls in love with her immediately. His friend tells him that the dancer is Alex (Jennifer Beals), one of his workers. In the end he wins her heart, but their love story is complicated by Alex's desire to improve her life by following her aspiration which is to enter a dance academy in order to become a professional dancer, although she has never had the money to attend a dance school. Only Hanna (Lilia Skala), a retired classical dancer, gives her technical suggestions to improve her art, and encourages her to work hard to reach her aims. The couple Nick-Alex and the latter's goal are echoed by the love story between Richie (Kyle T. Heffner) and Jeanie (Sunny Johnson), who both work with Alex at Mawby's Bar – the former a sous-chef who dreams of becoming a comedian, the latter a waitress who dreams of becoming a professional ice skater. Their relationship ends when Richie leaves for Broadway to try his luck, but does not succeed and goes back to work at the bar. Similarly, Jeanie must abandon her dream when during a competition for which she has been working hard for years, she falls down twice. The lucky relation Nick–Alex is repeated, but counterbalanced and turned upside down by the unhappy couple Richie–Jeanie.

The source-path-goal schema, dominated by the rhythm of suspense around the outcome of the protagonists' love story and of Alex's entrance exam, is slowed down by some erotic moments, during which eroticism is only subtly suggested, by the tragic scenes of Hanna's death and Jeanie's defeat on the ice rink and, mainly, by dance performances.

For example, when Alex and Nick are in the former's apartment, the camera remains still when Alex raises her skirt to sit down in front of Nick and slowly takes off her bra from under her jumper. In the following reverse shot Nick is clearly surprised and aroused by her behaviour, and in the next shot the zoom in on her emphasizes his state of mind. After shot-reverse-shots during their dialogue, in a close-up they kiss for the first time, but a fade to black prevents us from witnessing any development. The audience wonders whether something occurs between them, wait for their kiss, but suspense is slowed down by Alex's actions. She is provocative, apparently without realizing she is exciting Nick. Whereas in this case Alex acts like the girl next door, when she is having dinner with Nick at an elegant restaurant, she becomes a femme fatale. As before, during shot-reverse-shots between them they speak, but this time she provokes him while eating a lobster with her hands and sucking her fingertips:

Nick How is the lobster?

Alex It sucks.

Nick Want some of mine?

Alex I'm not hungry, thanks.

Nick Whatever turns you on.

Alex What turns you on?

There follows a detail of her foot, under the table, that taps his legs and then his groin:

Alex You like phone booths?

Nick Phone booths?

Alex You probably just like doing it in bed, right?

And there is another detail of her foot on his crotch. They are interrupted by the arrival of Nick's former wife, who is sarcastic and offensive with Alex. Alex responds in kind and takes off her jacket, wearing a shirt that covers her breasts only, leaving her arms and shoulders and her back bare – but with cuffs. This scene takes place when the protagonists have already made love, thus there is no suspense about the development of their relationship, as in the scene described above. There is suspense around the sardonic exchange of words between the two women, but it is eroticism that prevails. The trajectory of the source-path-goal schema briefly halts, leaving space for Alex's timeless play of seduction. Much like in *Foxes*, and unlike in the other Lyne films, we are never shown the protagonists making love; we can only deduce what is going to happen between them. For example, at the end of a montage sequence during which they spend their free time together, when Alex speaks of her love of dancing, a close-up of the couple is followed by a detail of Nick's hand that touches Alex's breast and by another close-up of them kissing, but the sequence ends with a fade to black.

The endless run of Newtonian time is momentarily halted by tragic scenes, too. When Alex finds out that Hanna died, details of the latter's ballet shoes that Alex keeps next to her face and of other objects that recall Hanna's passion for dancing, prolong and emphasize Alex's loss. At the beginning of the film, we are shown similar objects in Alex's apartment, when the camera slowly tracks along shelves of books about dance and other personal belongings. The similarity between these scenes increases the affective proximity between Alex and Hanna and, consequently, the former's grief. Moreover, in the next two scenes, Alex is first shown alone in her apartment, crouched on the floor, smoking, and the camera slowly zooms out, emphasizing her loneliness, and when she goes backstage at Mawby's Bar to collect her belongings, a colleague of hers confesses to having lost all her hopes and dreams:

> You know, when I started out I was seventeen. I used to work in these old movie theatres. Every cent I had, I spent on costumes. I had more fancy costumes and dresses than you do. When I went on that stage, I was looking so good. One day I just stopped buying them. I don't even know what happened. I thought about it a lot. I just can't seem to pin it down. The dresses got old and I just stopped wearing them.

If this dancer tells of her loss of faith in the future, a disillusionment which grew gradually, Jeanie's failure is abrupt and tragic. When Jeanie dances, details of her skates and long shots of her alternate with shots of the diegetic spectators. Suspense around the outcome of her performance is increased by shots of characters who care and are anxious about her, and who know that her future depends on this competition: her best friend Alex, her boyfriend Richie, her parents, and Nick. These diegetic spectators empathize with Jeanie, and our own empathy is mirrored and emphasized by theirs. Moreover, the music chosen by Jeanie is the pop song 'Gloria' (performed by Laura Branigan, and written by Giancarlo Bigazzi, Umberto Tozzi and Trevor Veitch), which is very fast, like her bold choreography. When she falls down for the first time, she manages to get up immediately, unharmed, and continues her ballet, but when she falls down for the second time she is no longer able to stand up (Figure 3.1). While the music plays, she remains alone on the ice rink, lit by a bright spot, until a man helps her to her feet and accompanies her outside the rink, going out of frame and leaving only a beam of light on the ice. Time is suspended first in the dim hope that she goes on dancing, then in our sorrow for her and, finally, in the void of the frame, a metaphor for Jeanie's broken, lost dream.

Flashdance comprises a lot of staged musical performances that occupy 24 per cent of the duration of the film, but only three can be considered important for the development of the fabula. In addition to Jeanie's competition, there are the first and last of Alex's performances that take place at Mawby's Bar and at the dance academy, respectively. Jeanie's competition seems, at the beginning, a *mise-en-abîme* of Alex's exam to gain access to the academy: Alex, like her girlfriend, chooses pop music – 'Flashdance … What a Feeling', performed by Irene Cara and written by Giorgio Moroder – instead of a classical piece, and her choreography is fast and spectacular. She falls but manages to stand up and begin her ballet again. Unlike Jeanie, she does not make any other mistake, and her liveliness and determination involve the examiners, who are bored at the beginning, whereas at the end they beat time with their feet and pencils, clap their hands and smile. This scene also involves us, as extra-diegetic spectators, because the other girls who attend the academy come from higher social

Figure 3.1 *Flashdance* (Adrian Lyne, 1983). Jeanie (Sunny Johnson) falls down for the second time and is eliminated from the competition.

classes and are rich enough to take dance classes and buy the necessary equipment. We enjoy Alex's exam, our suspense developed during the previous sequences, asking ourselves whether the girl will succeed relying only on her own strength, to make her dream come true. For example, the first time she is shown in front of the huge academy building, the camera, from a close-up of her, tilts down. In the next shot, it tilts up from the main entrance to the top of the building. There follows a high-angle, long shot of Alex who seems to be metaphorically crushed by the building and what it represents. When she enters the academy to take the form she has to fill in before the exam, she queues with other young dancers. From a detail of her old boots, the camera tracks left to show the other girls' new and clean shoes, and in the next shot, from a close-up of the first dancer, the camera tracks in the opposite direction to a close-up of Alex, comparing the other girls' hairstyles with Alex's naturally curly hair.

Throughout the film, shoes become a symbol of the social class to which the characters aspire. For example, Alex's sneakers when she first enters a church, her bare feet when she dances alone and fills in the academy form in her house; Nick's elegant shoes when he waits for her together with her dog, and the expensive and glaring shoes and boots of Johnny (Lee Ving), the disreputable and violent owner of a strip club. During the exam, details of Alex's simple, black dance shoes alternate with long shots of her and the examiners. Dance shoes symbolize the possibility of altering Alex's future, not through money, as in the case of Johnny, but through talent and commitment. The style, either during these three dance performances or during the other shows at Mawby's Bar and other places, is always the same. Diegetic music accompanies long shots, plans américains and medium shots alternated with close-ups, details of body parts, especially feet, and shots of the diegetic audience. These features are also adopted when the staged musical performances are montage sequences accompanied either by diegetic or extra-diegetic music, during which dialogue can sometimes be heard, and there may be a diegetic audience – e.g. when Alex, Jeanie and the other showgirls of Mawby's Bar are in a gym; when Alex and Jeanie look at two street dancers; and when the former mimics a policeman directing traffic.

The difference between the three dance performances analysed above and all the others is not in their style, but in the time the spectator experiences. When we watch the former three scenes, we take pleasure in seeing Alex's and Jeanie's muscles and stunning bodies, and the elegance of their movements, but we are also involved in the outcome of their performances. Whereas during the other staged musical performances we do not experience suspense, but only the pleasure of watching. *Flashdance* cannot be defined as a musical but, as we saw in the discussion of *2001: A Space Odyssey*, *A Clockwork Orange* and *Full Metal Jacket*, since the 1960s and especially during the 1970s and 1980s, cult non-musical films appeared in which musical performances were included within the fabula, hybrid films in which classical genre conventions were challenged by an MTV aesthetic (Conrich 2006: 115–16).[1] These staged musical performances, as in classical musicals, enrich the audience's knowledge of the development of the film and the characters' features (Conrich and Tincknell 2006: 5). In *Flashdance*, on the other hand, while dance performances are diegetically motivated – girls exhibit themselves because dance is their passion and work – the majority of their ballets are redundant from the point of view of the progression of the fabula. Much like in classical musicals, in Lyne's film: 'performance is usually transparent and expressive of sincere emotions or it is linked to the theatrical presentation of "talent" or star charisma [...] the performance itself is represented as authentic' (Tincknell 2006: 136). Gene Kelly suggests that music performances should arise from 'plot situation', 'character development' or 'incidents that enhance one of these two', and that should: 'be natural, expressive extensions of the film narrative, motivated yet not quite invisible components of the conventional classical narrative style' (Telotte 2006: 49). On the other hand, in classical musicals, characters often sing and dance in front of the camera, addressing directly the extra-diegetic spectator, and a diegetic audience, and are accompanied by extra-diegetic music. While in classical musicals performances are diegetically motivated, and give information about the development of the film and the characters, some of their stylistic features are anti-realistic (Grant 2007: 10).

In Lyne's film, staged musical performances are always realistic, both from the point of view of style and from that of narration, but the majority of them neither advance the fabula nor the characters' features. This is the main difference between *Flashdance* and classical musicals and non-musical films with staged musical performances produced from the 1960s to the 1980s. During most of the ballets in Lyne's film, narration is frozen to let the extra-diegetic and the diegetic audience contemplate the

---

[1] It is interesting that, after the release of the film, Lyne directed two music videos: *Irene Cara: Flashdance ... What a Feeling* (1983) and *Michael Sembello: Maniac* (1983). The song of the former music video was written by Giorgio Moroder for *Flashdance*, whereas the latter was written by Michael Sembello and Dennis Matkosky before the release of the film.

spectacle and enjoy the music. The soundtrack comprises both original pieces, written by Michael Sembello, and non-original music, but almost all of the songs are pop numbers. From the perspective of musical choices, *Fashdance* remains, once more, suspended between what usually happens in classical musicals – where there are 'diegetically produced and visibly performed numbers' – and what happens in 'soundtrack films' – 'that is a curious hybrid of the musical and the traditional classical Hollywood score', in which there are 'extramusical allusions', and that: 'consisting mainly of previously recorded material, are put together on the assumption that the audience will recognize the artist, the song, or, at a minimum, a familiar style' (Tincknell 2006: 134). In Lyne's films, the majority of the songs used to accompany staged dance performances are fast and filled with life, as if to underline the showgirls' determination, their grit in facing their challenging suburban context. As mentioned, this is one of the features of the new musicals that offer a momentary escape from the daily routine and problems of the diegetic world (Telotte 2006: 49).

The slowing down of the rhythm of suspense that we experience during the majority of the dance performances is repeated and emphasized at the end of the film, after Alex has passed the exam. She runs outside the academy where Nick, with a bouquet of roses, and her dog are waiting for her. The film, like *Foxes*, closes with a freeze-frame: a medium shot of Nick on the left and Alex on the right, who gives him a rose from the bouquet.

3.2 From staged musical performances to staged erotic performances: *Nine ½ Weeks* (1986), *Fatal Attraction* (1987), *Indecent Proposal* (1993) and *Unfaithful* (2002)

All four of these films, *Nine ½ Weeks*, *Fatal Attraction*, *Indecent Proposal* and *Unfaithful*, follow a source-path-goal schema, in which the protagonists find themselves moved by an uncontrollable passion: eroticism progressively leaves space to suspense when the passion overcomes reason, self-defence and the preservation of the characters' families and environments. With the exception of *Nine ½ Weeks*, the other three films present love triangles: a married couple is destroyed by the arrival of a third character who has an affair with the husband or wife. Why the male/female member of the couple, who seems to happily share his/her life with her/his partner, betrays her/him, is never verbally explained, but usually subtly suggested first by a secret, almost shy, exchange of glances, and then by an overwhelming passion, far from an enduring love, but untameable. For Lacan, the object that best matches the movement of desire is the gaze (Recalcati 2019: 27). Every time we experience desire, we lose the confident surveillance of ourselves, we are dragged away by a force that exceeds the power to control and govern the ego (ibid. 2012: 28). Human beings are not Aristotelian beings, are not rational animals who are satisfied with everyday life, they are pleasure beings who choose pleasure instead of life-preservation and defence. Freud speaks of the death drive and Lacan of pleasure (105). Lyne's films stage these family and couple dynamics. When the character who has been betrayed begins to suspect his/her partner's infidelity, suspense begins to take the place of eroticism until substituting it completely, thus begins a play of knowledge between what each character knows and what the audience knows.

Nine ½ Weeks is adapted from the autobiographical novel of the same title (1978) written by Ingeborg Day under the *nom de plume* Elizabeth McNeill. The fabula of the written medium is very similar to that of the cinematic. The first-person narration of the novel is partially adapted in the film where the audience shares only the female protagonist Elizabeth's (Kim Basinger) knowledge and never that of the male character John (Mickey Rourke). We know as much about John as Elizabeth does. When he tells her something about his past or present life, we share the information with her, and we always see him in the same diegetic space as Elizabeth, whereas we see her in settings where John does not appear, interacting with other characters. For example, when John and Elizabeth are alone for the first time in a one-bedroom apartment at the sea's edge and she asks him what he does, he answers that he buys and sells money. In a later scene, when he first invites her to his apartment, looking at stock exchange data on a screen, he comments that he risked a heart attack looking at them, adding that before living in that apartment he used to stay in a hotel. Judging from his standard of living – his house, his clothes, the presents he gives Elizabeth – and the few statements about his life, we deduce that he is a successful stockbroker. But Elizabeth and the audience do not understand the aims of his relation with her.

At the beginning he seems to be a gentleman. For example, he buys her a French shawl that she saw on a stall but that she did not purchase for its excessive price. Twice he sends a bunch of roses to the art gallery where she works; one morning he prepares her breakfast, lays the tray on the bedside table, prepares her dress on the bed and gently wakes her up. But some of his behaviour and requests, as well as some of his comments, sound strange and contradictory. In the one-bedroom apartment by the sea he plays the romantic 'Strange Fruit' performed by Billy Holiday (written by Lewis Allan), but without asking Elizabeth, he takes the blanket from the bed, and lays a clean white sheet and when she says to him that she is not going to make love, he scares her, claiming that she is alone in an isolated place with an unknown man. John's play of seduction, his romanticism and attention to her physical pleasure, progressively leaves space to his desire to dominate her, and their relationship becomes a sadistic bond between ruler and ruled, lived as a timeless obsession that soon destroys itself – as opposed to the happy ending of a very similar relationship in *Fifty Shades of Grey* (Sam Taylor-Johnson, 2015), *Fifty Shades Darker* (James Foley, 2017) and *Fifty Shades Freed* (James Foley, 2018). At her house, he asks her to undress, to be blindfolded and tells her that he will leave if she does not obey, but then he romantically and erotically plays with ice cubes on her body. When he gives her an expensive wristwatch, he asks her to touch herself every day at noon while thinking of him. In the scene in front of the fridge (which has earned cult cachet), she has to keep her eyes shut while he feeds her. When he leaves her alone in his apartment, she snoops around. When he returns, he scolds her, ordering her to turn towards the wall and lift up her skirt so that he can spank her. When she refuses, he becomes violent and drags her onto the table where he tears off her underwear and rapes her until she surrenders. He buys her an expensive dress at an elegant atelier, but when she asks him whether he would like to know if she enjoys it, he says he does not care. The decline of their relationship begins when the ruled agrees to the ruler stepping on basic norms. Elizabeth likes a necklace in a shopping centre, John suggests that she steals it and she does so. In Elizabeth's house, he says he can no longer get excited, and asks her to walk on her hands and knees to collect banknotes, and when she stops complaining that she does not enjoy the play, he becomes violent, takes off his belt and whips her. Finally, John asks Elizabeth to wait for him blindfolded in a hotel room. When she realizes that it is not him who is touching her, but a prostitute who then kisses and embraces John, she runs away.

John takes care of Elizabeth, but as if she was a little girl rather than a woman. When she tells him she is going to wash dishes, he replies:

> You don't do dishes. You don't ever have to do dishes. I'll do the dishes. And I'll buy the groceries. And I'll cook the food. And I'll feed you. And I'll dress you in the morning. And I'll undress you at night. And I'll bathe you. And I'll take care of you. And you can see your friends in the daytime. I just want the night-time from now on to be ours.

Similarly, when she is sleeping in his bed, he wakes her up because he has prepared hot soup for her:

Elizabeth   How did you know? How did you know I'd respond to you the way I have?

John   I saw myself in you.

When he is combing her hair, she asks him whether he behaved in the same way with other women, and he whispers something in her ear that we cannot hear: this is the only moment during which Elizabeth knows more than us.

While they are both free of other bonds, their love relation develops entirely in the present, without links to past or future projects. At Elizabeth's, when she listens to her former husband's phone message, she asks John whether he would like to know what she is feeling for him but he answers that he does not care. Similarly, when she asks him to go out with her friends, he replies that he does not want to know anybody and would like to stay only with her. The emphasis on the present moment is underlined in the dialogue between Elizabeth and an old painter for whom she is organizing an exhibition:

Elizabeth   I wanted you to know that your show opens in three weeks . . . and we still don't have all your paintings. And we were hoping you'd come. Do you remember about your show?

Mr. Farnsworth   I remember to eat when I'm hungry and I remember to sleep when I'm tired.

Elizabeth   I saw your work. It's wonderful. I don't know what it is. The way you manage to capture a moment.

Mr. Farnsworth   It's the moment a thing is so familiar. It is strange.

The erotic passion between Elizabeth and John is so deep and overwhelming that they do not understand that it is destroying itself, that the sadistic play of ruler–ruled is overtaking the borders of self-esteem and respect. It is only at the very end of their relationship, when she is collecting her belongings to leave his apartment, that John tells her something about his past and family, and confesses that he loves her more than he has ever loved anything in his entire life. It is too late, according to Elizabeth. When she leaves, shutting the door behind her, he claims, 'I love you' – this is the only time during which we know more than Elizabeth, sharing John's point of view – and there follows an alternated montage between her, walking and crying, and him, waiting in vain for her to come back. The film closes with a fade to black.

The present moment is also emphasized through eroticism, when the rhythm of the film, the alternation between suspense and curiosity, is frozen. There are two different kinds of erotic scene that are shot in different styles. When there is a desirous play of glances between Elizabeth and John, either there are shot-reverse-shots between close-ups or medium close-ups of them, or they are in-frame together, often facing the camera in medium close-up or medium shot, and either they speak or remain silent. Discussing *The Blue Angel* (*Der blaue Engel*, Josef von Sternberg, 1930), Maurizio Regosa claims that when there is a play of gazes between characters, close-ups and shot-reverse-shots represent the instant of an emotion that breaks space and time (2002b: 37). Similarly, of Max Ophüls' oeuvre, Regosa comments that the gaze is the main element of every seduction and attraction, it is a fact that transcends words and explicit awareness (2002a: 61).

Whereas when Elizabeth and John make love, or immediately before doing so they are in-frame alone or together, the camera is usually near them, and shots of them alternate with details of the woman's body and of the man's hands touching it. There is often a light blue backlight to emphasize their silhouettes. The style of these scenes is similar to that of the staged dance performances in *Flashdance* – with the exception of details that are more numerous in staged erotic performances, and of music that is usually extra-diegetic in staged erotic performances and diegetic in dance performances. The style is the same during the cult scene of the protagonist's striptease, when she undresses accompanied by Joe Cocker's *You Can Leave Your Hat On* (written by Randy Newman). The use of details is paramount in the Lacanian description of male sexual desire. For men, the woman's body is fragmented into little objects – called 'objects (a)' – because their desire has a fetishistic structure, i.e. it is a 'piece' of the body that causes their sexual desire (Recalcati 2012: 138).

Consciously or unconsciously, Lyne's style during erotic scenes embodies the mechanism of the arousal of male sexual desire. Moreover, during erotic scenes sometimes there is a diegetic audience, too. In a bar, close-ups of Elizabeth and John, during which he puts his thumb in her mouth and around her lips, alternate with details of their hands touching their groins, and medium close-ups of a man sitting next to them who stares at them. Similarly, when they are in an elegant restaurant and she is dressed as a man, he suddenly tears off her fake moustache and kisses her, and the other guests turn around to look at them. In the shopping centre, in front of the cashiers, first John asks Elizabeth to lie down on a bed and he lays on her, then he tries a whip and slowly flogs her legs. Finally, in the hotel room when the prostitute touches Elizabeth, John remains a diegetic spectator. Conversely, when he kisses and embraces the woman, it is Elizabeth who takes the role of the audience. She does not remain passive, hits them and runs away to a strip club, where everybody is watching a couple having sex. When John catches up with her, she kisses the man next to her and then John kisses her. Their relationship ends in a confused game, in which actors and diegetic spectators exchange roles, in which their passion has no more borders, becoming a spectacle within the spectacle and overwhelming the characters near them. A dangerous, timeless present with neither roots and curiosity in the past nor aims and suspense in the future, it is a present that swallows up the protagonists. According to the psychiatrist Eugenio Borgna, when we experience acute pain, either in our body or in our mind, our subjective experience of time changes, and we live, imprisoned, without emotion and imagination, in an Augustinian present made up of instants that succeed one another, isolated both from the past and the future, and in which we can only cry and scream, desperately seeking help to soothe our pain (2015: 116).

I have called some scenes 'erotic' without defining what can be considered erotic. The conventional difference between an erotic and a pornographic film is that in the latter, sexual intercourse is shown as excited sexual organs and details of penetration. While in erotic scenes we are not shown these details; if the characters are or seem to be aroused, their excitement should involve us, thrilling us (Menarini 2015: 76–7). And empathy, as defined within embodied simulation, reinforces these scenes. Erotic films usually stage the transgression of social taboos, a sexual drive that can only be provoked by vice (Caprara 2007: 6), and in *Nine ½ Weeks* the couple develops a sadistic relation of ruler–ruled that often plays out in front of a diegetic audience, whereas in *Fatal Attraction*, *Indecent Proposal*, *Lolita* and *Unfaithful* there are love triangles. But not every transgression is erotic and not all the erotic scenes stage a transgression. I believe that style and fabula increase our empathy, as in the case of the play of gazes, which often symbolizes the beginning of a relationship, and in the scenes and sequences that I will henceforth call 'staged erotic performances'.

Fatal Attraction, much like *Flashdance*, is a simple source-path-goal schema that does not present the features of objective and subjective verisimilitude – as *Foxes* and *Nine ½ Weeks* do – but in which the protagonists have opposite goals. Dan (Michael Douglas) remains alone in New York while his wife Beth (Anne Archer) and his daughter Ellen (Ellen Latzen) spend a weekend in the country visiting a new house they would like to buy. Although he seems to love and care for his family – like the protagonists of *Indecent Proposal* and, especially, *Unfaithful* – he gives in to the advances of one of his colleagues, Alex (Glenn Close), and has an affair with her. Unfortunately, Alex is metally ill, does not accept a one-night stand, and begins to stalk Dan and his family in a crescendo of madness and violence. The play of eroticism, of gazes followed by staged erotic performances, soon gives way to suspense.

Dan first meets Alex during a party. There are brief shot-reverse-shots between her and Dan and his friend Jimmy (Stuart Pankin) who makes comments about her gaze, emphasizing verbally the visual play. At the bar Dan finds himself next to Alex, they both face the camera in medium shot. Their dialogue is interrupted by Beth who summons Dan to go home. When he is leaving, there is a medium shot of Alex who stares at him, smiling. The next day, at a business meeting, Alex is a little late. The play of gazes between her and Dan continues, and they become more explicitly complicit when she indicates, without being seen by the others, that he has cream on his nose. When they leave the building, it is raining and Dan's umbrella does not open. Alex approaches him. They cannot find a cab and decide to have dinner together – not unlike what happens in *Unfaithful* where the female protagonist accepts her future lover's invitation because they do not manage to stop a cab. At the restaurant, their play of gazes continues – as in *Nine ½ Weeks*, there are either shot-reverse-shots between them or they are in-frame together – and their dialogue becomes more and more sexually allusive. There follow staged erotic performances – shot with the same style as those of *Nine ½ Weeks* – in Alex's house, in a club where they dance to Latin American ballets, and finally in the lift in Alex's building

The next morning, when Alex wakes up, Dan has already left, and when she calls him we begin to suspect, together with him, that she is crazy. The camera slowly zooms in on her, underlining her insistence, while on the phone she persuades him to spend the afternoon with her. At sunset, back at her home, she becomes aggressive, hits Dan and then cuts her wrists. When he goes to work, after having gone to pick up his wife and daughter in the country, he finds Alex waiting outside his office. She proposes that they go to the opera to see *Madama Butterfly* – in which the woman commits suicide for love, as she stresses in a previous scene during the day spent with Dan – but he refuses. In an alternated montage, we see Dan, Beth, Jimmy and his wife Hildy (Ellen Foley) happily bowling, and Alex alone in her apartment, sat on a chair, rhythmically switching the table lamp on and off, with her eyes fixed in a void off-screen behind the camera. She repeatedly calls Dan, even at home during dinner and in the middle of the night, until he has to change his phone number. When she manages to meet and speak with him, she tells him she is pregnant, wants to keep the baby and subtly menaces that she will act in accordance with how he treats the situation. Unable to find Dan's new phone number, she goes to his house pretending she is interested in buying it. Dan and Alex quarrel and fight violently in her house, and she begins to take her revenge: she pours acid on his car and records a cassette in which she menaces him; in his home, she kills the rabbit he bought his daughter and puts it in a pot to boil it; she kidnaps Ellen, and finally tries to kill Beth. As we have seen, it is not the ego that decides desire, but it is desire that decides for the ego, that burns, kidnaps and overturns it. The experience of desire is the experience of a force that comes from the ego, but goes beyond it, overwhelming and decentring the ego (Recalcati 2012: 28). Alex is the metaphor, the embodiment of this desire whose power, freed from any rule, becomes both destructive and self-destructive.

Alex's progressive descent into madness is staged through the increase of her violent actions, as well as through style and alternated montage sequences that increase suspense, as occurs in action movies. When characters fight, actor and camera movements and montage are more rapid. When Beth finds out that Ellen has been kidnapped, the point-of-view shots are made with a handheld camera to emphasize her anxiety. As regards simultaneity, while Ellen runs outside towards the rabbit's cage to find out that it is not there, Beth approaches the boiling pot in the kitchen where she finds the rabbit's corpse. Similarly, while Beth is driving to look for Ellen, the latter is with Alex at an amusement park, and when Beth and Alex are fighting upstairs in Beth's house, Dan is downstairs preparing tea, unaware of what is taking place. Alex's actions are the cause of the separation between members of Dan's family, of their physically being in different places rather than together. Relations between Alex and Dan begin because the latter is physically far from his family. The city is par excellence the location where Lyne stages his characters' prohibited sexual relations, while the countryside symbolizes family life. In *Indecent Proposal*, when the protagonists arrive at Las Vegas, they fall victim to the temptations of sex and money; and in *Unfaithful*, the female protagonist meets her lover almost every day in the early afternoon in New York to go back to the countryside in the evening.

Indecent Proposal is a source-path-goal schema and, not unlike *Fatal Attraction* and *Unfaithful*, it is based on a love triangle in which characters have different goals. Diana (Demi Moore) and David (Woody Harrelson) have been in love since high school, are happily married and building the house of their dreams. Both employed in the construction sector – he is an architect and she is a realtor – they have to deal with serious economic difficulties due to the recession. One night, unable to sleep, they decide to leave for Las Vegas to try their luck. After a winning, insufficient to pay their debts, they continue to gamble, losing everything. At that point, a fascinating millionaire, John Gage (Robert Redford), infatuated by Diana, and used to buying everything and everybody, offers them a million dollars to spend one night with Diana. The couple unwillingly accepts the proposal, but back home, jealousy and the discovery that John bought the land where they were building their house, cause their separation. John reappears to conquer Diana, and succeeds, but when David reaches them with divorce papers, the millionaire realizes that Diana will never gaze at him as she does at David and, consequently, he will never be able to entirely conquer her heart. The film ends with husband and wife back together. It is adapted from Jack Hengelhard's *Indecent Proposal* (1988), in which the Jewish protagonist Josh and his lover Jean go bankrupt and accept the proposal of Ibrahim Hassan, a handsome and rich Arabian Prince. Hassan shoots a video when he makes love with Jean, and Josh, fighting him, manages to take it and throws it into the ocean. Jealousy prevents Jean and Josh from living together, and Josh leaves to fight against Muslims. Jean first tries in vain to commit suicide and then reaches Josh. The rivalry between the two men is not only caused by love, as in the film, but also by sociopolitical differences. The complex context of the novel becomes a more straightforward economic recession in the film where, consequently, the love triangle is emphasized.

Unlike in *Fatal Attraction* and *Unfaithful*, staged erotic performances occur when Diana and David make love, whereas we are never shown intimate relations between Diana and John: the entrepreneur seduces the woman staring at her, paying her compliments, being romantic and anticipating her desires. This behaviour seems to counterbalance the way he persuades her to spend a night with him, taking advantage of her economic difficulties and bargaining with her as if she was a prostitute, and David and his lawyer her whoremasters. There are only two staged erotic performances: at the beginning of the film after Diana and David quarrel in their kitchen about David's disorder, and during the first night they spend in Las Vegas, after having won some money, on a bed covered in dollars. In the former scene, they are so aroused that they do not realize that David's underwear is near the stove which is left on for the kettle and begins to catch fire. This detail on the one hand underlines the couple's passion – as in *Fatal Attraction* when Alex and Dan have sex for the first time, she accidentally turns on the tap with her bottom – and on the other is evoked when David, after the adventure in Las Vegas, lights the stove with a match and realizes that the matchbox is labelled 'Griphon', the name of John's yacht, as Diana later confesses.

If these staged erotic performances interrupt the fabula, offering the audience a spectacle, the play of gazes introduces suspense about the protagonists' relations and the development of the fabula itself. Both the affair between David and Diana and that between John and Diana are introduced by a play of gazes. At the beginning of the film, there are montage sequences of enacted recounted flashbacks narrated either by David's or Diana's voice-over during which we are shown peculiar moments of their adolescence and young adulthood. Sometimes during these montage sequences, their voices-over ceases and we listen to their dialogue: from enacted recounted flashbacks, we pass to enacted flashbacks. At other moments, a montage sequence ends to show us an entire scene, as in the case of the first staged erotic performance discussed above. This alternation between montage sequences of enacted or enacted recounted flashbacks and scenes begins when David and Diana fall in love and end when, due to the economic recession, David is fired and Diana is no longer able to sell houses and their dream of building a house on the shore fades away. Diana's voice-over underlines that she fell in love with David's eyes during high school, when he used to drive her home from school, while we are shown him driving his car and Diana sat in the backseat, both exchanging glances through the rear-view mirror.

Similarly, in Las Vegas, the first encounter between Diana and John is staged through a play of gazes, but this time more charming and complex. When John first sees Diana, she is in a dress shop and does not notice him staring at her from the window; she sees him and exchanges gazes, smiling when he sees her stealing chocolates from a tray. Similarly, while she is looking at herself in a mirror holding an elegant black dress against herself, she does not see him until he claims that she should have that dress and that he could buy it for her because he enjoyed looking at her, but she replies that whereas the dress is for sale, she is not. Later, while David and Diana are wandering in the casino, they stop at the gambling table where John is playing: Diana and John exchange glances, and she keeps looking at him while kissing her husband. The day after, the three meet again in the casino, the couple has just lost all of their money, and

John asks Diana to throw the dice for him, betting a million dollars. She wins and he offers them a night in a suite, inviting them to a party in his penthouse and giving her the black dress. At the beginning, when the couple arrives at the party, they start to dance while John stares at her, unnoticed. In the first part of the film, Diana either does not immediately see John when he looks at her, or she is with her husband when she exchanges glances with him. The same play of gazes that explicitly stages their love triangle is repeated at the end of the film, when David reaches Diana and John, who are at a charity auction, to sign the divorce papers. The three of them sit at the same table – David and Diana dressed in white, John in black – the entrepreneur leaves them alone and, when it starts raining, everybody stands up to find shelter from the rain, except for David and Diana. Shot-reverse-shots between David and Diana alternate with shots of John staring at them. He is once more the vortex of a triangle that is disappearing as quickly as it appeared. As in the other Lyne films, the play of gazes is usually staged through shot-reverse-shots, during which either the camera progressively zooms in on the characters, or it moves closer and closer to them during each shot.

The source-path-goal schema is embedded in a container schema, indeed both at the beginning and at the end of the film we are shown David on a bench at the end of a pier and Diana on a bus. At the beginning, David's voice-over explains that losing Diana was like losing a piece of himself, and that he thought that nothing could have changed their relationship, that together they would have been invincible. Whereas Diana's voice-over comments that if you want somebody you have to set them free; if they return to you, they will be yours forever, if they do not, they were never yours. At the end of the film, Diana catches up with David and sits down on the other side of the bench, her back to David, while her voice-over explains that she is going there to remember their relationship – during the montage sequence that opens the film, we were shown David asking Diana to marry him on that same bench. Close-ups of them alternate with details of their hands holding the others', and the film closes with a freeze-frame of their hands – as in *Foxes* and *Flashdance*. The play of gazes is excluded at the end, dominated instead by the stillness of a freeze-frame that seems to emphasize that the entire adventure between Diana and John is only an analepsis that pertains to an already forgotten past.

During the film, suspense is also increased through other techniques. Following the development of the events, this first emerges in gambling, then from John's proposal. At the casino where David and Diana play, there are lots of details of chips and fingers moving and stacking them, and details of the roulette shot from above. Sometimes the camera quickly turns above the roulette wheel or whirls among the players, emphasizing their excitement. In other shots, slow motion is adopted to catch the ball inside the roulette wheel, and this technique is also used when Diana and David lose and Diana puts her hands on the chips in a last, useless attempt to save their money, when Diana kisses the dices that she throws for John and the camera follows them and, similarly, when the camera follows the balls when John and David play billiards before John's proposal. On the one hand, fast, circular movements of the camera emphasize the thrills, on the other, slow motion prolongs the players' suspense. This same play of first extending and then contracting temporalities is adopted when David tries to reach

Diana in vain before she spends the night with John. David is having a drink, but then begins to run and, when he enters a lift to reach the entrepreneur's penthouse, either the camera turns around, stressing the claustrophobic and suffocating space and situation, or there are details of the numbers of floors that seem to increase too slowly in comparison with David's anxiety. When he finally leaves the lift, both when he tries to reach the suite and then the roof, and when he goes back to the casino, rapid movements of him and the camera – often handheld – and fast editing stress his misery. Lyne plays with temporalities, moulding them, and translating both the characters' will to accelerate time – in the case of the gamblers and during David's attempt to reach Diana – and how, paradoxically, time seems to extend when characters would like it to contract.

A play of in-frame and out-of-frame is instead adopted when John makes his proposal and when Diana and David discuss it. At the beginning, during the billiards scene, when the proposal is only a hypothesis, the three characters are in-frame alone. Whereas when the proposal is no longer a joke and the couple feels outraged and insulted, John is in-frame alone and husband and wife are in-frame together. But when Diana and David are alone in their bed and begin to speak seriously about it, either the camera is above them and turns around, as in the lift, or is at the same height as the bed and they are in-frame together or alone: the discussion distances them. Finally, after having signed the contract, when David and his lawyer leave the penthouse, a zoom-out from Diana visually translates the physical and emotional distance between her and her husband.

If in *Indecent Proposal* there are only two staged erotic performances and, although we are not shown what happens between Diana and John, we know, as do all the other characters, that they make love, in *Unfaithful* there are lots of staged erotic performances and suspense is often due to a play between what we know and what the characters do or do not know. Connie (Diane Lane) and Edward (Richard Gere) are a happily married couple who live in the country with their son Charlie (Erik Per Sullivan). The husband is a successful businessman and Connie is a housewife. Connie meets by chance a young and fascinating librarian, Paul Martel (Olivier Martinez), and they begin a secret, sexual relationship. The reasons for Connie's behaviour are not verbally explained and are contradictory. On the one hand, she behaves like Elizabeth in *Nine ½ Weeks* because she cannot master her passion that soon overcomes her reason – whereas Connie betrays and deceives her husband, Elizabeth remains caught up in a sadistic relationship – on the other hand, her relation begins unexpectedly, as in *Nine ½ Weeks* and *Fatal Attraction* – but unlike Dan in *Fatal Attraction*, Connie seems to desperately look forward to leaving her country villa and go to her lover's apartment. Connie's confusion is made visually clear during a montage sequence, in which we are shown actions occurring in different spaces and times: the family at Charlie's party, and Connie alone, absentminded, or with Paul. It is only after several meetings with Paul that Connie calls him and, via a message on the answering machine, leaves him. Unfortunately, it is Edward who listens to the message, but it is too late. Having discovered his wife's adulterous relation, he goes to Paul's, where, losing his head, he kills the librarian. Like the other Lyne films discussed, *Unfaithful* is a source-path-goal scheme, but here, as much as in *Foxes* and *Nine ½ Weeks*, Connie's behaviour is unclear – consonant with the art film's subjective verisimilitude. Edward would like to be loved and desired by Connie, he supports and defends his family; Connie seems to care for her husband and son, but passion contradicts her previous aims.

In *Unfaithful*, eroticism slowly gives way to suspense, as in a fade in and fade out. Connie and Paul's relationship begins, as in the majority of Lyne's films, with a play of gazes that soon becomes an overwhelming sexual relation shot through staged erotic performances. Connie's behaviour with Paul is completely different from hers with Edward. She looks forward to meeting the former, whereas she avoids the latter, whatever he does to be kind and win her heart. This difference is underlined through style. For example, the first time she arrives at Paul's, before the beginning of their sexual relationship, he asks her to take off her coat. A detail of her neck, during which his fingers enter the frame, is followed by another similar detail shot in front of her, by another detail of neck and fingers and finally by a close-up of him. His fingers gently touch her neck while he helps her to undress. Through acting, details and editing, physical contact is emphasized and becomes erotic. After this sequence, Connie goes to her husband's office to give him a jumper she bought for him. As soon as he tries it on, their dialogue is interrupted by a phone call. There is a detail of her hands cutting the label from the neck of the sweater, but her fingers do not touch his neck. The contrast between the details of the two sequences could not be clearer: the desire to touch and be touched versus an innocuous act.

Except for at the beginning of the film when both the audience and Connie and Paul do not know whether Connie and Paul will make love, in *Unfaithful* suspense is always due to the difference between the spectator's knowledge and that of characters, that is, the audience knows more than the characters and wait for them to understand what is happening. When Connie and Paul meet for the first time, they cannot find a cab, but as soon as he invites her upstairs, she sees a free taxi but chooses not to hail it. Interestingly, at the end of the film, in Connie's enacted flashback mixed with her imaginings, she stops the cab and gets in. Suspense about their relations is prolonged during their first meetings, indeed she goes to his house three times before making love with him, and these encounters are dominated by a play of gazes and details of fingers and hands touching. The first time she meets him he gives her a book and when, back at her home, she opens it, a card with his phone number falls out. Next day at the station she does not know whether to call him. She begins to dial the number, but hangs up before entering all the numbers. When she manages to call, the answering machine answers, and when she is going to hang up for the second time, Paul answers and invites her to his apartment. Acting, together with close-ups and medium close-ups alternating with details of a coin, a keypad and a receiver, increase suspense, extending time. Hence, we feel Connie's hope and fear, her desire and hesitation. Similarly, when she is going to make love with Paul for the first time, there is a cut followed by a plan américain of her sitting on a train, smiling and crying at the same time. Is the director not going to show us what he implicitly promises us during the previous sequences? Is he going to forbid us from watching a scene of adulterous sexual relations as we see in *Indecent Proposal* and *Lolita*? On the contrary, he increases our suspense, alternating close-ups of Connie with enacted flashbacks of her and Paul making love and, moreover, he manages to stage all Connie's complex and contradictory feelings. In an interview, Lyne claims: 'You see the entire scene reflected in her face, you see her guilt to see her excitement and laughing and crying all at once' ('*Unfaithful* Interview' 2016).

We know that Connie and Paul have sexual relations and, from the beginning, Edward seems to suspect that something has changed. Clues help him and us to understand and follow his suspicions. For example, one evening, Connie continues to wash the same dish without realizing that Edward is near her, smiling at her. On another night, during which the husband is still working in his studio, his wife, having wished him good night, switches the studio light off. One afternoon, while Connie is sleeping, Paul draws on her groin a flower with a marker, and she sees it only when, back at her home, she takes a bath. Unfortunately, Edward joins her with a glass of wine and, in the bathtub, he tenderly touches her legs but she curls up before leaving on the pretext that she is cold. One morning, knowing that Connie has to go to the city, Edward asks her to travel there with him and have lunch together, but she refuses, saying that she would have taken too much time to get ready and she would have been late for her appointment at the beauty salon. But while she is in the bathroom, we see from Edward's point of view her sexy petticoats and high heels. Edward's suspicions become more concrete when he calls the beauty salon to find that Connie has no appointments that day. After the phone call, when he hangs up, the camera slowly tracks out from a close-up of him, and there is a superimposition with a long shot of Connie, walking in slow motion, below Paul's building. Similarly, some days before, Connie had justified being busy with the excuse that she had to organize a school auction and that a friend of theirs gave her money, but when Edward meets him, he does not know anything about the auction. The husband asks Frank (Dominic Chianese), a private investigator, to stalk his wife after having fired one of his employees, Bill (Chad Lowe), who tells him to open his eyes and better control his family instead of his company. Indeed, Bill had seen Connie kissing Paul in a restaurant. Thus, following the order of the fabula and film, the characters who come to know of the adulterous relationship are Bill, Frank and, finally, Edward.

As soon as Edward knows, suspense focuses on who comes to know that the husband is aware that his wife is unfaithful. Paul is the first to know. Edward knocks at his door and presents himself as Connie's husband. Suspense now switches to what is going to happen between them, and is increased through style and dialogue. The husband comes to know that his wife complains about living in the country and speaks with her lover about her husband. Edward definitely loses his temper when he sees, near the bed, the glass ball we had previously seen in Connie's hands at her villa. The lover explains that Connie gave it to him; the husband replies that he bought it for his wife. It is at this point that Edward, having repeated that he is not feeling good, hits Paul with the glass ball, killing him. Style emphasizes the crescendo of suspense through low angles and canted shots at the beginning of the sequence, and a shot from Paul's point of view of a knife on the table when he goes to take something to drink. When the situation begins to escalate, Edward's point-of-view shots are out of focus and shot with a handheld camera, and when he kneels down to see whether Paul is still alive they are canted and, again, a handheld camera is adopted. Before the husband enters Paul's building, there is a shot that, in my opinion, confuses spectators. Connie is still in Paul's apartment, and there is a shot from Paul's of Edward in the street below, followed by a long shot of the husband walking away from the building and of the wife running outside the front door in the opposite direction. We wonder whether Connie was near Paul, recognized Edward and got away so as not to be seen by her husband, but when the two men meet, our hypothesis is proved wrong because the lover is surprised when Edward tells him who he is. Connie comes to realize that her husband knows about her extramarital affair when she brings his clothes to the laundry and finds in a pocket the pictures of her with Paul shot by the private investigator.

After the first climax of the killing, there are two other questions that maintain the suspenseful rhythm of the film. When Edward realizes that Connie knows that he found out about her relations with Paul, and when and who come to know that Edward killed Paul. It is during a brief scene, at a party in the couple's villa, that Edward realizes that Connie realizes that he knows, and that Connie suspects that Edward is the killer. One of the guests lift a glass ball, and behind it is the glass ball with which the husband killed the lover: a zoom in on the ball is followed by a shot-reverse-shot, enriched with a zoom between Edward and Connie. A play of gazes is adopted here to stage the climax. Before this scene, a series of contretemps increases suspense: the lift in Paul's building stops when Edward is carrying his corpse; in the parking lot after the school play, a car crashes into the back of Edward's car – in which is hidden Paul's corpse – and, at the beginning, he cannot close it, and the police finds at Paul's a sheet with Connie's name and phone number on it – as usual, we are shown the leaflet before, after Edward kills Paul, so that we know the police are going to question Connie sooner or later.

If the spectator knows more or as much as the other characters during the entire film, with the exception of the beginning, when neither we nor Connie and Paul know whether they will have an extramarital affair, the end of the film is open. After a party, Connie and Edward speak about their situation in their car. She would like to go away with him and Charlie, he cannot forget what he did, and they kiss and embrace. In a long shot, we see their car stop at a traffic light, on the right the police station, and there follows another long shot of their car farther away.

Unfaithful is a remake of *La femme infidèle* (Claude Chabrol, 1969), but the two films are very different in terms of eroticism, rhythm and knowledge. In Chabrol's film we share the husband Charles, (Michel Bouquet) knowledge. We suspect, like him, that his wife Stéphane (Stéphane Audran) has an extramarital affair, and we come to know the truth together with him, after he asks a friend of his to stalk her. The gap between Stéphane's and her lover Victor's (Maurice Ronet) first meeting remains open, and we see them speak only once. The end is open, as in *Unfaithful*, but different. Policemen suspect that Charles is Victor's killer, but we do not know why and, at the end of the film, when they arrive at his house, we do not know whether they arrest him or drive him to the station to ask him questions. He is in a wood with his wife and son when two policemen arrive, and the film closes with a long take – a long shot of Stéphane and her son – that could be a shot from Charles' point of view – during which the camera first

tracks backwards away from the mother and her child, then forward towards them, but
turning right so that they remain half-hidden behind the leaves of trees.

3.3 *Lolita* (1997): Another adaptation, not a remake

Lolita, like *Fatal Attraction*, *Indecent Proposal* and *Unfaithful*, is based on love triangles,
but here these triangles change continuously, and the audience and characters have
different knowledge about them. The same is true of Vladimir Nabokov's and Stanley
Kubrick's *Lolita*, one of the few features, together with the main events in which the
protagonists are involved, that is common to the novel and its two adaptations. Here I
will highlight the differences rather than the similarities between the two adaptations.
As regards the fabula and the succession and simultaneity of love triangles, I refer to
Kubrick's *Lolita* in Chapter 2. In an interview, Lyne emphasizes how different his film is
from Kubrick's: 'I wanted the movie to be a road movie because I didn't feel in the other
film, in the Kubrick film and this was tough, I'm trying to avoid talking about the
enemy but it was a little tough. I wanted to get a feel of this pair travelling across
America' ('Adrian Lyne Interview' 1998).

Both Lyne's and Kubrick's films are source-path-goal schemas embedded in a
container schema, but the latter is slightly different in the two films. Whereas in the
opening sequence of the Kubrick adaptation we come to know that Humbert killed
Quilty because of Lolita, in Lyne's film we know that the protagonist (Jeremy Irons) is
a desperate killer, but we do not know either the identity of his victim or the cause of
the murder. His voice-over during this very first sequence introduces Lolita (Dominique
Swain), and while he drives, zigzagging and absent-mindedly, there are details of his
blood-stained fingers holding a gun and a hair clip. Even if the audience does not know
the fabula, we may deduce that Humbert killed somebody who destroyed his
relationship with Lolita. The first love triangle is traced, but the identity of the character
who constitutes one of the vortexes remains unknown: Humbert–Lolita–? The
spectator's curiosity focuses upon the third character. Unlike in Kubrick's first sequence,
where curiosity is suspended by comedy intertwined with tragedy, and where we share
Humbert's grief but, nonetheless, laugh with Quilty at him, in Lyne's film curiosity is
almost overwhelmed by drama.

A sad, melancholic, rather than tragicomic, mood also dominates the subsequent
sequence of Lyne's film. A title specifies 'Cannes, France, 1921', it is an external flashback
constituted by a montage sequence of the love story between the fourteen-year-old
Humbert and Annabel (Emma Griffiths Malin), that tragically ended with the girl's
untimely death. Humbert's voice-over explains or, better, tries to persuade us that there
would not have been Lolita if there had never been Annabel because he has been
looking for his lost love his entire life. This flashback, which appears in the novel but
not in Kubrick's film, provides a witty and touching explanation for the protagonist's
future behaviour. Lolita becomes the embodiment of Annabel, her replacement, the
mean through which Humbert stitches up his wound. But when the protagonist meets
Lolita, he is no longer 14, he could be and will become her stepfather. During this

montage sequence, Lyne adopts some of the techniques that he uses in love scenes in his other films: the camera is near the characters; there are details of body parts and dresses, and sometimes slow motion is used. Moreover, this particular sequence is dominated by a white *mise-en-scène*, fades in and out or fades from and to white. White seems to be a metaphor of the purity of the first love story, and contrasts with the pastel colours, faded by the fog, of the previous sequence: from innocence, perversity is born. The style, and especially the use of white, gives a dreamy, timeless atmosphere that imbues the protagonist's as well as the spectator's experience of Humbert's adventure. Much more than Kubrick, Lyne seems, from the very beginning, to stress Humbert's tragedy, downplaying the novel's humorous moments and emphasizing the tragic and erotic moments. The protagonist becomes a victim of a cursed past, of a teenager who first seduces and then abandons him, and of a remorseless playwright. His being a paedophile takes a back seat, even more so than in Kubrick's film. This montage sequence is followed by a scene that opens with the title, 'New England, 1947', and a train that enters from the right of the frame to exit left, as in Société Lumière's *L'Arrivée d'un train en gare de La Ciotat* (1986). Is it a nostalgic homage that references both France, where Humbert's first love story took place, and the beginning of Lolita, that is to say, Nabokov's protagonist and novel?

Three years after Lolita's disappearance, Humbert receives a letter from her, in which she writes that she is married to Richard Shiller (Michael Dolan), is pregnant and they have to pay debts before moving to Alaska. She asks Humbert for financial support. Moved by the desire to see her and probably, even more, to meet the man for whom she left him, he visits her. As soon as he sees Richard, who is working in the garden behind the house, he realizes he is not the man he has looked for over the years, checking all the registers of the motels where he had slept with Lolita until recognizing the unknown man's handwriting, but being unable to find out his real name. Richard seems too rude to cover his own traces in such a sophisticated manner. When Lolita naively reveals Clare Quilty's (Frank Langella) name, there follow Humbert's three internal flashbacks about the playwright's presence on the veranda of the Enchanted Hunters Hotel, in the theatre of Beardsley High School and at a petrol station. While the dreamer Humbert should open his eyes and understand how much he has been deceived by Lolita and Quilty, he declares his blind love in a pathetic, last effort. Our empathy for his tragedy increases when Lolita coldly claims that she has never been in love with him, but only with Quilty.

The film ends where it began. Hopeless, Humbert drives his car, holding a gun and Lolita's hair clip, and is followed by the police. The scenes of the chase alternate with those of the playwright's murder. The desperate quietness of the protagonist in his car, one of the main theatres of his dreamy love story, is counterposed with the fight with Quilty. When, with a jump, Quilty manages to disarm Humbert, they fight on the floor to reach the gun – quick movements of the camera and characters and fast editing – until Humbert reaches it and shoots the playwright to death, as seen in slow motion. If before the murder Humbert accused Quilty of not having allowed him to redeem himself, at the end of the chase with the police his voice-over admits that he stole Lolita's childhood. He tragically acknowledges his sins and his powerlessness to change the past. At the end of the film, two titles tell the audience that Humbert died in prison on 16 November 1950, and Lolita during childbirth on 25 December 1950. Thus, Humbert could not even have been able to change the future, and his character remains forever trapped in the tragedy of his sick love affair.

Unlike in Kubrick's film, in Lyne's the relationship between Humbert and Lolita is foregrounded through several techniques: secondary characters are less numerous, e.g. the Farlows, Vivian Darkbloom and the piano teacher do not appear; there are no scenes in which several characters are grouped, as in the graduation party or the school recital; Quilty is less present on stage and is not a comedian like Peter Sellers who focuses attention on his performance; and the relationship Humbert–Lolita is shot through with different features that tend to exclude the other characters. Lyne's Quilty is a ghostly presence, his face almost always concealed either in the dark or in the shadow of his wide-brimmed hat. He first appears in the lobby of the Enchanted Hunters Hotel, sitting in an armchair with a dog, in the restaurant – where Lolita recognizes him, then on the veranda when he speaks with Humbert and where the darkness of the night and the flashes of flycatchers prevent us from clearly seeing his face. He is present in a couple of long shots in the theatre of Beardsley High School, seen from a low-angle and with a backlight from the window behind him that allows Humbert to see only his silhouette, although a friend of Lolita's tells the Professor his name and role. Similarly, Humbert never recognizes him looking in the back rear mirror of his car when he chases them, nor when he speaks with Lolita at the gas station. Quilty utters a few words about his dog in the hotel lobby, and the exchange of dialogue between him and Humbert on the veranda is witty, but not as funny as that between Sellers and Mason:

Quilty   Where the hell did you get her?

Humbert   I beg your pardon.

Quilty   I said the weather is getting better.

Humbert   Seems so.

Quilty   Who is the lassie?

Humbert   Ehm. My daughter.

Quilty   You lie. She is not.

Humbert   What?

Quilty   I said the light was hot. Where's her mother?

Humbert   Dead.

Quilty   Oh, sorry. Why don't you two have lunch with me tomorrow? That clerical cradle will be gone soon.

Humbert   We'll be gone too, thanks. Goodnight.

Quilty   Sorry, I'm very drunk. Goodnight. That child of yours needs a lot of sleep. Sleep is a rose, as the Persian said. Smoke?

Humbert   Not just now, thanks.

Quilty   Enjoy.

He is a serious, menacing ghost who, in spite of his corpulence, manages to hide himself. If Sellers could be interpreted as Mason's diabolical, but funny, alter ego, Langella is the dark demon of Irons' consciousness.

Lolita is in-frame with Quilty only twice, and for few seconds: in the lobby and at the petrol station. Unlike in Kubrick's *Lolita*, there are no virtuoso long takes and camera movements in the hotel during which characters are in-frame together, exchanging positions and gazes. Similarly, these techniques are not adopted in Charlotte Haze's (Melanie Griffith) house. The triangle Charlotte–Humbert–Lolita is not emphasized through long takes or takes in which the three are in-frame together, and there is a different play of gazes among them. In Lyne's film, Charlotte is usually out of frame, excluded when Humbert and Lolita are in-frame: either there are shot-reverse-shots between the Professor and the girl, or the former peeps at her, without her noticing him. At the beginning Lolita is introduced by the male protagonist's voice-over and, being, in the first part of the film, only the object of his gaze, she seems to exist only through him. But little by little, through Humbert's desire, violence and selfishness, she begins first to innocently play with him, teasing him, and finally manages to dominate him. For example, we first see Lolita through Humbert's point of view shots: she is in the garden, looking at a magazine with pictures of Hollywood stars, and does not realize her mother and the new lodger are near until the end of the scene when she looks back at Humbert smiling. Zooms in on both Lolita and Humbert seem already a visual metaphor of the latter's desire to possess her. In the next shot the Professor, pretending to be reading a newspaper, peers at her over his glasses: she is hanging white laundry – and the white echoes the montage sequence with Annabel, subtly merging the two girls, the past with the present. She does not look at Humbert, but when she finishes with the laundry, we are shown a detail of her wet foot that steps onto the Professor's trousers; she bypasses him. Does she do so on purpose or for distraction? Does she want to innocently play or is she already seducing him? There are several other examples during which Lolita does not seem to realize that she is the object of Humbert's gaze – e.g. when he stares at her from his window while she is playing with a girlfriend; when at night she sits in front of the open fridge and eats food directly from it – a homage to *Nine ½ Weeks*?; when her image is reflected in the mirror while she is brushing her teeth, or when, on the toilet, she reaches out for toilet paper, or when she's lying on her bed; when she dances inside the house while Humbert sits with Charlotte on a swing and, to see her, he moves the swing right and left, instead of up and down, and turns back (Figure 3.2); when he goes to pick her up at the summer camp, it is he who first sees her, and the zoom emphasizes his desire to meet her after six weeks, and in the car he peers at her from the rear back mirror while she changes her shirt. Sometimes there are shot-reverse-shots between Humbert and Lolita, the

Figure 3.2 *Lolita* (Adrian Lyne, 1997). Lolita (Dominique Swain) dances inside the house while Humbert (Jeremy Irons) sits with Charlotte (Melanie Griffith) on a swing and, to see her, he moves the swing right and left, and turns back.

classical play of gazes that in the majority of Lyne's films precedes love relations or sexual encounters.

In *Lolita*, the female protagonist is mainly the object of the Professor's gaze, at least at the beginning of the film, as if she was in-frame only because of shots from his point of view. On the other hand, Charlotte is seldom in-frame, not being the object of Humbert's stare. Robert Stam claims: 'Both Kubrick and Lyne emphasize Humbert's voyeurism. But, in Kubrick, [...] he has us watch Humbert watching, often catching him in flagrante [...] Lyne, in contrast, rigorously identifies us with Humbert's perspective by having us look with Humbert through carefully constructed point-of-view shots. Countless shots show Humbert straining to get a glimpse of Lolita' (Stam 2005: 237–8).

More than a play of gazes, there are several moments during which the border between play and seduction becomes indistinguishable, although Lolita is a defenceless teenager because her father died and her mother has goals well beyond her care and education. She often seems to provoke Humbert on purpose, for example when she sits on his lap and puts a piece of the gum she is chewing on his diary, and then she shows him how she is able to move her chin. He smiles and is mesmerized by her, he lays his head on her shoulder, but Charlotte interrupts them and, to prevent a scolding from her mother, he puts Lolita's gum in his mouth. Interestingly, during the montage sequence in which we see moments of Humbert and Charlotte's marriage, Charlotte sits on Humbert's lap, not unlike Lolita, but he keeps writing, as if she was not there. During the scene on the swing, details emphasize Lolita's right leg pressing against Humbert's left leg, and when her mother goes inside to take another drink, Lolita puts her braces inside Humbert's glass and he tries to put it in Lolita's mouth before Charlotte notices her daughter's joke. One morning, when Lolita brings Humbert his breakfast, she touches his legs with hers and puts her feet on his feet. But the more significant scene of mutual play takes place the morning Lolita leaves for summer camp. Humbert sees her from the window of his room. Noticing him, she runs upstairs. When she reaches the first floor, in slow motion she runs and jumps into Humbert's arms and kisses him on the mouth. Details, slow motion, the alternate montage between Humbert and Lolita before and after they meet, increase the eroticism of this scene. As they say goodbye to each other with a kiss, the next time they meet at the summer camp they greet each other with another kiss. Lolita claims she had been unfaithful to him, but that he evidently does not care because he has not kissed her yet. He quickly turns into a side road, she sits on his lap and they kiss.

But if gazes, jokes, touching legs and feet and kisses can still be considered an innocent display of desire, what occurs at the Enchanted Hunters Hotel is the satisfaction of that forbidden desire that clearly becomes sex with an underage girl, which is transforming Lolita from a fourteen-year-old experimenting with her first relationships with friends into a prostitute. Humbert's voice-over admits his 'vulnerability', his incapacity to resist temptation:

> Gentlewomen of the jury, if my happiness could have talked it would have filled down that hotel with a deafening roar. My only regret is that I did not immediately deposit key number 342 at the office and leave the town and the country and the planet that very night.

But when he enters the room where Lolita is sleeping, editing translates the overwhelming power of his desire. He then enters the bathroom and returns in his pyjamas. Desire erases time. There follow point-of-view shots of Lolita and of details of her body, and he gently pushes her to gain a place in the double bed. This scene echoes his marriage, when he used to give Charlotte sleeping pills and, when she was asleep, he would roughly push her away. The next morning, Lolita tells Humbert she used to play with Charlie, a boy at the summer camp, and would like to repeat it with him. She whispers in his ear, then sits on his lap and begins to undo the belt of his pyjamas. From now on, she will lead, using sex as exchange. Pure sex desire, as when Lolita is reading comics on Humbert's lap, and moves back and forth until they both reach orgasm, soon gives way to a filthy bargain. To persuade him to let her take part in the Beardsley school play, with a foot she moves the rocking chair on which Humbert sits, with the other she touches his groin and with a hand she caresses his leg. In the meantime, she ups the ante and asks for an increase of her weekly pocket money. Soon, in exchange for sex with Humbert, she asks him for money and increases the price each time: we see them lit by a blue light, they are naked on the bed and fight to collect coins. When they quarrel because she did not attend her piano lessons, after a chase along the street at night she waits at home, upstairs, and begins to unbutton her shirt; the low-angle versus the high-angle of him visually translates her control of the situation. She asks him to leave on another trip, and he accepts.

Kubrick had to deal with the Production Code and the Catholic Legion of Decency, claiming that: 'because his [Humbert's] sexual obsession was only barely hinted at, it was assumed too quickly that Humbert was in love. Whereas in the novel this comes as a discovery in the end' (Connolly 2009: 162). Similarly, Lyne had to face the Child Pornography Prevention Act, approved in 1996, which criminalized pornography involving children as well as 'actors or altered photographic images that make it appear as if children were involved', and he had to edit the film following the suggestions of a lawyer specialized in this field (166). The result was that many shots with, for example, details of the breasts of Swain's double, had to be cut ('Adrian Lyne Interview', 1998). While both directors would have liked to underline eroticism and the protagonist's sexual obsession, they had to play it down, with the result that love, rather than erotic passion, comes to the fore.

Unlike in Kubrick's *Lolita*, in Lyne's humour is downplayed – there remain traces of it during the dialogue between Quilty and Humbert at the Enchanted Hunters Hotel, and when the Headmistress of Lolita's high school tells Humbert that he should explain sex to her daughter. Eroticism and tragedy are emphasized, and focus around Lolita and Humbert only, as if they lived in a dream world with only a few contacts with other people. On the other hand, we share only Humbert's perspective: the only voice-over is his, Lolita is often the object of his gaze, and she is never present when he is not with her. We share Humbert's inaccurate and partial knowledge of Lolita. While we know more than he about Lolita's meetings with Quilty, thus we are able to identify her secret lover, we are never spectators of their affair. Metaphorically, we are imprisoned in a house of cards made of desire, a sick and obsessed love and the tragedy of loss. If the ASL of Kubrick's *Lolita* is very high, and there are long shots and deep-focus compositions – usually features of slow movies – temporalities in Lyne's film seem slower because the diegetic world seems to collapse around Humbert, imprisoning him, from the beginning, with Annabel's death, to the end, with his own and Lolita's death. He is trapped in his own past, obsessions and nightmares. In a motel, when he finds Lolita with dirty feet and red lipstick all over her face, he has a hallucination in the middle of the night: he listens to somebody knocking at the door, to people chatting and laughing, he sees distorted faces with yellow hats, and his point-of-view shots of the washbasin and his image reflected in the mirror are equally distorted – a hallucination not dissimilar to those of *Jacob's Ladder*. He moves quickly, as the handheld camera takes and editing are rapid. The same style, together with canted shots, will be adopted at the hospital, where Humbert is told that Lolita checked out, that he lost her. His dreams and desires slowly become an obsession, a nightmare that closes around him, as the film closes where it had begun.

3.4 *Jacob's Ladder*: A change in Lyne's temporalities

Jacob's Ladder, according to Miklòs Kiss and Steven Willemsen's taxonomy, is a disorienting but solvable puzzle film during which the audience continually makes hypotheses to fill in curiosity gaps until the narrative twist discussed in Chapter 1. The twist fixes: 'an otherwise irrational and incoherent story into which the plot got gradually tangled up when presenting a subjective realist view of some untrustworthy, hallucinating, mad or simply fallible character' (2017: 57, 56–9). I do not agree with this classification, and see *Jacob's Ladder* rather as an impossible puzzle film, in which narration is very similar to that of deceptive, unreliable or twist films – such as *The Sixth Sense* (M. Night Shyamalan, 1999) and *Fight Club* (David Fincher, 1999) – in which, when a surprise gap is filled in, the spectator has to reformulate his previous hypotheses and knowledge (Kiss and Willemsen 2017: 52–6). Unlike deceptive unreliable films, in *Jacob's Ladder*, following the twist, several questions remain unanswered and possible hypotheses arise, even after several viewings and close analysis.

Jacob's Ladder opens with a sequence accompanied by the title 'Mekong Delta 6 Oct. 1971'. There is an alternating montage among helicopters, soldiers running and the soldiers of Jacob (Tim Robbins), the protagonist's platoon who, at the beginning chat and smoke, then some of them begin to feel sick and others to fight. To increase suspense, the montage and the camera and actor movements are rapid, and a handheld camera is deployed close to characters or their wounds. The sequence ends with a medium shot of Jacob who is stabbed and puts his hands on his chest – we are not shown the killer. The curiosity gap around whether Jacob is dead or alive is immediately filled in the next sequence that opens with another medium shot of the protagonist, sleeping in a subway train. He suddenly wakes up and puts his right hand to his chest. The order of representational time, and Jacob's gesture as he wakes up, suggest that he awakes after a nightmare or an external flashback that troubled his nap. The second hypothesis is confirmed when we see the second of Jacob's external flashbacks of his experience in Vietnam. What is interesting is that in the second sequence of the film we are already witnesses of a dreamlike reality characterized by nightmarish characters and events. For example, on the train there are a couple of point-of-view shots during which we see two advertisements: 'HELL. That's what life can be, doing drugs' and in the other we read 'NY' so that we come to know where the story is set. On the train, Jacob asks a woman whether they have already passed a station, but she stares at him, her eyes wide open, remaining silent. Before getting off, he sees a man who is sleeping, lying on seats, and from his coat a strange creature comes out: it seems to be a snake, but the two point-of-view shots are too brief and dark to identify it. At the station, the exit is closed, and Jacob has to cross the binaries to reach the other exit, but when he goes through them, a train comes in his direction. He cannot understand on which binary the train is travelling, and consequently in which direction he has to run, until the very last moment. He manages to save himself, but when he is still lying on the binaries, from his point of view, first we are shown men looking at him with their hands placed on the windows and then, on the last carriage, a faceless man who greets him.

In New York, Jacob lives in an apartment with his lover Jezzie (Elizabeth Peña) and they both work in a post office. Through dialogue and his external enacted flashbacks, we come to know that he was married to another woman, Sarah (Patricia Kalember), and they had three sons. When he came back from Vietnam, one of his sons, Gabe (Macaulay Culkin), was hit by a car and died. Sequences set in Jacob's and the other characters' diegetic present in New York alternate with Jacob's external enacted flashbacks about his past life with his family, his son's death and Vietnam. But the diegetic present is haunted by frightening, sometimes horrific creatures and events that implicitly pose questions to the audience: are these strange creatures and events real or are they figments of a Vietnam veteran's mind confused by memories of past atrocities? That is to say, is he a reliable or an unreliable character? When he meets one of his former war comrades, Paul (Pruitt Taylor Vince), Paul confesses that he is descending into hell, that he is hunted by faceless men who want to kill him. Outside the pub, as soon as Paul gets in his car, it explodes. During his wake, Jacob tells the other veterans what Paul said before dying. One of the comrades asks questions, as if he was living the same experiences, and a detail of his hand, trembling while holding a bottle of beer that finally falls, underlines his fear. These sequences confirm that Jacob is a reliable character because in his diegetic present his point of view is confirmed by other characters. The comrades decide to contact a lawyer, Geary (Jason Alexander), to find out the truth about what happened in Vietnam when Jacob was stabbed, and about what is happening now, whether the US Army is menacing them to conceal secret experiments. After some research, Geary tells Jacob that he and his comrades have never been in Vietnam, but in Thailand where they were discharged for mental disorder. At this point, the spectator, who could have believed the protagonist's visions because they were confirmed by other veterans, once more doubts Jacob's reliability.

It is towards the end of the film, when the protagonist meets the chemist Michael (Matt Craven), that it is at last explained what happened during that day in Vietnam that haunts Jacob's memories. Michael was ordered to create a drug able to increase aggressiveness to strengthen the soldiers' bravery and cruelty. They called it 'the ladder' because it was like throwing oneself headlong down a ladder, towards primal fears and wild rage. They tested it on monkeys, then on Vietnamese people and, finally, on Jacob's platoon: they all ended up killing everybody, without distinguishing between friends and enemies. This explains why some soldiers felt sick that day, why during Paul's wake some comrades commented that nothing had happened except for smoking bad pot and why the lawyer did not find out anything useful.

Even if Jacob's reliability is sometimes confirmed, strange events and, most of all, faceless men, make us wonder whether he experiences hallucinations. These creatures are called 'devils' by Jacob and Paul, and they experience a seeming descent into hell – it is interesting to recall that one of the two advertisements on the train in the second sequence links hell with drugs. At Jezzie's, when Jacob recovers after a high fever, we see him browsing books – e.g. *A Witches Bible*, *Demonology*, *The Roots of Evil* – looking for images of devils. Moreover, in his diegetic present, he suffers from backache and goes to the chiropractor Louis (Danny Aiello), who gives him advice about his flashbacks. The first time we see them together, Jacob defines Louis as his guardian angel. The second time, after Louis drives Jacob away from a hospital, he explains to him:

You ever read Meister Eckart? [...] Eckart saw Hell, too. You know what he said? The only thing that burns in Hell is the part of you that won't let go of your life;

your memories, your attachments. They burn 'em all away. But they're not punishing you, he said. They're freeing your soul. [. . .] So the way he sees it, if you're frightened of dying and holding on, you'll see devils tearing your life away. But if you've made your peace then the devils are really angels freeing you from the earth. It's just a matter of how you look at it, that's all. So don't worry, okay?

Similarly, at the end of the film when he enters Sarah's house, before meeting his dead son and going upstairs with him towards a blinding white light, he listens to Louis' voice-over repeating these sentences.

In an interview with Patty Spitler, Lyne confirmed the presence of demonic and angelic creatures, underlining that the screenwriter Bruce Joel Rubin 'the way he wrote it, it was very much in biblical terms', because he describes them with classical wings and horns. But Lyne sought to create something more realistic that, according to him, would have been scarier. For example, rather than using horns for the nurse at the hospital reception, they created 'bony things', 'something that had grown out of her skull'. As regards what I have called 'faceless men', he was inspired by Francis Bacon: 'who did kind of blurry smeared, kind of tortured imagery, and so [. . .] a lot of the demonic stuff is moving [. . .] the audience can't see it clearly and when they could see something clearly than it's less scary [. . .] it was something that worked at eight frames' ('1990 Director Adrian Lyne Talks with Patty Spitler about "Jacob's Ladder"' 2018 [1990]).

Apart from the fact that Lyne himself claims that in the film there are demons that he tried to represent as realistically as possible, Jacob sees them only in his diegetic present, they never appear in his enacted external flashbacks. The only other diegetic characters who see them are his war comrades and, moreover, the protagonist's reliability is continually questioned. I suggest that the spectator speculates about whether Jacob is haunted by devils that are real, that is to say, creatures that are present in his diegetic world, or by demons that his mind and those of his comrades created after having experienced 'the ladder' in Vietnam. According to Tzvetan Todorov, a fantastic text must fulfil three conditions:

> First, the text must oblige the reader to consider the world of characters as a world of living persons and to hesitate between a natural and a supernatural explanation of the events described. Second, this hesitation may also be experienced by a character [. . .] Third, the reader must adopt a certain attitude with regard to the text: he will reject allegorical as well as 'poetic' interpretations. These three requirements do not have an equal value. The first and the third actually constitute the genre; the second may not be filled.
>
> 1975: 33

In an uncanny text, the laws of the diegetic world coincide with the physical laws of our own world; by contrast, in a marvellous text they do not coincide. A text is fantastic-uncanny when, after a hesitation between a natural and supernatural explanation of the events, the reader chooses the former; on the other hand, it is fantastic-marvellous

Table 3.1 *Jacob's Ladder*. Differences among spectators' beliefs and how they read events.

Spectator's beliefs		Definition of *Jacob's Ladder*
Spectators who believe that demons and angels exist in our world		Uncanny
Spectators who do not believe that demons and angels exist in our world and	who think that devils exist in Jacob's mind	Fantastic-uncanny
	who think that devils exist in the diegetic world	Fantastic-marvellous

when at the end he chooses the latter (ibid., 44). Watching *Jacob's Ladder*, spectators fall roughly into two groups: those who believe in the existence of devils and angels in our own world and those who do not. The former considers the film uncanny because the laws of the diegetic and extra-diegetic world are the same. The latter group may define it either as fantastic-uncanny or fantastic-marvellous. At first, they hesitate between a natural and supernatural explanation of events and creatures, then some believe that demons exist only in the protagonist's mind, while others that they exist in the diegetic world like all the other characters (Table 3.1).

When the surprise gap is filled in, when the narrative twist arrives, and we understand that Jacob is still in Vietnam, is stoned and dying, and during moments of consciousness or unconsciousness he either dreams or thinks about his past, mixing memories and fantasies, the spectator who believes that devils do not exist but are present in the diegetic world, may change their mind and think that demons do not even exist in the diegetic world: he may pass from a definition of the film as a fantastic-uncanny narration.

According to the director: 'when you get to the end of the movie you have to reassess everything that you've seen because you weren't seen what you thought you were seeing. So it's a kind of like two movies in one. You know, it's a movie that you have to work at, it's not just something that will kind of wash over you and you'll forget immediately.' I believe that the film is even more complex: it can be uncanny, fantastic-uncanny, fantastic-marvellous or initially fantastic-marvellous and then fantastic-uncanny. Moreover, the twist may come before the end of the film, at different moments for diverse spectators, and when the surprise gap is filled in our perception of represented and representational time and their relation changes completely. Before the narrative twist, in the diegetic present, Jacob lives in New York with Jezzie and has external flashbacks about his previous life with Sarah and his three sons, which precedes his experience in Vietnam, followed by Geary's death (Table 3.2). After the twist, in the diegetic present, Jacob is in Vietnam with his comrades, and has external flashbacks about his family, his son's accident and his relationship with Jezzie (Table 3.3). The events of his past should follow the order in which I have listed them.

Unfortunately, the protagonist is unreliable because he is doped and is dying, thus his flashbacks can be a mix of memories and dreams, but we cannot appreciate the difference between what happened in the diegetic world and what Jacob is imagining.

Table 3.2 *Jacob's Ladder*. The order of events before the surprise gap.

Before surprise gap is filled in	Life with his family before his son's death	Vietnam	Death of his son	Life with Jezzie
Vietnam		X		
US – Subway and Jezzie's				X
Vietnam		X		
US – Jezzie's				X
US – Dead Son			X	
US – Jezzie's, Street, Post Office, Louis'				X
Vietnam		X		
US – Louis', Street, Hospital, Jezzie's, Party				X
Vietnam		X		
US – Jezzie's				X
US – Sarah's	X			
Vietnam		X		
Jezzie's				X
Vietnam		X		
US – Jezzie's, Bar				X
Vietnam		X		
US – Bar, Street				X
Vietnam		X		
US – Street, Churchyard, Paul's, Lawyer's Office, Jezzie's, Court, Hospital				X
Nightmare Hospital				
Vietnam		X		
US – Hospital, Louis'				X
US – Jezzie's				X
Vietnam		X		
US – Jezzie's				X
US – Dead Son			X	
US – Jezzie's				X
US – Dead Son			X	
US – Jezzie's				X
US – Dead Son			X	
US – Jezzie's				X
US – Dead Son			X	
US – Jezzie's, Street				X
Vietnam		X		
US – Street, Cab				X
Vietnam		X		
US – Cab				X
Vietnam		X		
US – Sarah's	X			
US – Dead Son and family – 6 different shots	X			
US – Sarah's	X			
Vietnam		X		

Table 3.3 *Jacob's Ladder.* The order of events following the surprise gap.

After surprise gap is filled in	Life with his family before his son's death	Death of his son	Life with Jezzie	Vietnam
Vietnam				X
US – Subway and Jezzie's			X	
Vietnam				X
US – Jezzie's			X	
US – Dead Son		X		
US – Jezzie's, Street, Post Office, Louis'			X	
Vietnam				X
US – Louis', Street, Hospital, Jezzie's, Party			X	
Vietnam				X
US – Jezzie's			X	
US – Sarah's	X			
Vietnam				X
Jezzie's			X	
Vietnam				X
US – Jezzie's, Bar			X	
Vietnam				X
US – Bar, Street			X	
Vietnam				X
US – Street, Churchyard, Paul's, Lawyer's Office, Jezzie's, Court, Hospital			X	
Nightmare Hospital				
Vietnam				X
US – Hospital, Louis'			X	
US – Jezzie's			X	
Vietnam				X
US – Jezzie's			X	
US – Dead Son		X		
US – Jezzie's			X	
US – Dead Son		X		
US – Jezzie's			X	
US – Dead Son		X		
US – Jezzie's			X	
US – Dead Son		X		
US – Jezzie's, Street			X	
Vietnam				X
US – Street, Cab			X	
Vietnam				X
US – Cab			X	
Vietnam				X
US – Sarah's	X			
US – Dead Son and Family – 6 different shots	X			
US – Sarah's	X			
Vietnam				X

For example, before leaving for Vietnam, was he still married to Sarah and was he having an extramarital affair with Jezzie? Does the chiropractor Louis exist in the diegetic world or only in Jacob's mind? The protagonist cannot have met his comrades in New York, Paul's car cannot have exploded and his wake cannot have taken place. These are only a few examples of how, after the narrative twist, we rethink the order of represented time and the authenticity of events.

One of the techniques that cheat us further, making us believe that Jacob's diegetic present is that in which he is living with Jezzie, is the duration of the sequences and scenes shot in different spaces and times: 0.4 per cent of the time represented consists of the protagonist's external flashbacks of his dead son; 1 per cent is about Vietnam; 12 per cent of his life with Sarah; and 74 per cent narrates his life with Jezzie (Figure 3.3). In classical Hollywood films, flashbacks are usually briefer than the diegetic present, or the whole present is presented as a flashback embedded in a frame, as in the case of Kubrick's *Killer's Kiss* and in both versions of *Lolita*.

What assists us more to understand that the order of diegetic time is different from that we thought, and that the protagonist's memories are mixed up with hallucinations and dreams, is the editing, particularly how the end of a sequence is linked to the beginning of the subsequent one when they are shot at different places and times.

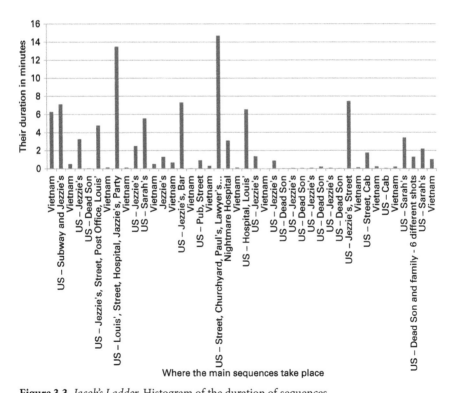

Figure 3.3 *Jacob's Ladder*. Histogram of the duration of sequences.

Usually, medium close-ups or close-ups of Jacob in different spaces and times are separated only by a cut, or a medium close-up or close-up of him is followed by his point-of-view shot in another time and place. For example, when Jacob attends a party with Jezzie, besides having frightening hallucinations, a palm reader tells him that his lifeline is strange because he should already have been dead. Gripped with a panic attack, Jacob faints and medium close-ups of him, during which the camera is above, alternate with shots from his point of view of the guests grouped around him. Colourful lights flash as in a discotheque. The sequence closes with a medium close-up of him and the next scene opens with a shot from his point of view of two soldiers in Vietnam lit by red lights and commenting that the protagonist's guts are spilling out. Time and space are different, but lights and the shot-reverse-shot technique merge the two sequences. Similarly, the subsequent sequence opens with a medium shot of Jacob in bed at Jezzie's, continuing the play of shot-reverse-shot. He has a high fever and when Jezzie calls the doctor, he tells her that to lower the temperature Jacob must be immersed in a bathtub full of ice. The last shot is a medium close-up of Jacob screaming in the bathtub. The next sequence opens with a detail of a desk, the camera then pans right until a medium close-up of Jacob in bed, at which he wakes and shuts the window. He is at Sarah's, in bed with her, and tells her he is cold and had a nightmare during which he lived with Jezzie, whom he defines as the woman who works at the post office, felt burned by ice and saw devils. In his dream, he mixes the party sequence with that at Jezzie's. When his dead son Geary arrives, he brings him to bed before going back to bed with Sarah, and the sequence closes with a close-up of him looking at the ceiling, the camera above him.

The next sequence takes place once more in Vietnam and opens with a handheld shot of the sky, as if it was Jacob's point of view while he is carried on a cot by other soldiers. Similarly, the subsequent scene opens with a detail of Jacob's eyes slowly opening, then a zoom-out reveals he is in the bathtub at Jezzie's. Later, after another scene shot in Vietnam, Jezzie tells Jacob that while he was sleeping he kept asking his former wife to shut the window and he spoke with his sons, even the dead son. These sequences merge not only through the editing, but also through Jacob's definition of two of them as nightmares and the protagonist's physical condition. At the party he has a panic attack, in Vietnam his guts are spilling out, at Jezzie's he has fever and is inside a bathtub full of ice and at Sarah's he is cold and closes the window. When we dream, physical stimuli can influence our sleep. It is, indeed, during these sequences that the narrative twist takes place, and the link between the first and second sequence of the film becomes a surprise gap. As discussed, this step can occur, for different spectators, before or after these sequences. It is explicit at the end of the film, as mentioned by Lyne himself during the interview cited above, when the shot in which Jacob and his dead son go hand in hand upstairs and disappear in blinding white light is followed by a shot of a light above Jacob's corpse in Vietnam and a couple of doctors commenting that he is dead.

It is interesting to note that, whereas the duration of the represented time of the doped, dying, often unconscious Jacob is approximately the same as the representational time, the duration of the represented time of his nightmares and hallucinations is much longer. Again, this difference in duration mimics that of our dreams. It is interesting to note that Salomon Resnik compares dreams with reactive psychosis. In both cases, the theatre of dreams is constituted by several acts or parts of acts that are not always connected to each other, but are always linked by an intrinsic coherence and can take place simultaneously (Resnik 2007: 50). This definition matches the succession of sequences analysed above, during which Jacob seems to be present in three different settings: in Vietnam, at Jezzie's and at Sarah's. Moreover, rather thinking than about Jacob as a dreamer who continually alternates sleep with waking states, we can, more realistically, think of him as a character who suffers from a reactive psychosis triggered by drugs and close combat. Reactive psychosis often causes hallucinations, unreal and persecutory beliefs as, respectively, during delirium and paranoia and speech disorders: an ensemble of Jacob's symptoms. During reactive psychosis, there is no distinction between sleep and waking states, dreams emerge from the oneiric scene and the dreamlike space merges with reality, confusing and changing it. The psychotic dreams, but cannot wake up: his delirium is an attempt to fit together fragments of a time that exploded, scattering its pieces in space (72). The psychotic worries about fundamental, ontological problems that often appear as mythic thoughts (73), much like Jacob who is anxious about devils and angels, death and life. From a phenomenological perspective, time in dreams is the present, while past and future experiences become a projection, from the present, in a point in space respectively called 'past' and 'future' (101). For a psychotic, the past is a way of being in the time that is always present, diachronic events are lived as synchronic ones, and all the pieces of the exploded time are scattered in the present space (125–6). In *Jacob's Ladder*, after the narrative twist, the succession of sequences shot in different spaces becomes a metaphor of the protagonist's present, in which past and present experiences are simultaneously present in his mind: succession becomes simultaneity, and editing is the means through which his psychosis is represented.

3.5 Conclusion

Lyne has developed peculiar temporalities through style and themes, alternating suspense with staged musical and erotic performances. Whereas during musical performances – as in *Flashdance* – usually the fabula does not advance and the spectator can appreciate the spectacle that develops before his eyes, erotic performances also stage different sexual relations, although they are shot with similar stylistic techniques. *Fatal Attraction*, *Indecent Proposal*, *Lolita* and *Unfaithful* are based on love triangles, in which two characters have a sexual affair and the third represents the obstacle to the former's relation, but also, paradoxically, the spark that fuels the fire of their passion. This occurs in Shakespeare's plays where the dramatic device necessary to give life to a true love is the presence of an impediment to its development. The rhetorical figure that is often used by the English playwright and that describes this situation is the oxymoron: a character's hate towards another increases, rather than decreasing the passion between them, expressing the despair of the rejected lover

(Girard 2012: 43–4, 52). In those Lyne's films that present a love triangle, passion between two characters is increased by the presence of a third character who represents the obstacle to their relation, while the third character's love for one of the other two increases when he/she finds out that she/he has another relation.

On the other hand, in twentieth-century novels, eroticism becomes a fight between two self-absorbed people, who are both obsessed by their independence and try to overwhelm one another. The first to confess his/her desire loses his/her freedom: he/she will be refused, becoming a puppet in the hands of the lover who still possesses her/his divine autonomy (129–34). In *Nine ½ Weeks*, whereas Elizabeth behaves with John as if they were a couple, speaking of her past and present life, he always maintains a detachment, excluding her from his past and from the moments during which they are not together. Through this behaviour, she progressively loses her independence, becoming his slave. René Girard claims that what looks more like possession is seeing without being watched: voyeurism, already omnipresent in Dostoevsky and Proust, becomes fundamental in contemporary culture and literature (129–34). In *Lolita*, this is first the case with Charlotte in her relationship with Humbert and of Humbert in his sexual affair with Lolita, and then of Lolita herself at the hands of Quilty. A similar mechanism plays out in *Fatal Attraction*: when Alex is refused, she becomes so obsessed with Dan that in the end she not only spies on him and his family, but also loses her mind.

In chivalric romance, a knight's heroism is the source of a female character's admiration and love, much like in our sociocultural context success in business, and social power and prestige are often the cause of a crush (17–18). Nick's, John's and John Cage's charm – in *Flashdance*, *Nine ½ Weeks* and *Indecent Proposal*, respectively – are certainly due to their success and prosperity, not only to their physical appearance, as much as Paul's glamour in *Unfaithful* is partly due to his knowledge of literature and antique books. In the story of Paolo and Francesca in Dante's *Divine Comedy*, the woman has an adulterous affair with her brother-in-law Paolo: they fall victim to temptation while reading of the adultery between Lancelot and Guinevere. Words often activate the desire (21, 35). This occurs when Paul asks Connie to take a book from his library, look for a specific page and read a romantic quote aloud: he knows it from memory and recites it with her, winning her heart.

During these love plays, suspense is not suspended, but temporalities slow down, echoing those timeless love stories that imbue our culture.

4

Temporalities

Conductors of Michael Bay's films

Lincoln Six-Echo   *I think they're going to kill you.*

Jordan Two-Delta   *I'm going to The Island.*

Lincoln Six-Echo   *Jordan, there is no island!*

The Island (2005)

Michael Bay is a contemporary action director: *Bad Boys* (1995) and *Bad Boys II* (2003), *The Rock* (1996), *Armageddon* (1998), *Pearl Harbour* (2001), *The Island* (2005), *Pain & Gain* (2013), *13 Hours: The Secret Soldiers of Benghazi* (2016) and *6 Underground* (2019); and the Transformer saga – *Transformers* (2007), *Transformers: Revenge of the Fallen* (2009), *Transformers: Dark of the Moon* (2011), *Transformers: Age of Extinction* (2014) and *Transformers: The Last Knight* (2017). Unlike in Chapters 2 and 3, in Bay's case, I do not analyse each film or group of films that adopt similar techniques separately, because in this oeuvre the narrative and stylistic choices used to create temporalities are almost always the same, with the exception of *The Island*. Moreover, apart from *Pain & Gain*, all his films are source-path-goal schemas. Thus, in each section, I concentrate on some of his peculiar narrative and stylistic techniques, focusing on remarkable examples.

In *The Rock*, when the protagonist Stanley (Nicolas Cage) goes home after having disarmed a bomb, risking his life and that of his colleagues, he tells his fiancée Carla (Vanessa Marcil): 'I really believe that anyone who's even thinking about having a child in this world is coldly considering an act of cruelty.' Carla replies that she is pregnant, and asks him whether he really believed that: 'seven and a half seconds ago'. The comments enclosed in the DVD[1] run, 'Technically it was forty-eight seconds ago, but who's counting?' stressing that if spectators are involved in what is happening on-screen they do not feel the passage of time. As Claudia Gorbman claims, usually spectators do not consciously hear film music; however, the comment above suggests that they usually do not perceive screening time if they are interested in what they are watching, unless temporalities call attention to themselves. Bay's temporalities,

---

[1]   DVD released on 3 December 1997 by Buena Vista Home Entertainment.

although not often consciously felt by spectators, are the principle that organizes the overall balance and rhythm of his films. For example, audience empathy with the characters' experience of time is obtained in different ways, such as camera movement, use of the Steadicam, slow-motion, close-ups and detail, soundtrack and ASL. In some films, the alternation of sequences shot with different techniques and of differing rhythms, or the use of cross-cutting, create a play between suspense and comedy – not unlike in Kubrick's *Lolita* and *Dr. Strangelove*. Moreover, during cross-cutting, when the characters watch or speak with other characters through radios and monitors, the spectator's role is mimicked and the characters' entrapment is highlighted. Audience appreciation of a character's race against time is also augmented towards the end of the films through a decrease in diegetic time in comparison with screening time and through countdowns. Furthermore, the *Transformers* films propose a diegetic time that continues throughout the pentalogy, increasing suspense, but also curiosity, presenting flashbacks that clarify and deepen the whole saga. *Pain & Gain* is narrated through a long-enacted flashback that ends where the narration begins, and is continuously suspended and enriched by external analepses narrated from the characters' points of view, creating a tragicomic choral narration. On the other hand, in *The Island*, past time and memories come to the fore because their importance and influence on the characters' present and identities become the main theme.

4.1 Empathy between spectators' and characters' experiences of time

When empathy between the spectators' and the characters' experience of time increases, for example when characters have to rush against time while facing a threat, temporalities are either accelerated or extended and almost frozen, although the effect is the same: an increase of suspense.

During the first countdown of *Bad Boys*, when a gang steals heroin from a police station, the voice-off that at the beginning advises, 'You got twenty minutes,' then, 'We got twelve minutes,' and finally, 'We got six minutes,' underlines the passage of time, and passing from the second person singular to plural, almost directly addresses the audience. Thanks to choices of *mise-en-scène* and cinematography, spectators understand, and are able to guess, the rapid development of the action. Indeed, when the gang members enter through the air-conditioning tubes, characters and objects move down, the camera tilts up and down, and the alternation of high and low-angles emphasize these vertical movements. Similarly, when they exit, characters and objects move up when they go up the tubes, and down when they get into the truck parked outside the police station, where there are again high and low-angles, the camera tilts up and down, and is mounted on electrical carriages alone or with characters. Whereas when the men are inside the room with the heroin, horizontal movements prevail: the camera pans or tracks right or left with or without characters. Alternation in the order of vertical, horizontal and again vertical movements help spectators to understand actions. Moreover, when a shot of a man on an electrical carriage is followed by a shot in which the camera is mounted on the carriage, the camera mimics a character's position and movement and spectator empathy increases. We are able to share feelings and emotions not only with characters, but also with a camera movement that simulates the presence of a human being (Gallese and Guerra 2015: 139–47). Thus, when shots of men on electrical carriages alternate with shots in which the camera is mounted on carriages, and in which continuity editing communicates the succession of shots and their relations, empathy between characters and spectators increases. Moreover, during this sequence, there are several close-ups and details of hands and feet that increase the haptic visuality of the shots, i.e. sight is in direct relation with touch, and it is as if spectators touch the film with their eyes (ibid., 232–3). Finally, the rapid editing is accompanied by the lively rhythm of the extra-diegetic music ('Bad Boys – Main Title' by Mark Mancina) that contributes to the audience's 'absorption', adding emotional information (Cohen, MacMillan and Drew 2006). Style increases audience empathy with the character's race against time, creating accelerated temporalities.

On the other hand, suspense can increase through an extension of temporalities. For example, whereas the ASL of *The Rock* is 2.5 seconds,[2] when Stanley, who is in front of John (Sean Connery), has to disarm for the very first time a rocket at Alcatraz, the ASL rises to 3.26 seconds. The camera moves in one shot only: in about half of the shots characters do not move, and in the other half they slowly and briefly move and there is no extra-diegetic music. Suspense is created by the dialogue between the two protagonists and by their close-ups: the chemist Stanley explains to John how easily the bomb can be inadvertently activated and how lethal it is, and John asks questions that betray that he is becoming increasingly anxious. The slow rhythm of characters' and camera movements and montage and the absence of music and noise expand temporalities. It is almost the same effect created as when slow motion is used to shoot dangerous actions.

In *13 Hours*, both before the first Libyan attack against the Special Mission compound where the US Ambassador is hidden and before the last Libyan attack at the US outpost, slow motion, extra-diegetic music and muffled noises expand temporalities, reproducing the quiet atmosphere that precedes the tempest. In the former case, the effect increases by slow panning to the right and left, and details of faces and feet, as if the unknowable enemy were everywhere. During these two attacks (after the titles '8:40 PM' and '5:23 AM', respectively), but also after the title '12:19 AM', the Steadicam advances among the Libyan militants mimicking them, as a threatening ghost – as do the handheld cameras in Kubrick's *Paths of Glory* and *Dr. Strangelove*, and the Steadicam in *Full Metal Jacket* and *The Shining*. In the first attack, after a shot during which the Steadicam moves outside the compound among Libyan men, it slowly advances towards Americans inside the Special Mission compound. The enemy is not yet inside, but the attack will soon begin as the Steadicam suggests. The camera mirrors the militants' positions and movements, increasing the spectator's empathy, which is further increased by the adoption of the Steadicam, whose movements are more

---

[2]   See http://www.cinemetrics.lv/database.php, submitted by Radomir D. Kokes on 21 July 2003. Last accessed 26 September 2016.

effective in evoking activation of the mechanism of mirror neurons (Gallese and Guerra 2015: 157–9). Temporalities are frozen thanks to slow motion, sound effects, details, slow camera movements and the Steadicam.

Bad Boys closes with a deadline defined by a forthcoming event: Mike (Will Smith) has to get into his Porsche, driven by Marcus (Martin Lawrence), before a hangar explodes. Temporalities are expanded but now mainly through repetitions and slow motion. At the beginning, when the Porsche comes to rescue Mike, there are jump cuts, and the car seems to repeat the same path four times: it always moves from left to right of the frame, and the camera does not move or pans right to accompany it. When Mike manages to get into the car, the camera pans left to accompany the Porsche that goes in reverse: the camera and the car move symmetrically, unlike at the beginning of the scene. While Mike is trying to jump into the car, Julie (Téa Leoni) and Marcus keep shouting at him to get into the car, and Marcus' 'This shit's going to blow' is preceded and followed by shots of explosions. These repetitions, stressing the dangerousness of the situation and delaying the conclusion of the scene, expand temporalities. The same effect is obtained through slow motion that is used during shots of a pained Mike who rolls on the ground and cannot stand up. According to the 'oddball effect', time seems to slow down in threatening situations. David Eagleman claims that time does not actually run in slow motion during dangerous events, but the episodes seem to last longer in retrospect because the protagonists' memories of these episodes are more densely packed.[3] Slow motion in this scene mimics the spectator's past experiences of threatening events, increasing their empathy with the protagonists and, once more, sharing their time experience.

Similarly, in *Bad Boys II*, slow motion is adopted when the two cops find themselves in dangerous circumstances, but their performance is sometimes so physically impossible that it becomes unbelievable. For example, at the beginning of the film, Mike, while throwing himself on the ground, shoots a bullet that passes through three glass bottles and Marcus' groin to hit the throat of the man who holds Marcus at gunpoint. This technique is widely used in the *Matrix* trilogy (Wachowski Brothers) to underline the characters' physical speed and strength. Slow motion emphasizes the extraordinariness of the actions, but in *Bad Boys II*, in which characters are not heroes with superpowers, and in which comedy and action scenes alternate, these shots become parodies.[4] It is interesting to note that *The Matrix* was released in 1999, and *The Matrix Reloaded* and *The Matrix Revolutions* were both released in the same year as *Bad Boys II*. In the *Matrix* trilogy, *Bad Boys* and *Bad Boys II*, slow motion is adopted to shoot dangerous situations, but whereas in the former films it increases audience empathy and suspense, in *Bad Boys II*, with its unbelievable situations, this technique transforms some scenes into a parody of action films, arousing the spectator's amusement.

---

[3] For a definition of oddball effect, and David Eagleman's theory (Frenzel 2008).

[4] According to Gérard Genette, hypertextuality is a relation that links a text, called a 'hypertext', to a previous text, 'hypotext', without being a comment (Genette 1997: 5–7). Given a hypotext with a respected subject and style, its parody is characterized by a vulgar subject narrated in the same respected style as the hypertext (ibid., 10–38).

4.2 Alternation of action scenes or staged action performances and comedy sequences

In the majority of Bay's films, narration is constructed through alternation of action and dialogue sequences that present different features and move to different rhythms. Action scenes are characterized by fast montage, loud extra-diegetic music, rapid camera and character movement, or slow motion. Lorrie Palmer stresses how many critics dislike the collective style adopted in action films, and branded since the 1980s by Jerry Bruckheimer, Bay and Tony Scott, because it 'has come to symbolize an abandonment of plot and character in favour of excess and spectacle, the centrality of surface over substance', where: 'bigger (and faster) is better' (Palmer 2012: 4). According to David Bordwell, intensified continuity, characterized by a rapid editing, bipolar extremes of lens length, reliance upon close-ups and wide-ranging camera movements: 'is the traditional continuity amped up, raised to a higher pitch of emphasis. It is the dominant style of American mass-audience films today' (Bordwell 2006: 120–1). Geoff King claims that big budget action films, through intensified continuity, reach an 'impact aesthetic', i.e. 'an aggressive approach to shooting and cutting' that seeks the audience's visceral response (Bordwell 2006: 158). Many critics sustain that, through these features, narrative is sacrificed in the name of spectacle, and the films become episodic. But: 'every action, however "spectacular," is a narrative event, and it can advance characters' goals and alter their state of knowledge'. As Murray Smith claims, in action films: 'the plot advances through spectacle' (Bordwell 2006: 104–5). In an interview, Bay underlines: 'It is only as the world quickens for the characters that the cuts get more intense and they start picking up. That's one of the ways I build up energy and keep this kinetic thing going' (Rodriguez 2005). ASL and other cinematic techniques increase the empathy between the audience's and characters' experience of time. As in Chapter 3, in which I discuss Lyne's staged musical and erotic performances, I now call Bay's action sequences 'staged action performances', during which, in the majority of cases, the fabula is not completely abandoned at the expense of spectacular scenes. Sometimes its development is only slowed to allow the audience to contemplate the extraordinary nature of the characters' action at the limits, or beyond, of human capability. Different spectators experience these sequences in diverse ways, as in the case of musical and erotic performances, mainly according to personal tastes. If the spectator enjoys these scenes and is involved in them, then the techniques used to increase empathy work; otherwise, boredom sets in.

In dialogue scenes, there are usually no camera movements – shot-reverse-shots or racking focus are used along with some characters' movements, editing is not as rapid as in action scenes and if there is extra-diegetic music it is not so loud as to drown out dialogue. *Bad Boys* and *Bad Boys II* offer two different types of dialogue sequence: when the protagonists Mike and Marcus, and their friends, relatives and colleagues are involved, dialogue is usually amusing and fast-moving. Whereas when members of the gang that the cops Mike and Marcus have to arrest speak among themselves, dialogue is slower and has more gravity. In *Armageddon*, too, dramatic and action scenes alternate with comedy sequences, and sometimes within a scene drama and comedy alternate thanks to different registers of dialogue. Generally, lines spoken by Harry Stamper (Bruce Willis) and his drillers are amusing, whereas those of Dan Truman (Billy Bob Thornton) and NASA operatives are serious. The techniques used to shoot comedy scenes and serious dialogue sequences are mainly the same, except for the content of the dialogue and the speed with which lines are spoken by actors, which is generally more rapid in the case of gags.

Sometimes, in both *Bad Boys* and *Bad Boys II*, the amusing dialogue does not add relevant information about the characters or the fabula. For example, in *Bad Boys*, when the two cops go to Maxie's (Fawn Reed) boxing gym to enquire her about stolen drugs, while Mike questions her and flirts with her, Marcus strains himself lifting weights. Mike does not obtain any information, Maxie will never appear again, and the spectator already knows that Marcus is a bumbling man whereas Mike is a Latin lover. These funny moments freeze the main line of action, suspending it almost *à la* Tarantino. *Bad Boys* was released in 1995, after Tarantino's *Reservoir Dogs* (1992) and *Pulp Fiction* (1994), in which characters often delay what they are doing to begin long, amusing conversations that usually do not deepen either our understanding of the characters or of the story. In *Bad Boys*, *Bad Boys II* and *Armageddon*, comedy scenes cannot be considered digressions, parentheses to the main line of action, because they are numerous, and the very peculiarity of the narration consists in the alternation between them and action scenes. The varying rhythm of these two types of sequence is not only due to the techniques adopted to shoot them, but also to how the spectator is involved in them. Usually in comedy sequences there are no gaps, and the audience is surprised and amused. Whereas in action scenes – although they often comprise action performances and might be disliked by some spectators – suspense prevails and the audience is oriented towards the future, guessing what will happen next, whereas during comedy sequences the audience enjoys the present, momentarily losing interest in the development of the fabula. While the rhythm is rapid because lines quickly succeed one another, the spectator remains anchored to the present. In action sequences, the rhythm drives a race towards the future.

4.3 Simultaneity through cross-cuttings

The Rock opens with a very interesting sequence. Shots of marines at a military funeral alternate with shots of General Francis X. Hummel (Ed Harris) at home in his military uniform, and with shots of a war. The whole sequence is accompanied by extra-diegetic music and, at the beginning, by noises and voices that recall a battlefield, then by voices reciting during a military funeral, until a close-up of Hummel as he claims: 'It has to stop!' The cross-cutting ends when at the military cemetery Hummel meets marines, the same soldiers who took part in the funeral, before going to his wife's grave. There are three lines of action: the funeral at the cemetery, Hummel in his house and then at the cemetery, and a war. Whereas the first two lines of action occur at the same time but in different places, and at the end blend in the same location, the line of action showing a war represents Hummel's memories, an external enacted flashback, thus events that occurred in another time and place. Similarly, noises and voices from the war are diegetic and off-screen when they accompany shots of the war, and non-diegetic when they accompany the other shots. Conversely, voices at the funeral are diegetic and on-screen when the cemetery is in-frame, and non-diegetic in all the other shots. Subjectivity governs the sequence because the spectator hears Hummel's voice-over and sees his memories.[5]

The Rock, *Armageddon* and the *Transformers* pentalogy mainly develop through parallel editing. As analysed in Chapter 1, there can be several types of simultaneity, and according to them we can distinguish polyphonic or ensemble, parallel, branched, repeated event and hub-and-spoke plots. I also briefly discuss chases and phone calls during which different characters or groups are in different spaces and, in the case of chases, usually meet following the cross-cut sequence. In the case of action films, the use of parallel editing needs to be further discussed using two other variables: the causal links among events and knowledge of different characters involved in the various lines of action (Table 4.1).

(A) When there is a phone call or the characters communicate by radio, and both speakers or group of speakers alternate on-screen, they are in different spaces but their

Table 4.1 Different types of simultaneity.

Possible features in two or more simultaneous shots or scenes: →	Characters	Space	Character's knowledge	Presence of causal links among the shots or scenes
(A) Phone calls	Different characters or groups of characters	Different spaces		Yes
(B)	Different characters or groups of characters	Different spaces, but after the cross-cutting they may meet and a group's decision influences that of the other group		Not at the beginning
(C) Chases	Different characters or groups of characters	Contiguous or different spaces; the different actions usually end in the same place	All the characters are aware of the chase	Yes
(D) Chases	Different characters or groups of characters	Contiguous or different spaces; the different actions usually end in the same place	A group of characters does not know that another group is chasing them	Not at the beginning

---

[5] For a definition of mental subjectivity, see Bordwell and Thompson (2001: 90–2).

two-way communication establishes cause-and-effect chains among them. (B) Lines of action can occur in different, not contiguous, places and there can be no cause-and-effect links between them. This occurs when characters or a group of characters lose contact and are shown accomplishing different tasks, unaware of the other characters' decisions and actions. At the beginning of *Armageddon*, there is a very long period of cross-cutting between the South China Sea where Harry finds out that A.J. (Ben Affleck) is his daughter's fiancé and runs after him with a gun, and Houston where Truman and his men find out that an asteroid will soon hit Earth. When NASA scientists decide on how to blow up the asteroid and find out that the best driller is Harry, they send a chopper to Harry's oil platform, and the parallel editing ends. As often occurs within the same scene and sequence, this cross-cutting links gags to Harry and his drillers, and suspense to Truman and the other NASA operatives. Similarly, in each of the *Transformers* films, the second sequence introduces the first parallel editing between a human protagonist, his close friends and relatives, and transformers. The line of action that follows the protagonist is dominated by a humorous mood, especially in the case of the first three *Transformers*, in which the protagonist is always Sam Witwicky (Shia LaBeouf), whereas the line associated with the machines is characterized by action and a dramatic and serious mood. In these cases, the characters in the two or three lines of action do not physically meet in the same place, they do not influence each other during the cross-cutting, although the decisions and actions of the characters in a particular line of action often influence the characters in other lines of action when the parallel editing ends. (C) Lines of action can occur in different or contiguous spaces, and can be linked by cause-effect chains, as when there is a chase. (D) The characters associated with a particular line of action can be initially unaware of the physical proximity of the characters in the other line of action. In these cases, the characters in two or three lines of action physically meet in the same place, and they influence each other during the duration of the cross-cutting (C) or only at the end (D).

Cross-cutting can create and increase suspense. Usually, during phone calls and chases (A and C) suspense is not as pronounced as when the actions and decisions of characters in different lines of action do not directly influence each other (B), or when they influence each other only at the end of the parallel editing (D), because the narration is unrestricted, that is, the spectator knows more than the characters. As Alfred Hitchcock claimed in interview, whereas with suspense the director can play longer with the audience's fears and anguish, with surprise he strikes the spectator with a more shocking, but less enduring, effect (Truffaut 1967: 50–2).

Moreover, during some sequences of cross-cutting, in *The Rock* and *Armageddon*, our role as spectators is mimicked within the film by characters in the Mobile Command in San Francisco and in Houston, respectively. According to Maarten Coëgnarts and Peter Kravanja, in cognitive linguistics, perception can be conceptualized through four conceptual structures (Coëgnarts and Kravanja 2016: 5–7), which can be expressed in film to embody characters' perceptions. The conceptual metonymy 'eyes stand for seeing' can manifest itself on-screen 'by showing enough distinctive bodily features of the character so as to enable the viewer to recognize or infer the eyes of the character', and: 'the character's body in front of the camera has to be intentionally

Table 4.2 Overview of cinematic strategies to elicit contact between S and O (Coëgnarts and Kravanja 2016: 14).

	Homospatiality	Non-homospatiality
Single shot	By showing S and O together in one shot (e.g. framing or *mise-en-scène*)	By moving from S to O (e.g. tracking, panning, tilting, zoom-function)
Two shots	By presenting S and O, each occupying a different shot, as co-present or homospatial entities in the same frame (superimposition, split screen)	By cutting from S to O (editing)

directed at [...] the object of his perception'. The scholars distinguish between four cinematic strategies to address manifestations of the conceptual metaphor, 'perception is contact between perceiver and object perceived', and summarize them in Table 4.2 where S stands for character and O for the outer event seen by S.

Finally: 'the conceptual metaphor visual field is a container can be elicited cinematically by the perception shot or the POV shot' (Coëgnarts and Kravanja 2016: 13–15). In *The Rock* and *Armageddon*, the characters in the Mobile Command in San Francisco and in Houston remain, for most of the films, in spaces where there are monitors that show in real time what, respectively, Stanley and John and the drillers and astronauts are doing. The characters/spectators S are shown watching monitors that are in-frame with them or not (conceptual metonymy 'eyes stand for seeing'). In the former case, S are shown in the same shot together with monitors (conceptual metaphor, in film 'perception is contact between perceiver and object perceived', a case of homospatiality in a single shot). In the latter, S and monitors can be linked within the same shot through a camera movement (case of non-homospatiality in a single shot), or they can be connected through editing thanks to an S point of view shot that first shows S in one shot and the event O either through a monitor or not in the subsequent shot or vice versa, or thanks to cross-cutting that shows first S in a group of shots, and then the event O either through a monitor or not in a group of shots. Thus, in the case of non-homospatiality in two shots: there can be cutting between S and an image of O, that is to say, S and O can occupy the same space, or there can be cutting between S and O, O being in a different, not contiguous, space to that of S. Moreover, there can be non-homospatiality in more than two shots in the case of cross-cutting (see Table 4.3).

To embody character emotions in film, the metonymy, 'the physiological and expressive responses of an emotion stand for the emotion' can be elicited: 'by providing the viewer with a vivid representation of the physiological and expressive responses of the character. [...] There are many tools to achieve this goal, albeit shot size and lighting probably come up as the most important ones'. The metaphor, 'emotions are containers', can be elicited: 'by relating the image schema of containment to two kinds of frames: (a) the filmic frame and (b) the (second) frame within the filmic frame'. Thus, emotional intensity can either increase when the spatial distance between the character and camera decreases, or when the character is framed by a window or a door frame.

Table 4.3 Overview of cinematic strategies to elicit contact between S and O when they are not in the same frame, and O is shown through a monitor or not, and shots of S and O constitute a shot-reverse-shot or there is cross-cutting between shots of S and shots of O.

Non-homospatiality	Contiguous spaces	Non-contiguous spaces
Two shots	Cutting from S to monitors showing O	Cutting from S to O
More than two shots	Cutting from S to monitors showing O	Cutting from S to O

Consequently: 'a scene of great metaphorical intensity involves both moving the camera towards the character's facial expression (as standing for the emotion), as well as blocking the character's facial expression in a second frame' (Coëgnarts and Kravanja 2016: 16–20). There is a particularly interesting scene in which all these techniques interact: the parallel editing at the end of *Armageddon* when Harry speaks for the very last time with his only daughter Grace (Liv Tyler) before manually detonating the nuclear bomb that will disintegrate the asteroid, but will kill him. During this scene, Harry can be seen by Grace and all the other men in the same room with her, but can also be heard by the other drillers and astronauts who are on the shuttle *Freedom*; whereas Harry can only see and hear Grace through a tablet. The conceptual metonymy 'perceptual organ stands for perception' is manifested on-screen because: Grace and all the characters in the room with her stare motionless at the monitors; Harry looks closely at the tablet through which he sees Grace or watches directly in the camera; and A.J. and Chick (Will Patton) on *Freedom* listen to Harry's words and are touched by them. The conceptual metaphor 'perception is contact between perceiver and object perceived' is manifested both by showing in one single shot the monitors through which Harry is visible and Grace and the other men in the room with her, or via shot-reverse-shots between Harry and Grace or the other spectators. Moreover, monitors constitute frames within the filmic frame, and whereas we see Grace on Harry's tablet in two shots only, in the majority of the shots in which Harry is in-frame we see him through monitors. Furthermore, in three of these shots, the camera zooms in or tracks forward towards the monitor, as if to underline Harry's unchangeable destiny. The protagonist's fate and our empathy increase when, in three shots, the camera moves around the room, showing monitors around the walls, as if to underscore a feeling of imprisonment (Figure 4.1). The scene closes with three shots, during which Harry's image has disappeared from the monitors: a detail of Grace's hand that touches the monitor in front of her is followed first by a low-angle medium shot of her (Figure 4.2), and then by a long shot of her during which she keeps her hand on the monitor and the camera slowly moves backwards. It seems that our haptic visuality is evoked to be negated: a detail of a hand that tries to grasp an image that is no longer there becomes, thanks to camera movement and editing, a long shot of a woman alone surrounded by monitors without images.

Figure 4.1 *Armageddon* (Michael Bay, 1998). Graces and the other scientists surrounded by monitors that show Harry.

Figure 4.2 Graces' hand touches the monitor in front of her that does not show Harry anymore.

In *13 Hours*, during the Libyan attacks at The Annex, spectators are often shown the images visualized by CIA men via a drone, especially towards the end of the film: in the outpost, in the middle of nowhere and circled by militants, and American attempts to hide. The frame within the frame emphasizes the Americans' feeling of imprisonment. Their loneliness is further increased by titles that give spatial references underlining their distance from the team that will rescue them: 'Tripoli, US Embassy, 400 miles from Benghazi', 'Tripoli Airport 400 miles away' and 'Benghazi International Airport 12 miles away'.

4.4 Countdowns

Countdowns are developed aurally through dialogue and visually through an on-screen clock. They increase empathy between the spectator and the characters' during the latter's race against time. Several techniques are adopted to raise suspense: repetitions of a time, either verbally or aurally; briefer countdowns embedded within a longer countdown, or unexpected countdowns that substitute another countdown; and diegetic time that slows down towards the end of the countdown, sometimes equalling screening time, expanding temporalities.

The diegetic time of *Bad Boys* is six days and it contains four countdowns. During the first, when a gang steals heroin from a police station, there is time expansion towards the end of the scene (Figure 4.3). Then the murderous drug dealer Fouchet (Tchéky Karyo), before killing Julie's roommate and realizing that Julie is hiding, claims that the stolen heroin will be sold in four days. Measuring screen time, the last day is the second longest and, within it, the last four hours, which constitute a countdown – since Fouchet, having kidnapped Julie, calls Mike, claiming: 'I'm keeping your friend for four hours' – that occupies almost half of the screen time of the last day (Figure 4.4). Thus, towards the end of the film, diegetic time, compared with screen time, is briefer. As discussed, the film closes with a deadline that is not an explicit countdown because it is defined by a forthcoming event: Mike has to get into his Porsche before the hangar explodes.

The Rock, not unlike *Bad Boys*, opens with three countdowns before the beginning of the longest countdown that leads to the film's end. Indeed, when Hummel and his mercenaries enter the Naval Weapon Depot to steal nuclear warheads, having put

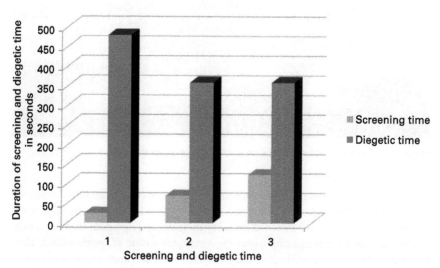

Figure 4.3 Comparison between diegetic and screen time in the first countdown of *Bad Boys*. Both screen and diegetic time are measured in seconds.

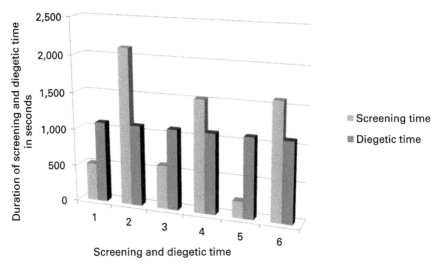

Figure 4.4 Comparison between diegetic and screen time in *Bad Boys*. Screen time is measured in seconds. Each histogram of diegetic time indicates a day, and its value is the average screen time of the entire film (seconds of the entire film divided into six, because the whole film develops over six days).

military men to sleep, a character claims: 'We've got thirty minutes till those darts wear off.' Then when a lethal green ball falls, before the gas disperses, they run away and shut the door of the warehouse. Thus, a first countdown in which time is explicitly mentioned is nullified and substituted by another, given by the necessity of escaping from a dangerous situation as soon as possible. Later, Stanley will have to disarm a bomb with a timer at the FBI. During this countdown, diegetic and screen time are very similar (Figure 4.5), and suspense also increases thanks to repetition because both the timer is shown on-screen and the same time is mentioned in dialogue three times. The longest countdown begins when Hummel promises his men that in less than 48 hours they will evacuate the island. In this countdown, diegetic time is longer than screen time, except for at the end when it is briefer (Figure 4.6). At the end of the film, this countdown is substituted by another: the FBI will launch rockets at Alcatraz in 17 minutes. The race against time restarts at the very end, as at the beginning of the film and in *Bad Boys*.

In *Armageddon*, countdowns are more complex, and all of them are embedded within the longest countdown without substituting it. This great countdown starts when a NASA scientist discovers that an asteroid will hit the Earth in 18 days, and ends when Harry detonates the nuclear bomb. As with the cases of the longest countdowns in *Bad Boys* and *The Rock*, diegetic time is longer than screen time at the beginning of the film, whereas it is briefer or equal to screen time at the end (Figure 4.7). The empathy between the characters' experience of time and the audience's is maintained throughout because spectators are constantly reminded of the passage of time through dialogue and, more often, by a huge digital clock that tells how much time is left until the asteroid hits Earth. In the countdown there are two mistakes,

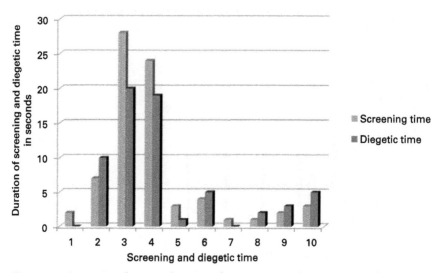

Figure 4.5 Comparison between diegetic and screen time in the countdown of *The Rock* when Stanley has to defuse a bomb at the FBI. Both screen and diegetic time are measured in seconds.

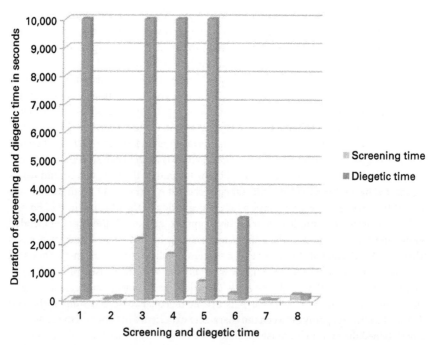

Figure 4.6 Comparison between diegetic and screen time in *The Rock*. Both diegetic and screen time are measured in seconds.

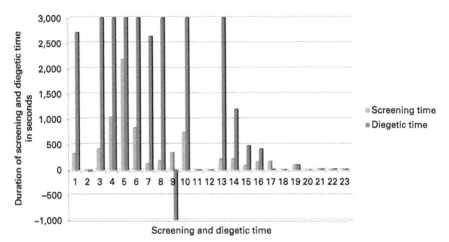

Figure 4.7 Comparison between diegetic and screen time in *Armageddon*. Both diegetic and screen time are measured in seconds. There are two mistakes in time references that are visualized using negative values.

which in Figure 4.7 are visualized using negative values. A detail of the clock that marks '17 23 14 48', meaning 17 days, 23 hours, 14 minutes and 48 seconds, is followed by a shot, over which Truman claims: 'That's 431 hours, 15 minutes, and 18 seconds.' There are no ellipses between the two shots, thus time should have remained the same or at least diminished. Similarly, we are shown a detail of the clock that marks 5 hours and 12 minutes (at 1 hour, 37 minutes and 4 seconds of screen time), but later a clock appears that says 6 hours, 49 seconds and 50 minutes (at 1 hour, 42 minutes and 54 seconds of screen time). Within the longest countdown are embedded several other countdowns. Before the shuttles *Freedom* (Figure 4.8) and *Independence* take off, and before Houston loses radio contact first with the shuttles, when they burn around the Moon, and then with *Freedom* when it has already landed on the asteroid and the Moon's rotation has changed. In the sequence during which the men of the US President receive the order to remote-detonate the bomb, there are five countdowns, and the longest is recalled, too, if only once, when the digital clock appears in-frame. In the order, the spectators are advised of how much time is left until: the bomb can be remote-detonated; the astronauts can drop the bomb out of *Freedom* and get off the asteroid; Truman's men can get radio contact with *Freedom* before the men of the US President remote-detonate the bomb; and the astronauts have to disarm the bomb twice before it explodes. The first countdowns introduce the last, progressively increasing suspense. The last countdown is developed visually, through the clock, and verbally, through dialogue. Diegetic time is almost always slower than screen time, and at the very end diegetic time stops: the countdown clock is in-frame twice and marks 2 seconds, although 4 seconds have passed according to screen time, and characters in-frame keep moving (Figure 4.9). Diegetic time expands until it freezes (Figure 4.10).

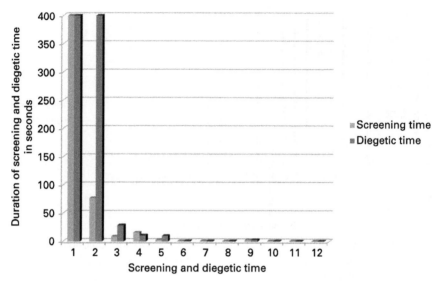

Figure 4.8 Comparison between diegetic and screen time in the *Armageddon* countdown before the shuttle *Freedom* takes off. Both screen and diegetic time are measured in seconds.

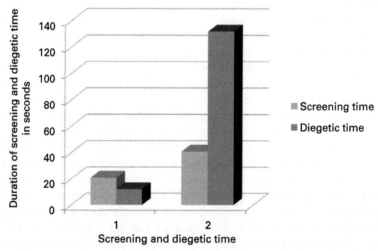

Figure 4.9 Comparison between diegetic and screen time in the *Armageddon* countdown when the bomb is remote-detonated for the first time. Both screen and diegetic time are measured in seconds.

As discussed in Chapter 1, according to Conceptual Metaphor Theory, our abstract idea of time is structured through the mappings of attributes and relations from the source domain space onto the abstract target domain time (Coëgnarts and Kravanja 2012: 86). Interestingly, in *Armageddon*, countdowns are often translated into space

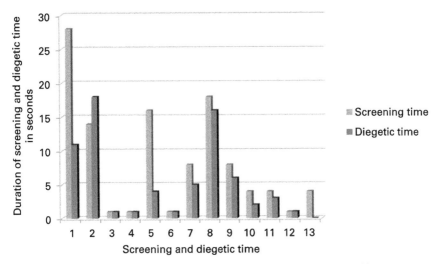

Figure 4.10 Comparison between diegetic and screen time in the *Armageddon* countdown when the bomb is remote-detonated for the second time. Both screen and diegetic time are measured in seconds.

countdowns – as in Kubrick's *Dr. Strangelove* analysed in Chapter 2. For example, when *Freedom* and *Independence* are approaching the Russian space station, the countdown is measured in how many feet divide the two shuttles from the station. When the shuttles are burning around the Moon, the countdown is measured in miles per hour and Gs. Finally, when Harry's men have to dig the hole on the asteroid, the countdown is measured in how many feet they have dug and still have to dig.

In *13 Hours*, there is a lot of chronological information given by titles and clocks that appear in-frame. From the beginning of 11 September, the ellipses in diegetic time are no longer than hours, and the fabula develops from 7:20 a.m. on 11 September to 10:30 a.m. the next day, encompassing 27 hours. The 13 hours of the title refer to the period from about 9 p.m. on 11 September, when the first ambush begins, to 10 a.m. on 12 September, when the Americans are rescued. Diegetic time is always longer than screen time, but they are more similar in the middle of the film where there are more ambushes (Figure 4.11). As in *Armageddon*, there are several mistakes in the time marked by the clocks that appear in-frame, which can be visualized by negative values in Figure 4.11. Unlike in *The Rock* and *Armageddon*, in this film the chronological information does not remind the audience that a task must be accomplished within a precise time span, but emphasizes the feeling that time passes inexorably, leaving CIA contractors more and more exhausted. The choice to constantly remind spectators of the passage of time, when the men remain barricaded in the outpost fearing the next ambush, underlines the drama of their situation, trapping them. While the title suggests that this situation will end in a few hours of diegetic time, there is no countdown from when CIA contractors are saved, and time passes irregularly because from one title to the next there can be a few minutes or tens of minutes.

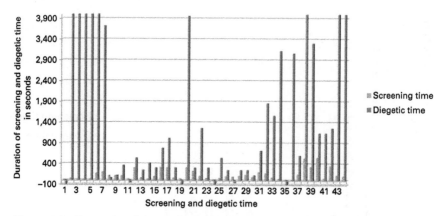

Figure 4.11 Comparison between diegetic and screen time in *13 Hours*. Both diegetic and screen time are measured in seconds. Mistakes in the time recorded by the clocks that appear in-frame can be visualized using negative values.

4.5 Expanding diegetic time through sequels and flashbacks

Transformers is a media franchise and, considering the relations between the stories narrated in the films, comic books and animated television series and those underpinning toy lines and video games, would require a long, accurate study that is beyond my means. Here, I analyse only the relations between the diegetic timeframes of the five films (Table 4.4).

In all the *Transformers* films, during the first sequence a voice-over explains part of the past story of the transformers: their origins; the wars between Autobots and Decepticons; their role in the Universe; and their relations with human beings. The main line of action of each film begins where that of the previous film ends (Table 4.4). In the first three films, continuity is assured by the presence of the same protagonist Sam Witwicky, who grows from a teenager in high school to a graduate looking for a job. The same trajectory occurs in the last two films, in which the protagonist is Cade Yeager (Mark Wahlberg): through street signs and TV news, in the last but one film of the saga, the audience understands that five years have passed since the Chicago battle with which the third film ends; and in the last film, Cade is still defending and taking care of Autobots. Like the two *Bad Boys*, in the five *Transformers* films some elements of the thematic of the first films are developed and expanded in the subsequent films. But in each film of the pentalogy, the origin of the story has ancient causes, old wars among transformers – with the exception of the last, in which Autobots, called by the magician Merlin, help King Arthur to defeat the Saxon invaders. Suspense briefly abates to leave space for curiosity that, in turn, increases suspense because each fight, becoming more deeply rooted within the story, acquires a more profound cause. Each flashback adds a new building block in the story of the pentalogy, although those spectators who have never read the comic books and seen the animated television

Table 4.4 The narratives of the five *Transformer* films ordered chronologically.

***Transformers* (2007)**	Before time began, there was the Cube		Origin of transformers	War between transformers				Sam in high school				
***Transformers: Revenge of the Fallen* (2009)**					17,000 BCE Humans and transformers first meet				Sam at college			
***Transformers: Dark of the Moon* (2011)**							1961–9 CE – War between transformers			Sam looks for a job after college		
***Transformers: Age of Extinction* (2014)**		65,000,000 BCE – Origin of transformers and our world destroyed to create them									Five years after the Chicago battle	
***Transformers: The Last Knight* (2017)**						The Dark Ages						Nowadays

series, are not aware of the missing element until it is revealed. Spectators who watch the films in the order of release are not only engaged to reorder the events of a single film in a chronological chain, but also to rearrange the episodes of all the previous films following cause-and-effect links.

If the five films constitute one film only, the flashbacks of the first *Transformer* would be external because they develop before the narrative starts, whereas those of the subsequent four films would be internal because they refer to an earlier point in the narrative. Carolyn Jess-Cooke notes that: 'Deriving from the Latin verb *sequi*, meaning "to follow", a sequel usually performs as a linear narrative extension, designating the text from which it derives as an "original" rooted in "beforeness"' (2009: 4). Similarly, Genette claims that the hypertext sequel exploits the success of a hypotext that in its own time was often considered complete (Genette 1997: 162): 'it continues a work not to bring it to a close but, on the contrary, in order to take it beyond what was initially considered to be the ending' (206). The story of each *Transformer* film is closed, but if spectators watch the other films, each story expands, encompassing new flashbacks, aside from whether the audience is familiar with the comic books, animated television series, toy lines and video games.

If each film plays with a long, explicatory flashback that introduces curiosity, increasing suspense, and these analpses of the pentalogy reconstruct the *Transformers* saga before their own origin, and through their numerous encounters with human beings, *Pain & Gain* is a source-path-goal schema embedded in a container schema – as in the case of Kubrick's *Killer's Kiss* and *Lolita* and Lyne's *Indecent Proposal* and *Lolita*. *Pain & Gain* is a long-enacted flashback that ends where it begins, adding a coda, and is enriched with several enacted, recounted or simply enacted external analepses. The story begins with Daniel Lugo's (Mark Wahlberg) arrest, and a title advises the audience that this occurred on 'June 17, 1995'. When the title 'Six Months Earlier' appears, Daniel is shown at the gym where he works as a personal trainer, and meets for the first time Victor Kershaw (Tony Shalhoub), a rich man whom the protagonist and his friends will kidnap, oblige him to register all his properties in their names and try in vain to kill. The end of the film repeats and complements the beginning, adding an epilogue and increasing suspense. At the end and at the beginning, the audience is shown three identical shots: Daniel does push-ups; when he sees the police arriving, he runs away; and finally, he is hit by a police car. Among these shots, at the beginning of the film, we follow the police chasing the personal trainer, whereas at the end we are shown the police arriving in other places to arrest the protagonist's accomplices. During the coda, Daniel manages to escape to the Bahamas, where he is finally arrested, and all the members of the gang are tried and found guilty. While, from the point of view of the fabula, the end is richer than the beginning, the conclusion does not change and overturn the beginning with a twist. Moreover, the characters' sentences seem to be announced by the freeze-frames used whenever one of them is arrested, as if to underline that their activities have been prohibited.

At the beginning of the film, during the police chase, there are point-of-view shots from Daniel's perspective, and a Steadicam often mimics his movements: perceptual subjectivity creates empathy between the protagonist and the audience. Throughout

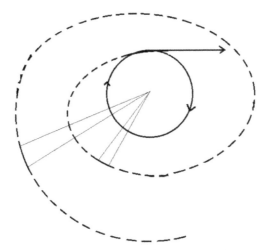

Figure 4.12 Scheme of the narrative structure of *Pain & Gain*. The main narration is represented by a circle that ends when it begins, and then continues. External flashbacks are visualized by arches along the spiral that represent the imaginary past of the story, which is not comprehended in the diegetic story.

the film, the spectator alternates between his point of view and that of the other characters. The enacted external analepses are all presented via montage sequences accompanied by the characters' voices-over, with the exception of Victor's that is only recounted. This access to different characters' mental subjectivity creates a kind of tragicomic choral narration of characters who, having trained for years to develop perfectly sculpted bodies, think that they can, and deserve, to profit from their exertions.[6] Moreover, these flashbacks within the analepsis that constitutes almost the entire film, slows the narration: the suspense of the main line of action is briefly frozen, then increased by the curiosity induced by the flashbacks. The film's narrative structure can be visualized through Figure 4.12, where the main line of action is represented by a circle in which the beginning and end coincide, whereas the epilogue continues outside the circle. The external flashbacks can be visualized through arches selected from the spiral that represents the imaginary past of the fabula outside the diegesis.

4.6 Temporalities come to the fore

In the films discussed up to now, with the exception of countdowns during which diegetic time is emphasized, temporalities remain unfelt, although they are the principle that accounts for the overall harmony and balance of the films, modulating audience empathy. On the other hand, in *The Island*, the theme of time, especially memory and imagination, comes to the fore.

---

6   For a definition of perceptual and mental subjectivity, see Bordwell and Thompson (2008: 90–2).

Thousands of people live in a facility following strict rules. They cannot leave because they believe that the environment outside is contaminated, but they have a hope of winning a lottery for which the prize is moving to a pure, paradisiacal island. But there is neither contamination nor an island, they are all clones, commissioned by rich sponsors so as to have spare parts for their bodies. When the clones are born, they are extracted from liquid sacks that resemble placenta, and are obliged to watch images and listen to a voice-over that 'summarizes' and 'represents' their childhood and adolescence and the island, thus their past and future purposes. James McCord (Steve Buscemi) helps the clones Tom Lincoln (Ewan McGregor) and Sarah Jordan (Scarlett Johansson) to escape. When Sarah recounts her memories before the contamination, James comments: 'Memory imprints. I see them. My buddy is a programmer at the Institute. He showed me. There's only, like, 12 stories. They change around little details. But they're all pretty much the same.' Sarah's past memories are defined as 'stories'.

As discussed in Chapter 1, we make sense of our lives by adopting 'familiar plot lines, archetypal characters, and significant remembered episodes' to select experiences and link them in: 'a coherent narrative that creates a sense of unity over time and a defined purpose for future action' (Singer and Bluck 2001: 93). Significantly, when Dr. Bernard Merrick (Sean Bean), who controls the proper functioning of clones, is asked about what they know of the outside world, he replies: 'We control them with the memory of a shared event. A global contamination. It keeps them fearful of going outside. The island is the one thing that gives them hope. Gives them purpose.' Indeed, our: 'self-narratives consist of a set of temporally and thematically organized salient experiences and concerns that constitute one's identity'. If we select from our memories some events to define who we are, to give unity and purpose to our lives, our identity is a product of choice (McAdams 2001: 110). The identities of the clones are the products of Merrick's choices. But in the case of the clone Tom, something goes wrong. When he dreams, we are shown montage sequences comprised of: images from his fake childhood and adolescence; shots presumably of his real past, from his birth in the water during adulthood (Figure 4.13); images of the island and of a paradisiacal world outside the facility given by memory imprints and the images that are continually projected on monitors inside the facility; shots illustrating his own imagination, such as those of him together with Sarah; and images from a past that is neither his own real past, nor his fake memory imprint. Remembering is just imagining the past because episodic remembering is a matter of generating: 'self-centred mental simulations about possible events that we think may happen or may have happened to ourselves'. 'Novel scientific work on mental time travel has repeatedly confirmed the existence of some strong similarities in the patterns of neural activity associated with the sorts of cognitive procedures employed in thinking about our past and imagining our possible futures' (Hutto 2016: 13). The mix in Tom's dreams of remembered events, whether real or imprinted, and imagined future episodes, is normal for human beings. It is true that clones have no choice but to select certain events from their memories, but it is also true that human choice is modulated by sociocultural models (4), and that when we remember something from earlier than age 3 it is usually a brief fragment, enriched

Figure 4.13 *The Island* (Michael Bay, 2005). The birth of Lincoln Six Echo (Ewan McGregor).

and modified by what our parents and relatives recount (14). What is uncanny in the case of Tom's dreams are the images that, as will later be revealed, come from his sponsor's memory. Their presence confuses and disrupts the unity and purpose of his life, his identity: in his mind, the island is overshadowed by other priorities and its existence is questioned.

4.7 Conclusion

The empathy between spectators and characters in Bay's films leads the audience to share the characters' experience of time that, although it is often not consciously felt by the spectator, is the principle that organizes the films' overall balance and rhythm. The audience's empathy with the characters' experiences of time, consequently the feeling that temporalities are accelerated or slowed down, is achieved through different techniques, such as camera movements that mirror those of characters, use of a Steadicam, slow-motion, close-ups and details, the soundtrack and ASL. In some action films, the alternation of sequences shot with different techniques and presenting different rhythms or cross-cutting, create a play between suspense and gags, in which suspense carries the main line of action, leading the audience to make hypotheses about the future and simultaneously enjoy the spectacle, whereas gags suspend it, leaving the spectator free to take pleasure in the present moment. Audience empathy with the character's race against time is usually augmented through parallel editing and, towards the end of the films, through a decrease of the diegetic time in comparison with screen time and through countdowns. The effect of the countdown is often multiplied through repetition, countdowns embedded within a longer countdown or substituted by other countdowns, and a decrease of diegetic time in comparison with screen time towards the end of the countdowns. The *Transformers* films propose a diegetic time that continues throughout the pentalogy, increasing suspense, but also curiosity, offering flashbacks that clarify and deepen the whole saga. *Pain & Gain* is narrated through a long flashback that ends where the narration begins, and is continually suspended and enriched by external analepses narrated from the characters' points of view, creating a tragicomic choral narration. Finally, in *The Island*, past time and memories come to the fore because their importance and influence on the characters' present and identities become one of the main themes.

Quentin Tarantino

Master of temporalities

Jules *The path of the righteous man is beset on all sides by the inequities of the selfish and the tyranny of evil men. Blessed is he who in the name of charity and goodwill shepherds the weak through the Valley of Darkness. For he is truly his brother's keeper and the finder of lost children. I will strike down upon thee, with great vengeance and furious anger, those who attempt to poison and destroy my brothers. And you will know my name is the Lord when I lay my vengeance upon thee.*

Jules *Maybe it means that you're the evil man and I'm the righteous man. This gun is the shepherd protecting my ass in the valley of darkness. Or it could mean that you're the righteous man and I'm the shepherd and it's the world that's evil and selfish. I'd like that, but that shit aint the truth. The truth is that you're the weak and I am the tyranny of the evil man. But I'm trying, Ringo. I'm trying very hard to be the shepherd.*

Pulp Fiction (1994)

In Quentin Tarantino's feature films temporalities are foregrounded, becoming one of the main themes and their structuring principle. *Reservoir Dogs* (1992), *Pulp Fiction* (1994), the segment 'The Man from Hollywood' in *Four Rooms* (1995), *Jackie Brown* (1997), *Kill Bill: Vol. 1* (2003) and *Vol. 2* (2004), *Death Proof* (2007), *Inglourious Basterds* (2009), *Django Unchained* (2012), *The Hateful Eight* (2015) and *One Upon a Time . . . in Hollywood* (2019) are either jumbled plots or present several enacted flashbacks or enacted flashbacks of simultaneity, mainly due to Tarantino's aesthetic choices – with the exception of his segment of *Four Rooms* in which diegetic and screening time perfectly match, thus temporalities are highlighted, while through a different technique. Owing to Tarantino's unique style, some new concepts, complementing those discussed in Chapter 1, need to be introduced.

Regarding jumbled plots and many enacted flashbacks, the order of events of the fabula is altered mainly by the director's choice; it is Tarantino himself who decided to edit the sequences in non-linear succession. Indeed, usually flashbacks are internal or mixed, they are hardly ever external – unlike in the case of Bay's *Pain & Gain* where they usually introduce a character through a montage sequence of his/her more relevant past experiences. On the other hand, in the case of enacted flashbacks of simultaneity, as in the case of repeated event and hub-and-spoke plots, if one action or event is shown from different characters' points of view, the filmmaker chooses the order of points of view, but it is the fabula that imposes a choice. While the director, rather than adopting enacted flashbacks of simultaneity, could have chosen to show the events via a split screen – as Mike Figgis did in *Timecode* (2000) – or superimpositions, Tarantino adopts this technique only occasionally. Thus, in jumbled plots, it is the director himself who decides to play with the order, and the audience strives to reorder the sequences following a cause-and-effect chain, and to understand and reconstruct the artistic order chosen for stylistic and thematic reasons. The causal logic among episodes and within them is usually 'strong' to assist the audience to reconstruct the story. In the case of enacted flashbacks of simultaneity, it is the fabula that imposes alterations in the succession of events. Causal logic is strong within each character's point-of-view scheme, but is often 'weak' between them – unlike in Kubrick's *The Killing* where cause-and-effect links between different flashbacks of simultaneity is strong.

I have already discussed the differences between suspense/prospection, curiosity/ retrospection and surprise/recognition, introduced the new concept of strong surprise and listed in which films they appear most often. To better analyse Tarantino's films, and those of other directors such as Robert Rodriguez, or particular films such as Gaspar Noé's *Irréversible* (2002), surprise and strong surprise must be distinguished from 'shocking surprise', that is, the shock of the unexpected scene which is not due to temporary or permanent gaps. During sudden gore-and-splatter shots and scenes, temporalities expand because the spectator's attention, rather than oriented towards disclosure of the past or future, is focused, almost trapped, in the present. Unless there is no empathy between spectators and characters, spectators experience enjoyment and pleasure, or loathing and revulsion, during scenes of shocking surprise. As discussed, close-ups and details of body parts increase the haptic visuality of the shots (Gallese and Guerra 2015: 232–3), and during gore-and-splatter scenes there are usually several close-ups and details of wounded or cut limbs that increase spectator's empathy with a present that is so shocking that it prevails over both curiosity and suspense. I use the expressions 'staged musical' and 'staged erotic' performances in the case of Lyne's oeuvre, and 'staged action performances' when discussing Bay's work. In the case of Tarantino, I can speak of 'staged violent performances', during which the narrative often gives way to a cruelty that is so emphasized as to appear unreal. According to Franco La Polla, Hollywood cinema has always exploited violent scenes – e.g. in Martin Scorsese's *Goodfellas* (1990), and in films by William A. Wellman, Howard Hawks, Robert Aldrich, Sam Peckinpah and others – but this is often motivated by diegetic events and constitutes their climax. Whereas in Tarantino violence is a regular feature that often appears unexpectedly (Gatti 1995: 3) – with the exception of *Once Upon a Time . . . in Hollywood* where the staged violent performance is the awaited climax at the end of the film. Similarly, the Director of the Toronto Film Festival, Piers Handling, in September 1992, when *Reservoir Dogs* was shown, claimed that Tarantino found an original way to embed violence in his film, as Arthur Penn, Francis Ford Coppola and Sam Peckinpah did in the 1960s and 1970s (Bernard 1996: 155).

Considering Kubrick's *2001*, *Barry Lyndon* and *Eyes Wide Shut*, in Chapter 2, I have discussed slowness. In slow films, characters restrain their emotions and take little action, uttering few words or remaining silent. There are no, or few, events, information is often withheld and the films remain open to interpretation and experience. There are many long takes during which the camera is still or moves slowly, and often does not follow the events. Characters are framed in long shots to prevent the audience from guessing what they are feeling and thinking, or there are landscape *tableaux*. These features foreground temporalities and determine our experience of them: the stillness of the present moment is emphasized. Tarantino creates a 'new slowness' through dialogue scenes that expand temporalities. These scenes consist of long takes, or a slow or regular editing pace, characters and camera remain still or move slowly, and dialogue does not offer useful information for the development of the fabula, and often does not add significant clues to the characters' introspection. Dialogue often revolves around trivial, mundane and everyday issues, and the seriousness and emphasis with which characters take part in these discussions, as if they pertain to relevant and substantial matters, freeze the development of the fabula. These amusing digressions unexpectedly change the rhythm of the film, and a hermetic, nonsensical present is emphasized to entertain spectators. While some of the features of 'classical' and new slowness differ, the effects are similar: spectators are suspended, mesmerized by a timeless present that is difficult to interpret owing to the customary absence of dialogue and long shots of characters in slow films, and to lots of vulgar, trivial jokes quickly succeeding one another and related by passionate characters who are often framed in medium close-ups or close-ups in new slow films. I have not introduced the concept of new slowness in discussions of Bay because in his oeuvre dialogue is not as long, absurd, almost insane as in Tarantino's, and is shot with different stylistic techniques that maintain a faster rhythm – shot-reverse-shots or racking focus.

5.1 Narrative schemas

5.1.1 Playing with narrative schemas – Jumbled and repeated event plots: *Reservoir Dogs* (1992), *Pulp Fiction* (1994), *Jackie Brown* (1997), *Kill Bill: Vol. 1* (2003) and *Vol. 2* (2004)

Reservoir Dogs has a jumbled plot in which the source-path-goal and the part-whole schema are intertwined. The first sequence, where the 'reservoir dogs' are having breakfast in a diner, the subsequent scene that takes place after the robbery, during which Mr. White (Harvey Keitel) drives Mr. Orange (Tim Roth), who is fatally wounded and all the sequences shot in the warehouse follow a chronological chain. The linearity that leads to the future is inverted by flashbacks. There are two types of internal analepsis: those enacted or enacted recounted that are introduced by a character's dialogue explaining to another character what occurred in the past and are causally motivated by the choice of a temporary gap; and those enacted due to the director's stylistic and thematic choices. For example, Mr. Pink's (Steve Buscemi) enacted recounted flashback about how he managed to run from the cops and survive the shooting, is a visual answer to a question that Mr. White asks him when they are in the warehouse. Almost all the other analepses are due to editing and announced by titles. After the two titles 'Mr. White' and 'Mr. Blonde', we are shown respectively these two characters at Joe's (Lawrence Tierney) office. After the title 'Mr. Orange', this character appears in a diner with his colleague Holdaway (Randy Brooks), and after Mr. Orange's flashbacks we see the sequences during which Joe assigns names of colours to the 'reservoir dogs'; Mr. Orange and Mr. White are in front of the jewellery store they are going to rob; Mr. Orange, Mr. White and Mr. Brown (Quentin Tarantino) run from the cops; and the latter is shot to death. The end of this sequence is an enacted flashback of simultaneity of the beginning of the second scene of the film, when we are shown Mr. Orange, wounded, lying on the back seat of the car driven by Mr. White.

There are two cross-cut narrative schemas. By and large, the former regarding the events after the robbery, and the latter concerning the episodes that precede the hold-up. The first narrative schema is a source-path-goal schema that, with the exception of the very first sequence shot in a diner, takes place entirely in the warehouse at which all the characters progressively arrive, evoking a drama thanks to its setting and choral quality. Whereas the second narrative schema, see the titles 'Mr. White', 'Mr. Blonde', 'Mr. Orange' and the events shown, is a part-whole schema, in which each part is mainly dedicated to one of the three characters' experience, the whole narrates the preparation for the robbery. Thus, the linear path towards the future is complicated by a vertical path focused on particular characters (Table 5.1). The spectators are able to reconstruct the fabula via the chronological development of the source-path-goal schema, its setting, the warehouse, the titles and costumes, indeed, the 'reservoir dogs' wear black suits only immediately before – at the diner – and after the hold-up. The cross-cutting of the two schemas displays Tarantino's montage. The director's choices are exhibited also by the selection of titles: why do only 'three reservoir dogs' deserve a title? Why is not a title dedicated to Mr. Pink, for example, who has a role as important as those of Mr. White, Mr. Blonde (Michael Madsen) and Mr. Orange?[1]

The cross-cutting of schemas, of horizontal and vertical movements, is emphasized by camera movements. During the first scene, when the 'reservoir dogs' sit round a table in a diner, the camera turns around them, mainly to the right and sometimes it pans left at the end of the shot, while cuts are disguised by characters' backs. These movements confuse spectators who cannot understand where the characters are in relation to each other and the camera. These circular movements are interrupted by a shot-reverse-shot between Joe and Mr. White, followed by a long take during which the camera turns to the right around the table until Joe stands up. A classical dialogue scene, during which shots of the characters who are speaking are divided by cuts, is followed by the first establishing shot: the camera is behind Mr. Blonde, but his head is not in-frame thus, once more, the camera position cheats the spectator. This scene is emblematic of the narrative structure and the gang's organization. The camera's circular movements are interrupted twice, both times by Joe, who is the leader. Although each character stands out from the others thanks to dialogue – each of them expresses his

---

[1] See Morsiani (2016: 37) for a discussion of the play between restricted and unrestricted narration.

Table 5.1 The scheme of *Reservoir Dogs*. The setting of the episodes (bold, first line), a brief description of each (subsequent lines) and the titles (bold, capital letters). F indicates a character's flashback, motivated by dialogue.

Episode	At Joe's	Outdoors	At Orange's	Out doors	In a bar and in a toilet	At Joe's	Indoors	At Orange's	Outdoors	In a bar	Outdoors	Breakfast	Robbery	Outdoors	Warehouse
Reservoir Dogs, Joe and Eddie in a diner												x			
Mr. Orange and Mr. White by car														x	
Mr. Orange, Mr. White and Mr. Pink															x
Mr. Pink's flashback									F		F				
Mr. Orange, Mr. White and Mr. Pink															x
MR. WHITE Mr. White and Joe	x														
Mr. Orange, Mr. White, Mr. Pink and Mr. Blonde															x
MR. BLONDE Mr. Blonde and Joe						x									
Mr. Orange, Mr. White, Mr. Pink, Mr. Blonde, the policeman and Eddie															x

Table 5.1 Continued.

	At Joe's	Outdoors	At Orange's	Out doors	In a bar and in a toilet	At Joe's	Indoors	At Orange's	Outdoors	In a bar	Outdoors	Breakfast	Robbery	Outdoors	Warehouse
MR. ORANGE Mr Orange and Holdaway in a bar										x					
Mr. Orange's flashback					F										
					F										
Mr Orange and Holdaway in a diner					F										
Mr. Orange's flashback								F	F						
									F						
Reservoir Dogs, Joe and Eddie (names)							x								
Mr. Orange and Mr. White in front of the jewellery store											x				
Mr. Orange, Mr. White and Mr. Brown by car														x	
														x	
Reservoir Dogs, Joe, Eddie															x

ideas about several topics – circular camera movements confuse them, and privilege their being members of the same gang rather than unique characters. In the next sequence, shot in slow motion outside the diner, the camera tracks with the characters to the left, but slower than them, so that they progressively enter in-frame from the right. Then it tracks backwards to precede them, and whenever one of them is in-frame, a title with the actor's name appears. These two shots seem to distinguish between them, but the sequence ends with a shot during which the camera remains still behind them, framed in long shot, walking away from the camera, once more almost undistinguishable in their black suits. Similarly, when Joe assigns a colour to each of the 'reservoir dogs', he is distinguished from all of them because he stands up while they sit on chairs. Moreover, when he is in-frame the camera remains still, whereas with a ping-pong effect the camera tracks to right or left, and sometimes it pans in the opposite direction at the end of the shots when the other characters are in-frame, although each distinguishes himself from the others through dialogue. These two sequences offer an example of how style mirrors narrative structure.

Style and structure determine the rhythm and the expansion or compression of temporalities. Usually in heist films, suspense around the hold-up grows progressively until the end, sometimes intertwined with the shocking surprise caused by particularly violent content and the surprise generated by unpredictable events. In *Reservoir Dogs*, the robbery is never shown, only recounted through characters' dialogue, and the film is dominated by curiosity about the robbery, soon substituted by that around the presence and identity of a spy among the 'reservoir dogs'. In both cases, curiosity is satisfied by strong surprise because spectators come to know that the robbery went wrong when they are shown, in the second sequence of the film, Mr. White who drives Mr. Orange, who is wounded, to the warehouse. Similarly, they know that Mr. Orange is the spy when the police officer Marvin Nash (Kirk Baltz), kidnapped and tortured by Mr. Blonde, speaks with him after Mr. Blonde's death. The film is dominated by curiosity, strong surprise, shocking surprise and new slowness, and is thus more oriented towards the past and the present than the future. Following the order of editing, suspense revolves around the cop's and Mr. Orange's destiny, and in the last sequence the fate of the surviving 'reservoir dogs'. Significantly, these scenes are mainly shot using long takes,[2] and the ASL of the sequences shot in the warehouse is longer than that of the other scenes:[3] temporalities are expanded to extend suspense, increasing it. The scene during which Eddie (Chris Penn) reaches the warehouse where Mr. Orange, Mr. White, Mr. Pink and Mr. Blonde are waiting for him with the cop tied to a chair, consists of nine

---

[2]   Long takes are present: when Mr. White and Mr. Orange, who is wounded, drive towards the warehouse (seven long takes); when Mr. Blonde reaches Mr. Orange, Mr. White and Mr. Pink at the warehouse with the cop (seven long takes); when Mr. Blonde tortures the cop and is finally shot to death by Mr. Orange (nine long takes); during Mr. Orange's flashbacks (three long takes) and during the last sequence when the Mexican standoff is staged (three long takes).

[3]   The ASL of the opening sequence is 7 seconds, of the robbery aftermath 4.8 seconds, of the back-story 8.6 seconds and of the warehouse 10.4 seconds (Cinemetrics, data submitted by Eric T. Jones on 7 September 2009. Last accessed 19 September 2019).

Figure 5.1 *Reservoir Dogs* (1992). Mr. Blonde (Michael Madsen) speaks into Marvin's (Kirk Baltz) severed ear.

long takes and eight of them stage Marvin's torture and Mr. Blonde's death. The camera lingers on the preparation of the torture and its effects, but the more violent acts occur out of frame. The camera remains still both when Eddie, Mr. White and Mr. Pink leave and Mr. Blonde takes off his jacket and approaches the cop, and when Mr. Blonde speaks to Marvin. Then the camera follows Mr. Blonde who approaches Mr. Orange after having switched on the radio and begins to dance. When Mr. Blonde cuts the cop's ear, the camera pans to frame the exit to another room and, after the violence, Mr. Blonde comes into the frame, goes out of frame and re-enters, speaking into Marvin's severed ear (Figure 5.1). From suspense, increased by the slowness with which the enforcer prepares for the torture, the film moves to black humour, from extended temporalities during which spectators await the future outcome, to the dissolution of tension attendant upon an amusing act that lets the spectator enjoy the present.

A similar play of suspense versus shocking surprise is organized in the subsequent scene, in which in a long take a Steadicam follows Mr. Blonde outside where he takes a petrol can from the trunk of his car, re-enters the warehouse and again starts to dance. After he has poured the petrol over the cop and flicked his lighter, we see Mr. Orange in a long take who unexpectedly shoots Mr. Blonde. The camera then turns 180° around him until Mr. Blonde, who is dying, appears in long shot. As the robbery is not shown in the whole plot, the cutting of the ear and the bullet that hits Mr. Blonde are not shown in this sequence. Camera movements, especially the pan left to leave Mr. Blonde out of frame, and the turn around Mr. Orange to frame Mr. White, who is dying in long shot, manifest the film's self-referentiality.

This feature is also underlined by Mr. Orange's flashback. After the title 'Mr. Orange', Orange is shown in a diner with his colleague Holdaway who asks him whether he recounted the commode story. There follows four of Mr. Orange's enacted flashbacks. During the first, Holdaway proposes that Mr. Orange tells the commode story to win the trust of the 'reservoir dogs', and explains how to recount it roughly following Stanislavsky's method: 'An undercover cop has got to be Marlon Brando. To do this job you got to be a great actor [. . .] You remember what's important, and the rest you make your own. The only way to make it your own is to keep saying it [. . .] The things you gotta remember are the details.' The cop's lessons lay bare the artificiality of the fiction within the fiction that will be staged. Furthermore, this flashback and the two subsequent ones underline their self-referentiality because Holdaway asks his colleague whether he recounted the commode story, whereas we are shown how Mr. Orange practised alone and with him to rehearse the story. Why should he tell him what they both already know? Mr. Orange's first three enacted flashbacks are shot for the spectator, not for Holdaway, whose question seems to motivate them, thus they also disclose the extra-diegetic level. During the fourth flashback there is interesting cross-cutting between the diegetic and the intra-diegetic level: Mr. Orange, who tells Joe the commode story, Eddie and Mr. White in a bar, and the staging of the story in a public toilet, respectively. But while Mr. Orange is in the toilet, he keeps recounting the story, whereas the *mise-en-scène* is intra-diegetic, Mr. Orange's character is diegetic, and the use of slow motion underlines the self-referentiality of the scene (Figure 5.2).

The technique adopted in *Reservoir Dogs* to present characters when they are having breakfast is exploited in *Pulp Fiction* to encompass the whole narration. We become acquainted with characters as we meet people by chance while waiting for somebody or something, and have begun to speak with them about banalities to kill time and satisfy our inexplicable need to break silence – as Mia (Uma Thurman) says to Vincent (John Travolta) at Jackrabbit Slim's:

> **Mia** Don't you hate that? [. . .] Uncomfortable silences. Why do we feel it's necessary to yack about bullshit to be comfortable? [. . .] You know you've found someone special when you can shut the fuck up and comfortably share silence.

The dialogue is abundant and funny, but through it we do not get a glimpse of the characters' past and memories or of their future goals – could Butch's (Bruce Willis) flashback, as well as Jules' (Samuel L. Jackson) decision to wait for God to tell him where to go and what to do, be considered the only partial exceptions? While dialogue does not add important information either about the characters or events in which they are involved, it accompanies the spectator from the beginning to the end of the film, entertaining them but also guiding them in this jumbled plot. Dialogue often increases both suspense and curiosity about, respectively, the effects and causes of the events seen, and links the sequences in a play of cross-reference. It offers a path through which the audience can enjoy the film, a flux that flows beyond the narrative schemas that dominate it. The peculiarity of *Pulp Fiction* is not so much the unusual exploitation of jumbled plot in a mainstream film, or the alternation of staged action and violent performances with dialogue, or the adoption of nonsense and humorous dialogue – new slowness – but the very mix of all of these features.

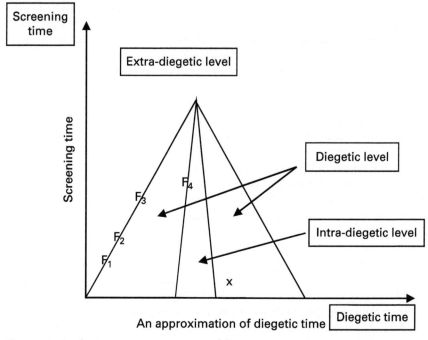

Figure 5.2 On the x-axis an approximation of diegetic time, on the y-axis screening time. The biggest pyramid represents the diegetic level, the smallest the intra-diegetic level, and all the space outside the pyramid the extra-diegetic level. X stands for the scene during which Mr. Orange and Holdaway are talking in a diner. F_1, F_2, F_3 and F_4 stand for Mr. Orange's subsequent flashbacks. F_1, F_2 and F_3 are written on the perimeter of the biggest pyramid-diegetic level because they lay bare the extra-diegetic level. F_4 is represented on the perimeter line of the smallest pyramid-intra-diegetic level because it manifests the intra-diegetic level.

Much like in *Reservoir Dogs*, in *Pulp Fiction*, the source-path-goal and the part-whole schema are mixed. A horizontal movement that leads from the beginning to the end of the fabula, linking its different parts, is intertwined with a vertical movement that privileges different characters' stories. Moreover, choices regarding the order of the episodes and other stylistic decisions lay bare the self-referentiality of the film, introducing a movement in a third dimension, from which the spectators can view the film from their extra-diegetic perspective, detecting both the horizontal and the vertical movement.

The film consists of three stories, each one a part of the whole, and introduced with a title: 'Vincent Vega and Marcellus Wallace's Wife'; 'The Gold Watch'; and 'The Bonnie Situation'. The first two parts follow a source-path-goal schema. In each, the order follows that of the fabula and, according to diegetic time, the second episode follows the first. The only exception is Butch Coolidge's external enacted flashback about his childhood, when Captain Koons (Christopher Walken) gave him his father's gold watch. This analepsis is motivated diegetically because at the end of it, following a cut, we see the adult Butch sit up suddenly as if awaking from a nightmare. On the other hand, 'The Bonnie Situation' can be divided into three main episodes that challenge the order of the fabula. Following the editing, the first event ends when Honey Bunny (Amanda Plummer) and Pumpkin (Tim Roth) begin to rob the diner where they are having breakfast, and the second when Jules Winnfield and Vincent Vega, after the former has recited the famous false quotation from the Bible, shoot every character but the last boy in the room. The third episode begins a little before the end of the second, and ends when Honey Bunny and Pumpkin leave the diner after the hold-up (Table 5.2). Spectators are assisted to reconstruct the fabula not only thanks to titles, but also through: dialogue, because before Vincent goes out with Mia, he speaks of this meeting with Jules; events, because Vincent is killed by Butch at the end of 'The Gold Watch'; and settings.

At the end of the second and at the beginning of the third episodes of 'The Bonnie Situation', we see three identical shots followed, in the former case by shots of Jules and Vincent, and in the latter by shots of a boy hidden in the bathroom of the apartment while we listen to Jules' voice-off repeating the last part of the fake excerpt from the Bible. In this latter case, the spectator has a chance to experience how duration can appear differently. To explain why we feel that a journey is briefer when we already know it, and longer when it is the first time we make it, Aristotle adopts the differences between limited and unlimited, and determined and undetermined. If the length of a path is

Table 5.2 The scheme of *Pulp Fiction*. The time of the episodes (bold, first line), a brief description of each (on subsequent lines) and the titles (bold, capital letters).

Years before	First day, 7.22 a.m.		From 8.00 a.m. to 9.30 a.m.			Second day, night	Some days after, night until the morning of the day after
Honey Bunny and Pumpkin							
				x			
Vincent and Jules and the suitcase							
	x	x					
VINCENT VEGA AND MARSELLUS WALLACE'S WIFE							
						x	
Captain Koons and Butch							
x							
THE GOLD WATCH							
							x
THE BONNIE SITUATION							
		x	x	x	x		

known, determined, limited, we experience the journey as briefer, whereas if the length is unknown, undetermined, unlimited, we experience it as longer. Similarly, when we watch a film for the first time, it is undetermined, open in several directions, our experience of it is more intense, and our attention and mental involvement mean we lose a sense of the passage of time. On the other hand, when we rewatch a film, it is determined, every sequence becomes a known passage that progressively leads to a familiar end (Ghislotti 2012: 21–2). Curiously, when in the last sequence of *Pulp Fiction* we see the diner that we have already seen in the very first sequence, we recognize the setting, and then we are explicitly shown Honey Bunny and Pumpkin. During this last sequence, Vincent stands up to go to the toilet. When we watch the film for the second time, we can recognize, during the first sequence, Vincent from behind who walks past Honey Bunny. It seems as if the director inserted a detail to let the spectators enjoy a second viewing, maintaining a feeling of indeterminacy and openness that usually characterizes the first viewing. Moreover, he plays with durations, cheating us (Table 5.3).

While the spectator should experience a second viewing as being briefer, they do not realize that screen time is compressed in the last sequence because they are shown the scene from different characters' point of view: in the first sequence from Honey Bunny and Pumpkin's, in the last from Jules and Vincent's.

Regular flashbacks and flashbacks of simultaneity, together with style, determine the play of rhythm and the expansion and compression of temporalities. Unlike *Reservoir Dogs*, *Pulp Fiction* is oriented more towards the future than the past, but like the previous film, the past is emphasized through strong surprise, and the spectator's enjoyment of the present moment dominates through shocking surprise and new slowness. The spectator feels curiosity when: at the beginning of 'Vincent Vega and Marcellus Wallace's Wife', they see Vincent and Jules dressed in shorts and T-shirts, whereas in the previous sequence they wore black suits; when Vincent and Jules tell about what happened to the man who gave Mia a foot massage; and when the spectator sees the suitcase first in the apartment and then in the diner, but not its content. Only the curiosity about the gangsters' outfits is due to montage. Suspense is caused by the outcome of: Pumpkin's and Honey Bunny's robbery; Vincent and Jules' presence in the apartment; Butch's behaviour during the boxing match and his subsequent escape; his and Marsellus Wallace's (Ving Rhames) destiny in the shop; Vincent and Mia's meeting and her overdose; and the Bonnie situation. Owing to the order of the episodes, suspense is left undefused for a longer period in the hold-up at the diner, and the result

Table 5.3 Comparison between screen time in the shots that maintain the same diegetic time in the first and last sequence of *Pulp Fiction*.

	First sequence Seconds	Last sequence Seconds
From Pumpkin: 'People never rob restaurants, why not?' to Vincent going to the toilet.	35	24
From Vincent going to the toilet to Pumpkin: 'I love you, Honey Bunny.'	55	24

of Butch's match. On the other hand, suspense is usually substituted by strong and shocking surprise. Strong surprise is caused by restricted narration because the audience shares only one character's point of view. For example, spectators, rather than being shown Butch's match, come to know of his victory when he, escaping from the gym, speaks with the taxi driver Esmarelda Villalobos (Angela Jones) about the match. Similarly, Butch meets Marsellus unexpectedly, while driving away from his house after having killed Vincent, and the spectator realizes only during a flashback of simultaneity that there is somebody else in the boys' apartment ready to kill Vincent and Jules. Shocking surprise often takes the place of suspense, too. The first time that Jules shoots a boy in the apartment he does so all of a sudden, when Vincent and Marvin (Phil LaMarr) die it happens abruptly and Mia's reawakening and her standing erect is so rapid that it almost scares the audience. Unlike in *Reservoir Dogs*, in which violent scenes are often preceded by a crescendo of suspense, but finally happen out of frame, in *Pulp Fiction*, rather than emphasized through a progressive increase of suspense until a final climax, violence is almost downplayed by being shown abruptly.

Furthermore, suspense is often introduced by dialogue, more than by the development of the fabula, as if expectations of the future were created by chance. The enjoyment of nonsense, funny dialogue, momentarily interrupts the trajectory of the source-path-goal schema, leaving space to amusing scenes and shots. For example, given the narrative position of Butch's flashback, the audience cannot know that the scene occurred in the diegetic past and that it is a Butch's enacted external analepsis, thus the flashback cannot satisfy curiosity. It introduces suspense about the future role of the watch, but mainly it presents a gag that could almost be enjoyed alone. When Mia and Vincent enter Jackrabbit Slim's, during a long take lasting more than one minute, the camera tracks forward to follow Vincent, and pans right or left when he stops to stare at something, moreover when he points to the right, the camera pans right, and when a waitress dressed as Marilyn Monroe comes into frame, he points at her. Suspense around Mia and Vincent's meeting is interrupted, and present time expanded to let spectators enjoy the *mise-en-scène*. The spectator has the impression of sharing Vincent's point of view thanks to the track forward to follow him, the pan right and left and Vincent pointing, but these very techniques lay bare the artificiality of the film. Another example is the Bonnie situation in which suspense is created by dialogue alone, and nonsense and funny dialogue delays development of the actions. Indeed, nobody is worried because Marvin has been shot to death accidentally, but because Jimmie's (Quentin Tarantino) house must be cleaned thoroughly before his wife Bonnie comes home.

The play between suspense, future, drama, compression of temporalities, versus enjoyment of the present, comedy, expansion of temporalities is usually resolved in favour of the latter features, except for the scenes concerning Mia's overdose and Marsellus' and Butch's adventure in the shop. After Mia overdoses in her house, in a long take we see Vincent's car that comes into frame from the right and goes out of frame from the left in Lance's (Eric Stoltz) garden, and a Steadicam follows Lance outside his house. Indoors, in another long take, a Steadicam keeps Jody (Rosanna Arquette) in-frame while she goes from the bedroom to the living room, and then with a ping-pong effect it pans right and left following her, or Vincent, Lance and Mia, and finally it follows Lance who looks for a medical book while quarrelling with Jody. The shot is delayed, both increasing suspense and allowing the spectator to take pleasure in the nonsense actions and dialogue. Similarly, when in the shop basement, Maynard (Duane Whitaker) and Zed (Peter Greene) enter a room with Marsellus, slow motion and extra-diegetic music increase suspense. When Butch manages to free himself and decides to help Marsellus, in a long take we see him looking for the best weapon. When he chooses a sabre, he looks directly into the camera, breaking the fourth wall, as if to assure the spectator that they are allowed to laugh. In these cases, stylistic features that expand temporalities both increase suspense and, during the narrative rush, leave space for amusing gags.

If in *Reservoir Dogs* the immediate aftermath of the hold-up is shown three times following different characters' points of view and, similarly, in *Pulp Fiction* the beginning of the robbery in the diner and the end of the shooting in the apartment are shown twice according to different characters' perspectives, in *Jackie Brown* this technique comes to the fore at the end of the film. The third Tarantino film is a repeated event plot, or better a hub-and-spoke plot, in which, once more, the source-path-goal and the part-whole schema are intertwined.

The incipit of the film is emblematic of this narration. In a long take, the protagonist Jackie (Pam Grier) enters frame from the right, and remains on the right of the frame during the title sequence: she is still, on a moving walkway that moves to the left, and the camera, anchored to the moving walkway, frames her in a medium shot via a straight angle (Figure 5.3). According to CMT, two major metaphors conceptualize time. In the time-moving metaphor, the spectator is stationary, whereas time moves and events flow from the future to the past (Coëgnarts and Kravanja 2012: 87). In this case, the character is stationary and the camera either tracks in a particular direction or pans, and its movement coincides with a flashback or a flashforward (90–2). The other metaphor is the ego-moving or time's landscape metaphor: while the observer moves, time is stationary, the spectator: 'move[s] over various location[s] in a landscape, where each location in the observer's path represents a time' (88). In the metaphor, time is a location, the camera is stationary and the character moves. In the metaphor motion of the observer, the camera tracks with the character through different temporal locations (93–5). At the beginning of *Jackie Brown*, movement and, consequently, time become relative because the shot can evoke either the time moving or the motion of the observer metaphor. We could either imagine that Jackie and the camera are still, while the background flows past on the right, or that Jackie and the camera move to the left, while the background remains still. The former hypothesis summons the time-moving metaphor because the observers, both the spectator and Jackie, are still, whereas the events flow from the past to the future. On the other hand, the latter hypothesis evokes the metaphor motion of the observer because the camera tracks with the observer who moves from the past to the future. In cognitive linguistics, the source-path-goal schema is known as the ego-moving metaphor: 'the "ego" or the observer's context (in this case the plot) progresses along the stationary time-line toward the past or the future' (Coëgnarts and Kravanja 2016: 115). Thus, the very first shot of the film evokes both the metaphor motion of the observer, a source-path-goal

Figure 5.3 *Jackie Brown* (Quentin Tarantino, 1997). Title credits. Jackie Brown (Pam Grier) on a moving walkway.

schema in which the timeline is still and the film advances towards the past, and a time-moving metaphor in which the timeline moves towards the future while the film is stationary. The time-moving metaphor seems to foreshadow the repeating event form and, consequently, the part-whole schema, during which the diegetic time does not progress, but each flashback of simultaneity constitutes a part of the whole ensemble of events that take place in the same time. The very first shot seems to announce how the source-path-goal and the part-whole schema will intertwine.

The repeating event form could have been substituted by parallel editing, but the play between suspense and curiosity would have changed. Indeed, during a sequence of cross-cutting, spectators usually know more than the characters involved in the events, and unrestricted narration arouses suspense. However, during a repeating event form the narration is restricted and the spectator shares the point of view of the characters they are shown. Suspense is mixed with curiosity or surprise because almost each part of the whole, whenever the event is shown from different characters' points of view, leaves either hidden or not temporary gaps.

There are several instances of cross-cutting in the film (Table 4.1) which are adopted to show events that occur either in different spaces but at the same time, or in different spaces and times. For example, during phone calls (case A in Table 4.1), the spectator sees characters speaking in different spaces but at the same time, and the narration is unrestricted. Similarly, at Del Amo Mall there is cross-cutting between Jackie and Ordell Robbie (Samuel L. Jackson) who speak in a cafeteria, and Max Cherry (Robert Forster) who comes out of the theatre and meets them (case B). This is followed by more cross-cutting between Jackie and Max speaking, and Ordell spying on them (case B). Interestingly, before Max meets Jackie and Ordell by chance, a title underlines that Del Amo is the 'largest indoor mall in the world', which is not true because Del Amo is not even the largest mall in California. Probably the goal of the title is to underscore how far the fortuitous encounter is due to the director's power and will. Other instances of cross-cutting during which events occur at the same time but in different spaces take place when Jackie, Max and Louis Gara (Robert de Niro) and Melanie Ralston (Bridget Fonda) travel by car to the mall before the exchange of money (case D), and when Jackie is in Max's office waiting for Max and Ordell who are coming by car (case D). In the former case, narration is unrestricted because we know more than Louis and Melanie who still do not know that Max will participate in the exchange. On the other hand, in the latter case, narration is restricted because we do not know that Ray Nicolette (Michael Keaton) is at Max's office with Jackie. Narration is also restricted during the cross-cutting between Jackie and Ordell in a restaurant, and she and Max at her house. The cross-cutting begins in the restaurant, and it is not until Ordell calls Jackie, who is home with Max, to tell her that Melanie will substitute Simone (Hattie Winston) during the exchange, that the spectators realize that the enacted flashback relates to the discussion between Jackie and Ordell, and not that between her and Max. All these instances of cross-cutting seem to progressively introduce the final flashbacks of simultaneity.

Jackie Brown is the only Tarantino film adapted from a novel, Elmore Leonard's *Rum Punch*, first published in 1992. Both the cross-cutting of characters driving to the mall and the repeated event plot of the money exchange are translated from the book, although the narrative structure of the written medium is more complex due to the adoption of several techniques (Tables 5.4 and 5.5). For example, whereas in the film during the exchange we follow first Jackie, then Melanie and Louis and, finally, Max from the beginning to the end of their roles, in the novel these different characters' points of view are continuously intertwined. Actions are either foreshadowed through characters' fluxes of conscience or narrated by the omniscient third person narrator (Leonard 2004 [1992]: 234–53). The narration goes back and forth through analepses and prolepses, and this greater fragmentation paradoxically gives the reader the feeling that the narration proceeds towards the future according to an undisturbed source-path-goal schema, as opposed to being strongly divided in parts as in the film.

While the part-whole schema in the cinematographic medium arouses curiosity and surprise together with suspense, curiosity and shocking surprise seem to dominate the spectator's experience. For example, when Ordell and Jackie are in her house after she is released from prison, the camera follows the woman in the living-room in a long take, as if it were the man's point-of-view shot, but then the camera tracks backwards till Ordell reappears in-frame. The camera was not anchored to the man, who remains still, increasing the suspense and cheating the spectator. In the same long take, the camera follows Ordell who, armed, gets near Jackie to menace her. A swipe to the right

Table 5.4 The scheme of *Rum Punch*. When the episodes take place (bold, first line), a brief description of each of them (subsequent lines) and the characters' points of view from which the events are narrated. F indicates a character's flashforward or an event related by the narrator.

Thursday:		04:10		04:30					
Jackie's p.o.v.: On the plane									
x									
Jackie's p.o.v.: She is with Ray in the airport parking lot									
	x								
Max's p.o.v.: Before entering the mall									
		x		F	F				
Jackie is trying a dress on									
			x						
Louis' p.o.v.: Louis and Melanie before and when she enters the fitting room									
			x	F x					
Jackie's p.o.v.: Jackie and Melanie exchange bags									
					x	F	F	F	
Melanie and Louis try to exit the mall									
						x			
Max's p.o.v.: Before going to the salesgirl									
					x	x	F	F	F
Louis' p.o.v.: Melanie and Louis cannot find their car and he shoots her									
							x		
Jackie's p.o.v.: She looks for Ray and exchanges bags with Sheronda									
							x		
Max's p.o.v.: Exits the mall									
								x	
Jackie's p.o.v.: She finds Ray									
								x	

creates a split screen and we are shown Max, in his car, who realizes that Jackie has stolen the gun in his glove box (Figure 5.4). Another swipe to the left abolishes the split screen. Now the spectator knows that the woman is armed: unrestricted narration increases the suspense of the shot. Similarly, when Jackie goes back home after having discussed the plan with Ordell in a bar, in another long take the camera movements seem to mimic a presence because the camera pans right and left with the protagonist, and does not follow her when she enters the kitchen and bedroom going out of frame.

Table 5.5 Scheme of *Jackie Brown*. When the episodes take place (bold, first line), a brief description of each (subsequent lines) and the characters' points of view from which events are narrated.

		03:30	03:47		03:52	04:04	04:12	
Jackie is on the plane								
x								
Jackie is with Ray at the airport parking lot								
	x							
Max is in his office								
		x						
Louis and Melanie receive Ordell's phone call								
			x					
Jackie is travelling by car								
				x				
Max is travelling by car								
				x				
Jackie is travelling by car								
				x				
Louis and Melanie are travelling by car								
				x				
Jackie's p.o.v.								
					x	x	x	x
Melanie and Louis' point of view								
							x	x
Max's p.o.v.								
						x	x	x

It is as if somebody is hiding in her apartment, but the scene ends with a cut. These camera movements and long takes increase suspense, extending temporalities. The same effect occurs after the money exchange, when Jackie runs and looks for Ray. In two long takes, the camera revolves around her, increasing her feeling of anxiety and confusion, but she is acting for the sake of the success of the plan, thus the camera takes part in her make-believe with two opposing effects: increasing suspense and laying bare the film's self-referentiality.

As in *Pulp Fiction*, when suspense comes to a climax or progressively increases, it is abruptly substituted by shocking surprise that almost freezes temporalities. Beaumont Livingston (Chris Tucker), Melanie, Louis and Ordell are all shot to death unexpectedly. After several long takes during which Ordell and Beaumont discuss their affairs,

Figure 5.4 *Jackie Brown* (Quentin Tarantino, 1997). Split screen. Max's glove box on the left, Jackie Brown (Pam Grier) and Ordell (Samuel L. Jackson) on the right.

adopting colourful language rich in similes and curse words, the former persuades the latter to enter his car trunk and in a long take a crane follows the car until it stops. Ordell gets out, opens the boot and shoots Beaumont in long shot. Similarly, there is a long take when Melanie mocks Louis because he cannot find his car in the parking lot, so he shoots her but the spectator is not shown her corpse. When Ordell and Louis are in Louis' truck after the money exchange the camera remains still, behind them, and after a series of long takes during which either they talk or remain silent, Ordell shoots Louis. The spectator knows that the boss is going to kill Louis, but the violence is unexpected because the two protagonists continue to speak and the camera remains still, not moving to frame the corpse. Similarly, after a sequence of cross-cutting that increases suspense between Max and Ordell who are going to the former's office, and Jackie who is waiting there for them, as soon as they enter in the former's office Jackie calls Ray, hidden in the back, and shoots Ordell. In these cases, long takes or cross-cutting, which increase suspense, are suddenly followed by violent acts that provoke shocking surprise and whose effects are not shown.

Kill Bill: Vols 1 and *2* are jumbled plots in which the source-path-goal and the part-whole schema are intertwined, as in *Reservoir Dogs* and *Pulp Fiction*. Both *Kill Bill: Vols 1* and *2* are divided into chapters that often do not follow the order of the fabula (Table 5.6).

Table 5.6 Scheme of *Kill Bill: Vols 1* and *2*. The setting of the episodes (bold, first lines), a brief description of each (on subsequent lines) and the titles (bold, capital letters). F indicates a character's enacted or enacted recounted flashback diegetically motivated.

	At Pai Mai's	In a hotel	In the Church	At the hospital	At the airport	At Hattori Hanzo's	At the airport and in Tokyo	At the House of Blue Leaves	Outside the hospital	In the hospital	At Vernita's	At Buddy's and in the desert	Towards Bill	At Bill's
VOL. 1 Bill shoots Beatrix			x											
CHAPTER 1 (2). The Bride and Vernita											x			
The Bride's flashback			F								x			
The Bride and Vernita											x			
CHAPTER 2. THE BLOOD-SPATTERED BRIDE. Four years and six months earlier.			x											
Elle is ready to kill the Bride				x										
The Bride, Buch and another name. **Four years later.**				x										
The Bride's flashback: Bill shoots Beatrix			F											
The Bride, Buch and another name. **Four years later.**				x										

The Bride's flashback: Beginning of rapes		F	x		
The Bride, Buch and another name and the Pussy Wagon. **Four years later.**			x		
The Bride's flashback	F				
CHAPTER 3. THE ORIGIN OF O'REN.	F	F	F		
The Pussy Wagon. 13 hours later.			x		
To Okinawa, Japan				x	
CHAPTER 4. THE MAN FROM OKINAWA.				x	
One month later.					x
CHAPTER 5. SHOWDOWN AT HOUSE OF BLUE LEAVES.	F?	F?			
	F	F			
	in	in			
	F?	F?			
	F?	F?			

(Continued)

Table 5.6 Continued.

To Tokyo, Japan										x								
Beatrix's flashback		F																
In Tokyo								x										
Showdown							x											
Beatrix's flashback		F					x											
Showdown							x											
Outside the hospital, Beatrix and Sophie									x									
In the hospital, Sophie and Bill													F	x				
														F	x			

By airplane																								x					
Hattori Hanzo's sword																							x						
By plane																								x					
Beatrix's flashforward about Buddy																													x
By plane																								x					
Beatrix's flashforward about Elle																													x
By plane																								x					
Beatrix's flashback about Bill																													
F																													
In the hospital, Sophie and Bill																x														

(Continued)

Table 5.6 Continued.

	At Pai Mai's	In a hotel	In the Church	At the hospital	At the airport	At Hattori Hanzo's	At the airport and in Tokyo	At the House of Blue Leaves	Outside the hospital	In the hospital	At Vernita's	At Buddy's and in the desert	Towards Bill	At Bill's
VOL. 2 Bill shoots Beatrix														
			x											
Beatrix goes by car to kill Bill													x	
CHAPTER 6. MASSACRE AT TWO PINES.														
			x x											
Bill speaks with Buddy														
CHAPTER 7. THE LONELY GRAVE OF PAULA SCHULTZ.														
												x x		
CHAPTER 8. THE CRUEL TUTELAGE OF PAI MAI.														
	x											x x x		
Beatrix comes out from the grave														
CHAPTER 9. ELLE AND I.														
												x		
Elle's flashback about Pai Mai.														
F?														

LAST CHAPTER. FACE TO FACE.

																			x
Beatrix's flashback about her pregnancy																			
F																			
End																			x

Without considering the characters' diegetically motivated flashbacks, and splitting some chapters into parts that regard different represented time, the fabula order of *Vol. 1* can be briefly summarized as follows:

Chapter 3. The Origin of O'Ren (1): O'Ren's childhood and adolescence.
Opening: Bill shoots Beatrix.
Chapter 2. The Blood-Spattered Bride.
Chapter 5. Showdown at the House of Blue Leaves (1): O'Ren becomes the boss.
Chapter 3 (2): Beatrix from the hospital parking lot to Okinawa.
Chapter 4. The Man from Okinawa.
Chapter 5 (3): Beatrix from Okinawa to Tokyo.
Chapter 5 (2): Beatrix against O'Ren and her entourage.
Chapter 1 (2).

Apart from Chapter 1, which is at the end of the fabula, and Chapters 3 and 5 that are divided into sections that take place at different diegetic times, the other chapters are presented chronologically. Moreover, the first part of Chapter 3 precedes the second, and stands out clearly from the other sections because it is an external enacted analepsis and a Japanese anime. Similarly, the third part of Chapter 5 differs from the others because it mimics the montage sequences that often appear at the end of each episode of a television series to disclose the main events that will be shown in the next episode. Beatrix is on board a plane travelling from Okinawa to Tokyo with her sword and writes the 'Death List Five', that is to say the names of the five people that she is going to kill. The spectators have already seen this list, which is a helpful device to reconstruct the fabula because Beatrix has already killed, according to the order of editing, Vernita (Vivica A. Fox) and O'Ren (Lucy Liu). Indeed, the spectator is not shown the Bride writing the names of these two characters. But when she writes '3 Buddy' through a superimposition, we see Buddy (Michael Madsen); when she writes '4 Elle', there is a cut to a close-up of Elle (Daryl Hannah); and when she writes 'Bill', a superimposition shows Beatrix looking directly into the camera and speaking to Bill (David Carradine) and it is a Bill's point-of-view shot. These shots of Budd, Elle and Beatrix will appear in *Vol. 2*.

Unlike in *Vol. 1*, in *Vol. 2*, representational time follows more closely represented time:

Chapter 8. The Cruel Tutelage of Pai Mai (1): Beatrix and Pai Mai.
Chapter 6. Massacre at Two Pines (1): the slaughter in the church.
Opening (1): Bill shoots Beatrix.
Chapter 6 (2): Bill speaks with Buddy.
Chapter 7. The Lonely Grave of Paula Schultz.
Chapter 8 (2): Beatrix comes out from the grave.
Chapter 9. Elle and I.
Opening (2): Beatrix goes by car to Bill's.
Last Chapter. Face to face.

Apart from the opening and Chapters 6 and 8, all split into two sections, the order of montage is similar to that of the fabula. Moreover, the title of Chapter 8 advises the spectator about what will happen, and the episodes in the opening and the first part of Chapter 6 are shot in black and white, unlike all the others. They regard, respectively, the massacre in the church during the rehearsal of Beatrix's marriage, and the Bride who addresses directly the spectator to explain that she is driving towards Bill's.

If we reorder the sections of both volumes according to diegetic time, we obtain the succession in Table 5.7.

If we consider all the sections, *Vols 1* and *2* are perfectly alternated. On the other hand, if we bear in mind that Chapter 3 (1) and Chapter 8 (1) are external enacted analepses, if we regard the massacre during the wedding rehearsal the beginning of the story, then all the episodes of *Vol. 1* precede those of *Vol. 2*, with the exception of the slaughter at the church that is divided into several flashbacks of simultaneity in both volumes.[4] The editing order assists the audience to watch and understand the two films separately, not necessarily one after the other in the same session.

The source-path-goal schema is emphasized in both volumes through Beatrix's will to avenge what happened during the slaughter at the church. The Death List Five and the majority of characters' enacted flashbacks highlight the theme of revenge. In *Vol. 1*, for example, there are thirteen analepses, nine of which are Beatrix's enacted flashbacks, and among them six regard the massacre during the wedding rehearsal. The other four enacted recounted flashbacks concern O'Ren's past, and all are introduced and/or accompanied by the Bride's voice-over, as if to reinforce the audience's empathy with the heroine. Moreover, many analepses are introduced by a zoom in on Beatrix's face or

Table 5.7 The order of the fabula of *Kill Bill: Vol. 1* and *Vol. 2*

Number of Chapters and Openings	Kill Bill Vol. 1 or Vol. 2
Ch. 3 (1)	*Vol. 1*
Ch. 8 (1)	*Vol. 2*
Ch. 6 (1)	*Vol. 2*
Opening (1)	*Vol. 2*
Opening	*Vol. 1*
Ch. 2	*Vol. 1*
Ch. 5 (1)	*Vol. 1*
Ch. 3 (2)	*Vol. 1*
Ch.4	*Vol. 1*
Ch. 5 (2)	*Vol. 1*
Ch. 5 (3)	*Vol. 1*
Ch. 1	*Vol. 1*
Ch. 6 (2)	*Vol. 2*
Ch.7 (2)	*Vol. 2*
Ch. 8 (2)	*Vol. 2*
Ch. 9 (2)	*Vol. 2*
Opening (2)	*Vol. 2*
Ch. 10	*Vol. 2*

---

4   Cf. Menarini (2009: 91–110) for another analysis and comparison of represented and representational time.

eyes, or by fades in and out, or superimposition, as if to underline that her past, the massacre, guides her vengeful present. In *Vol. 2* there are only three enacted flashbacks: two of them are Beatrix's analepses introduced by her voice-over and one of them is Elle's flashback about her experience with Pai Mei (Chia-Hui Liu), which is diegetically motivated by the Bride's question about what happened between Elle and the Sensei. There is also an interesting insert, a mix of past and imagination, when Elle, on the phone with Bill, pronounces the name 'Beatrix Kiddo' for the first time – because up to now her name had been censored through an extra-diegetic beep[5] – the spectator sees the Bride, as an adult sitting in an elementary classroom among children. The difference

Figure 5.5 *Kill Bill: Vol. 1* (Quentin Tarantino, 2003). Split screen. Elle (Daryl Hannah; right) and Beatrix (Uma Thurman; left).

Figure 5.6 Split screen. In the middle O'Ren's (Lucy Liu) picture, on the left as a young girl and on the right the boss.

---

[5] Her name is written on her air ticket to Okinawa at the end of Chapter 3 of *Vol. 1*, and on her ticket to Tokyo in Chapter 5. But it is readable only if the spectator uses the pause function.

between the number of flashbacks in the two volumes is probably due to the fact that in *Vol. 2* an entire chapter is dedicated to the slaughter in the church – 'Chapter 6. Massacre at Two Pines' – and the source-path-goal schema prevails.

The majority of instances of cross-cutting in both volumes link different times, with the exception of those that join events that play in different spaces but at the same time, such as phone calls and chases. In *Vol. 1*, after Beatrix has defeated O'Ren and her entourage, there is cross-cutting between the Bride who, before leaving Sophie outside a hospital, explains to her what she should tell Bill, and Sophie, inside the hospital, recounts to Bill what happened. At the end of this volume, as mentioned, there is cross-cutting between the Bride in the present and Budd and Elle in the future and Bill in the past. In *Vol. 2*, there is cross-cutting between Beatrix and Elle who both get to Budd's caravan at different times and in various ways, while Elle's flashback about her relationship with Pai Mei is presented as cross-cutting between past and present. It is worth noting that split screen is adopted in both volumes to cross-cut between two antagonists who are going to fight. In *Vols 1* and *2*, this technique shows both Elle and the Bride, Bill's new and old lovers respectively (Figure 5.5), and in *Vol. 1* the screen is split into three to show in the middle O'Ren's picture, on the left as a young girl and on the right the boss who is going to kill her parents (Figure 5.6).

The part-whole schema is foregrounded thanks to titles that often cite a character, and to those sections that focus on a peculiar character, the best example being 'Chapter 3. The Origin of O'Ren'. This schema is more evident in *Vol. 1*, where, thanks to representational order and the focus on characters other than Beatrix, the source-path-goal schema is sometimes deprioritized. Moreover, in this volume, the style of a scene or chapter often evokes that of another sequence or section, stressing links between different episodes, thus the part-whole schema. For example, both Chapters 1 and 5 are similar in their alternation of styles, whereas Chapters 3 and 4 are different from all the other chapters. Chapter 3 is an anime, and Chapter 5 is characterized by long takes or regular shot-reverse-shots during which characters remain silent or speak slowly, and before Beatrix asks for Hattori Hanzo nonsense dialogue dominates between the Bride, Hattori and his assistant Johnny Mo (Gordon Liu). These stylistic differences lead to a succession of differing ASL[6] and temporalities.

During Chapter 1, when Beatrix and Vernita Green fight in the latter's house, the editing of shots of the Bride or of Vernita or of both of them or details of their arms is rapid. When the school bus stops outside the house and Nikki Bell (Ambrosia Kelley), Vernita's daughter, boards, a slower montage prevails, ending with a long take when the two enemies decide when and where they are going to fight. Then, after Vernita shoots Beatrix, and before the latter throws a knife killing her enemy, we see the Bride who kicks over her coffee cup in slow motion. There follows a regular shot-reverse-shot between Beatrix and Nikki when Nikki enters the kitchen after her mother's death.

---

[6] The ASL during the opening is 38.5 seconds, Chapter 1's is 3.8, Chapter 2's 5.5, Chapter 3's 3.6, Chapter 4's 9.2, Chapter 5's 2.9 and the ending 6.6. Apart from the opening and the ending, Chapter 4 is the slowest (Cinemetrics, data submitted by Eric T. Jones on 10 September 2009. Last accessed 25 September 2019).

Temporalities are compressed during action scenes through a quick succession of shots during which the camera and characters move and slow motion increases suspense. This rhythm alternates with pauses during which temporalities are expanded owing to a slower editing rhythm when characters speak.

The same occurs during Chapter 5. This complex sequence is introduced by a succession of slow-motion shots inside the House of Blue Leaves, during which the camera tracks backwards to precede O'Ren and her entourage, until the last shot during which the camera tracks forward to follow them and, finally, with them. The sequence's self-referentiality is emphasized not only through slow motion, but also because the montage follows the rhythm of the diegetic music, and O'Ren, Gogo Yubari (Chiaki Kuriyama) and Sofie Fatale (Julie Dreyfus) often look directly at the camera. This scene evokes the shots in slow motion at the beginning of *Reservoir Dogs* when the camera first tracks backwards to precede the gang members who walk outside the diner in slow motion, and then remains still while they walk away from the camera. The scene of *Kill Bill* is followed by a long shot during which the camera keeps O'Ren and her entourage in-frame until, entering a room, they go out of frame. Then, without cuts, the camera frames, in order, the three girls singing on the stage, the two owners of the House and Beatrix at the bar. During this long take, the camera is not anchored to a particular character, as in the shot of *Pulp Fiction* when Vincent enters Jackrabbit Slim's, but in both cases camera movements allow us to explore the setting, almost in a 360° view. As the previous scene introduces the main characters of Chapter 5, the following long take is an establishing shot that presents the setting where the action will take place. In the following scenes different rhythms alternate. During fights, temporalities are compressed through close-ups, medium close-ups and medium shots, and details of arms and cut limbs that rapidly succeed one another, and alternate with long shots of characters during which both the camera and characters move.

These violent staged performances increase suspense and shocking surprise. Suspense further increases when slow motion is adopted, and when there are jump cuts during the fight between the Bride and the leader of the Crazy 88. These violent scenes are often introduced by zooming in on characters, or on details of the eyes of Beatrix or of other characters. Among these scenes are shots that do not present violent actions and have a slower rhythm. For example, both before fighting Gogo and the Crazy 88, a regular shot-reverse-shot is accompanied by a slow and nonsense dialogue. When the Crazy 88 advance upstairs there is a pause in their slaughter by Beatrix, and before killing the leader of the Crazy 88, the Bride spanks the last member of the squad who is still alive. Moreover, there are long takes when the Bride takes Sophie hostage, before the final fight against O'Ren and at the end of the sequence.

In Tarantino's first four films suspense precedes violent acts, but in *Reservoir Dogs* violence occurs out of frame and the spectator is shown its effects, in *Pulp Fiction* and *Jackie Brown* brutal acts often occur unexpectedly, while in *Kill Bill* brutality is exhibited. But through several techniques – camera movement, zooming, slow motion, jump cuts, a montage that follows the rhythm of the music, nonsense dialogue, characters who look directly at the camera, etc. – these bloodbaths lay bare the self-referentiality of the sequences, violating empathy with the characters and allowing the spectator to take pleasure in a spectacle that explicitly manifests itself as a show.

In both *Vols 1* and *2*, temporalities expand through new slowness, freeze-frames and slow motion. Moreover, in *Vol. 2*, the camera often lingers on useless details, creating pauses in the narration, such as when Budd and Elle are in the former's caravan and the spectator is repeatedly shown glasses and a mixer. On the other hand, temporalities are usually compressed thanks to rapid motion and editing of shots during which both the camera and characters move. Both volumes alternate between dialogue and action scenes. But in *Vol. 1* action prevails, whereas in *Vol. 2* dialogue comes to the fore, as in previous Tarantino films. In both cases, there is enjoyment of the present moment, but whereas in *Vol. 1* it prevails through the pleasure of staged violent performances, in the latter it arises from new slowness. Another difference between *Vol. 1* and *Vol. 2* is that the former focuses upon Japan, dominated by Hattori Hanzo – played by Sonny Chiba who is also the choreographer of Kenjutsu in the film – and the latter by China, represented by the legendary martial arts expert Gordon Liu Chia-hui (Morsiani 2016: 90–1).

Thanks to montage, in both films curiosity prevails because in *Vol. 1*, when Beatrix fights the nurse Buck (Michael Bowen), we already know that she will be the winner because she has already killed Vernita, and when she is at the House of Blue Leaves we know that she will kill O'Ren because the latter's name has already been struck through on the Death List Five. At the beginning of *Vol. 2*, Beatrix, addressing us directly while driving, explains that she is going to kill Bill, her last enemy still alive. What we want to know is not the effect, the end (that is already well known), but how, the path to the goal. This desire on the one hand mixes curiosity with suspense because, while we know that Beatrix will survive, we do not know the other characters' fates, but on the other it allows us to enjoy the spectacle without being afraid for our heroine. *Vol. 1* ends with a series of flashforwards that increase our desire to see *Vol. 2*, and to see Bill, who has never been shown in *Vol. 1*, and to know the Bride's fate. As often happens in Tarantino's work, the suspense created is not prolonged until a final climax, but unexpectedly satisfied and substituted by strong surprise. We see Bill, and come to know that Beatrix has already killed everybody, and is going to find her former boss and lover at the beginning of *Vol. 2*, after waiting for about a year – the time span between the release of the two films.

5.1.2 Towards classical temporalities: *Death Proof* (2007), *Inglourious Basterds* (2009), *Django Unchained* (2012), *The Hateful Eight* (2015) and *Once Upon a Time . . . in Hollywood* (2019)

Death Proof is dominated by the source-path-goal schema. The film consists of two separate episodes that are very similar, except for the end. Unlike *Pulp Fiction*, which is a jumbled plot consisting of different stories linked by more than one character, in *Death Proof* the order of editing follows that of the fabula, and the only character who appears in both episodes is the protagonist Mike (Kurt Russell). This film could have been divided into chapters or volumes, like *Kill Bill*, but unlike the previous film, the two episodes are very similar. Regarding narrative structure, *Death Proof* seems to edge towards classical narration, a trend that subsequent films will confirm, with the exception of *Once Upon a Time . . . in Hollywood*.

In each of the two episodes, two groups of female characters – Jungle Julia (Sydney Tamiia Poitier), Shanna (Jordan Ladd) and Arlene (Vanessa Ferlito); and Abernathy (Rosario Dawson), Lee (Mary Elizabeth Winstead) and Kim (Tracie Thoms) – are shown in a car talking and outside and/or inside Güero's and Texas Chili Parlor, and Potheads and a diner, respectively. The groups are joined by other female characters – Marcy (Marcy Harriell) at Güero's, Lanna Frank (Monica Staggs) and Pam (Rose McGowan) at Texas Chili Parlor and Zoë Bell (Zoë Bell) outside Potheads – whereas other women leave – Marcy is present at Güero's only, Pam is killed during the first accident, and Lee is left at Jasper's (Jonathan Loughran) when her friends drive the Dodge Challenger. In each group, only one of the female characters notices Mike's car – Arlene outside Güero's and Texas Chili Parlor and Abernathy outside Potheads – and he joins the group of women either inside or outside Texas Chili Parlor and a diner, respectively. In both episodes, the accident is divided into two segments: Mike kills Pam in his own car, and then provokes the death of Jungle Julia, Arlene, Lanna and Shanna in the first part; he runs after Abernathy, Kim and Zoë, and is finally chased by them in the second.

The two episodes are also shot using similar techniques and follow the same rhythm. A few long takes alternate with classical editing during dialogue scenes, in which nonsense and amusing talk succeed one another. The only exception in camera movement being when the camera turns around Arlene while she is lap dancing in front of Mike, and when it turns around the table at which Zoë, Lee, Abernathy and Kim sit talking, as in the scene shot in the diner at the beginning of *Reservoir Dogs*. The spectator gathers information about characters mainly through their dialogue, much like in *Pulp Fiction* and *Reservoir Dogs*, and often the camera lingers on details of their bodies, especially feet, as often occurs in *Kill Bill* and *Pulp Fiction*. This dialogue and these details slow the narration, expand temporalities and let the spectator enjoy the present moment. Moreover, narration is further decelerated and the two parts separated by a scene that is useless to the development of the fabula. When Mike is admitted, two policemen, Earl and Edgar McGraw (Michael and James Parks), speak alone and with Dr. Dakota Block (Marley Shelton) about Mike without adding new information about the stuntman. During this scene, the characters' nonsense dialogue is shot in long takes. It is an amusing insert and, at the same time, the film's self-referentiality becomes foregrounded even further because the policemen appear with the same names and roles in *Vol. 2, From Dusk till Dawn* (Robert Rodriguez, 1996) and *Planet Terror* (Rodriguez, 2007).

On the other hand, suspense hovers over the female characters' fate as soon as one of them notices Mike's car, and accompanies the car chases that often, as in *Vol. 1*, end with shocking and gory surprise. Action scenes are characterized, as in *Kill Bill*, by a quick montage during which characters and objects are in-frame and the camera moves rapidly. There are a couple of exceptions. During the second accident of the first part, the collision of the girls' car with Mike's is shown four times, each time from the point of view of one of the women, as in the exchange scene in *Jackie Brown*. And during the last accident of the film, when the female characters hit the stuntman, there are freeze-frames – as at the beginning of *Pulp Fiction* when the robbery begins – and the film ends with a freeze-frame. These features expand temporalities, prolonging and emphasizing the shocking surprise derived from violent staged performances and, in the meantime, lay bare the techniques of the medium.

The narration of *Death Proof* alternates between suspense, shocking surprise and enjoyment of the present moment. Only Mike's face, shown just after about 20 minutes' screen time, as in the case of Bill in *Kill Bill*, elicits our curiosity. Before the spectator can see the stuntman's face, his details are visible: the written 'husk' on his jacket and his right hand bringing food to his mouth.

Like *Death Proof*, *Inglourious Basterds* is dominated by the source-path-goal schema, although there is often cross-cutting between past and present, a narrative technique introduced in *Kill Bill* that seems adopted here to highlight similarities between the style and theme of different episodes. Like *Kill Bill*, *Inglourious Basterds* is divided into chapters, each one of them focusing on different characters that finally meet and are gathered together during 'Chapter 5. Revenge of the Giant Face' (Table 5.8).

Following the order of editing, the first enacted flashback narrates the ambush of some German soldiers by the 'inglourious basterds', introduced by the dialogue between Hitler (Martin Wuttke) and Pvt. Butz (Sönke Möhring) – Pvt. Butz is left alive by the enemies to recount their brutality to Hitler. Within this analepsis, there is another enacted flashback about Sgt. Hugo Stiglitz (Til Schweiger) that lays bare the film's self-referentiality because it begins with a freeze-frame of a long shot of Hugo, and a title with his name, accompanied by extra-diegetic music, followed by shots of newspapers with articles about his cruel exploits and a voice-over that introduces a montage sequence of his past. Then there is the first instance of cross-cutting between the diegetic present, represented by Pvt. Butz who recounts to Hitler what the 'inglourious basterds' did to him and his companions, and the diegetic past, during which the spectator sees what the German soldier is telling his leader. Present and past alternate, offering two different ways of narrating the same episode and arousing and increasing the spectator's curiosity about the legendary brutality of the 'basterds'. The other two occasions of cross-cutting between events that happen in different spaces and times, respectively open and close the last chapter. At the beginning, the spectator sees a montage sequence of Shosanna (Mélanie Laurent) getting ready for the night of the premiere in the diegetic present, alternated with another montage sequence of her and her fiancé Marcel (Jacky Ido) in the past, during the production and post-production phase of the short that they will project at the premiere. At the end, there is very interesting cross-cutting between the massacre in the theatre and Col. Hans Landa (Christoph Waltz), who dictates the terms of the operation before the slaughter. We believe that the cross-cutting is between events that occur simultaneously until we see Landa, who should be with Lt. Aldo Raine (Brad Pitt) in a bar, whispering something in Joseph Goebbels' ear, and leaving an explosive under his seat in the theatre. What we thought was unrestricted narration, is instead restricted narration, anchored to Col.

Table 5.8 The scheme of *Inglourious Basterds*. The setting of the episodes (bold, first line), a brief description of each (subsequent lines) and the titles (bold, capital letters). F indicates a character's flashback diegetically motivated.

At Perrier LaPadites	In England	In a wood in France	In Germany	In France	In England		In a tavern	In the cinema	In a tavern
CHAPTER 1. ONCE UPON A TIME . . . NAZI-OCCUPIED FRANCE									
x									
CHAPTER 2. INGLOURIOUS BASTERDS									
Introduction of Lt. Aldo Raine									
	x								
Introduction of Hitler									
			x						
Inglourious basterds against German soldiers									
		x							
Introduction of Sgt. Hugo Stiglitz									
	x								
Inglourious basterds against German soldiers									
		x							
Cross-cutting between present and past									
			x						
		x							
			x						
		x							
			x						
		x							
CHAPTER 3. GERMAN NIGHT IN PARIS. JUNE.									
Shosanna meets Fredrick Zoller, Joseph Goebbels and Col. Hans Landa									
				x					
Shosanna's flashback									
F									
Shosanna and Col. Hans Landa, then Shosanna and Marcel									
				x					
CHAPTER 4. OPERATION KINO.									
Cpl. Wilhelm Wicki meets General Ed Fenech and Churchill									
					x				

The inglourious basterds meet Bridget von Hammersmark											
								X			
Hugo's flashback											
	F										
The inglourious basterds and Bridget von Hammersmark											
								X			

CHAPTER 5. REVENGE OF THE GIANT FACE.

Cross-cutting between present and past											
									X		
								X			
									X		
								X			
Before the massacre											
									X		
Col. Hans Landa and Lt. Aldo Raine											
											X
Before and during the massacre											
										X	
											X
										X	
											X
										X	

Landa's knowledge that we do not share, much like almost all the other characters, until we see him in the theatre. This latter shot constitutes a gap created at the very moment in which it is filled, which provokes strong surprise because we realize that the colonel dictates his terms after having cheated his German companions. Narrative misleads us, much as Landa deceives all the other characters.

There are only a couple of characters' flashbacks which are motivated diegetically by their experiences and the development of the fabula. When Shosanna is in a restaurant with Fredrick Zoller (Daniel Brühl) to meet Goebbels, after a close-up of her there is a funny shot during which Goebbels and his secretary Francesca Mondino (Julie Dreyfus) are shown having sex. This insert is amusing, and its content contrasts with Goebbels' historical reputation of depravity as the Reich Minister of Propaganda of Nazi Germany, and similarly with how he is depicted in the film. Whereas this shot can be thought to arouse from Shosanna's imagination, and slightly mitigates the suspense of the scene, the subsequent girl's internal enacted analepsis increases suspense. Indeed, when Landa arrives in the dining room to find Shosanna, Fredrick, Goebbels and Francesca,

Shosanna does not turn around to look at Landa whom she recognizes from his voice, and loud extra-diegetic music accompanies camera movements that link the Nazi and the Jewish girl: from a close-up of Shosanna the camera tilts up to frame Landa and then down to frame Shosanna once more. They are not shown in-frame together, and camera movements delay their face-to-face meeting, extending temporalities. Then Shosanna's close-up introduces the internal enacted flashback of her desperate escape from the house where her family had been wiped out. Finally, there is a long take during which Shosanna is in-frame on the right in medium shot, whereas Fredrick and Landa talk on the left of the frame, their heads out of frame, and the camera zooms in on a close-up of Shosanna. Once more, suspense increases because *mise-en-scène* defers a direct confrontation between the man and the girl. Similarly, during 'Chapter 4. Operation Kino', when Sgt. Hugo Stiglitz and the other 'basterds' meet Bridget von Hammersmark in a bar and are joined by the German Walter Frazer (Sönke Möhring), who could blow their cover, a zoom in on Hugo who looks directly into the camera, loud extra-diegetic music and fades in and out introduce his external enacted flashback: we see him tied to a pole and whipped by Frazer. This analepsis, given the tension among the characters and Hugo's history of violence, expands temporalities because the possibility that Hugo loses control and the situation degenerates become more likely.

Thanks to the source-path-goal schema and the rhythm of narration, suspense prevails, as does unrestricted narration, with two exceptions discussed above during which curiosity and strong surprise dominate. Usually, suspense either increases through a compression or an expansion of temporalities. Much like in *Kill Bill*, the former effect is generally obtained during action scenes thanks to rapid montage, camera and character movements and loud extra-diegetic music. These scenes are often introduced by rapid editing or zooms in on details. For example, in Chapter 1, a succession of zooms in on Landa and Perrier LaPadite (Denis Ménochet) precedes the long take during which LaPadite stands up and walks above the hiding place of Shosanna's family, and in Chapter 2 zooms in on Sgt. Rachtman alternate with those on the dark cave from where the Jewish bear, nickname of Sgt. Donny Donowitz (Eli Roth), is expected to come. In Chapter 4, a rapid succession of shots of the characters' guns precedes the shooting, and in the last chapter details of Bridget's feet and her shoes announce and accompany her death.

On the other hand, temporalities are usually expanded during dialogue scenes through slow editing of shots or long takes during which the camera and characters remain still or move quietly, and nonsense dialogue, either rapid or slow, delays development of the fabula. These scenes elicit two contrasting feelings: on the one hand pleasure in the present, a wish that the waiting will not end, and on the other desire to learn about the future. New slowness not only results from dialogue, but also from other techniques, such as slow motion and freeze-framing, lingering on details and peculiar camera movements.

As regards camera movement, two of them have already been discussed, and respectively precede and succeed Shosanna's internal enacted flashback. When Landa enquires of Perrier about Shosanna's family, during a long take, from a close-up of LaPadite who is telling the girl's age, the camera moves down vertically, passing the pavement, until Shosanna's close-up as she keeps her hand on her mouth. Thanks to this slow camera movement, narration becomes unrestricted, increasing suspense. Moreover, this movement announces the tilting up and down that precedes the face-to-face meeting between Landa and the Jewish girl at the restaurant. During this latter dialogue scene, the camera moves around the table twice, as in *Reservoir Dogs* and *Death Proof*, but this time evoking a feeling of imprisonment. Also, when the camera turns around Landa and Bridget when he asks what has happened to her feet, and when, from a long shot high-angle of Shosanna, the camera turns around to follow her, revealing the top of walls, how the set is constructed, as in *Kill Bill: Vol. 1* when Beatrix and Vernita go into the latter's kitchen, and before Beatrix takes Sophie hostage in the bathroom of the House of Blue Leaves (Figure 5.7). A ping-pong effect slows down temporalities when Pvt. Butz decides to collaborate with the 'inglourious basterds', showing them on a map where Nazi troops are hidden. Here, the camera pans

Figure 5.7 *Kill Bill: Vol. 1* (Quentin Tarantino, 2003). The House of Blue Leaves.

Figure 5.8 *Inglourious Basterds* (Quentin Tarantino, 2009). Shosanna's theatre. The two locations are architectonically similar.

continuously right and left to frame the German soldier, Lt. Aldo and Sgt. Hugo who translates from German to English what Butz is saying, and the map when the soldier points at it. At the beginning of the last chapter, a long take joins all the main characters who will be involved in the final sequence, and offers an establishing shot of the theatre hall, much like the long take at the beginning of the last chapter of *Kill Bill: Vol. 1*. The camera keeps Shosanna in-frame while she goes downstairs to meet Fredrick, Goebbels, Francesca and Hermann Goering, then it tracks with an usher and goes up and right to frame Landa, finally tracking with him downstairs where he joins Bridget and the 'basterds'. The architectonic structure of the theatre hall evokes that of the House of Blue Leaves: the ground floor is connected to the first floor by two flights of stairs and the doors of the rooms on the first floor overlook a balcony, to which the stairs lead, and which dominates the ground floor (Figure 5.8).

Suspense, especially that experienced when temporalities are expanded, and sometimes almost frozen, dominates *Inglourious Basterds* and its climaxes are characterized by shocking surprise and violent staged performances. Characters fight with arms or bare hands. For example, when Nazi soldiers shoot Shosanna's family, when the 'basterds' and the German soldiers exchange shots at the tavern, when the 'basterds' shoot the spectators at the theatre, when Sgt. Donny hits Sgt. Rachtman on the head with a bat, when Lt. Aldo dips his finger into Bridget's wound, when Landa strangles her and when Lt. Aldo unexpectedly shoots a Nazi soldier, apparently without reason, as often occurs in *Reservoir Dogs*, *Pulp Fiction* and *Jackie Brown*.

Django Unchained, like *Death Proof* and *Inglourious Basterds*, follows a source-path-goal scheme, and presents several instances of cross-cutting, especially between episodes taking place at different times, as in the previous Tarantino's film (Table 5.9).

There are few enacted analepses and prolepses, owing to the director's stylistic and narrative choices, that slightly disrupt the chronological order of the fabula. During the night, when the hooded men led by Big Daddy (Don Johnson) gloriously gallop down a hill until they reach Dr. King Schultz's (Christoph Waltz) carriage, they are accompanied by the extra-diegetic *Ride of the Valkyries* by Wagner. Then, following the order of montage, they begin to discuss how poorly made and uncomfortable are their hoods. But in the previous scene they had already arrived at the carriage, whereas in this dialogue scene they have not left yet, thus the latter scene is an enacted flashback. The dialogue is nonsense and funny, and the comedy increases thanks to the contrast with the heroic tone of the music over the previous shots. Interestingly, the following enacted prolepsis and analepsis are cross-cut with the diegetic present. 'After a very cold and profitable winter,' Dr. King and Django (Jamie Foxx) are in a saloon where, having consulted the slaves' register, they find out that Broomhilda von Shaft (Kerry Washington), Django's wife, was sold to Calvin Candie (Leonardo DiCaprio). Dr. Schultz's voice functions as a sound bridge, and in the subsequent shot the spectator sees him and Django knocking and entering Calvin's house. But then they are shown again in the saloon and finally in Candie's house. Thus, the scene during which the two of them are outside the house is an enacted flashforward. Curiously, in the next sequence, Dr. Schultz, Django, Calvin and his entourage are going towards Candie's Land, but at the beginning these shots of their travel are cross-cut with enacted flashbacks of them at Calvin's house, and it is Candie's voice that functions as a sound bridge to link two shots recording different times. Thus, from the point of view of the editing, the first encounter among King, Django and Calvin occurs first in the future and then in the past, but never in the diegetic present, and it is always cross-cut with other events as if to foreshadow how long and complex, and full of unexpected developments, the negotiation with Calvin will be.

There are several flashbacks to events involving Django: about his former owner Old Man Carrucan (Bruce Dern); cross-cutting between Django and his wife escaping from the plantation and their subsequent punishment; about Broomhilda's burnt face; and at the very end about Django training to shoot in the snow with King. With the exception of the last analepsis, all the flashbacks are external and concern Django's and Broomhilda's past as mistreated slaves, reinforcing the goal – much like Beatrix's flashbacks about the slaughter in the church in *Kill Bill* – Django's desire to set Broomhilda free and avenge the atrocities they suffered as slaves. Along with these analepses, there are five shots of Broomhilda that seem to come from Django's imagination and further underline his aim: he is shown looking at something, and in the subsequent shot the spectator sees his wife from his point of view. King's flashbacks also underline his goal. Indeed, at Candie's Land there is cross-cutting between Broomhilda, Django, Calvin and Stephen (Samuel L. Jackson), who are signing the contract that enshrines Broomhilda's freedom, and in the next room where a girl plays the harp King sits in an armchair with a thoughtful expression on his face. His internal enacted flashbacks are about the boy D'Artagnan (Ato Essandoh), who had been mangled alive by dogs that morning. King cannot be fully satisfied about Django and his wife's future and in the next scene, first he refuses to shake hands with Calvin and, finally, he shoots him to death. Dr. Schultz's goal now becomes broader than Django: not simply avenging the brutalities experienced by Broomhilda and Django but those suffered by all the slaves.

As discussed, there is cross-cutting between episodes that occur in the future and in the present, or in the present and in the past, or in two different past moments, or present moments, such as when the funeral procession for Calvin is cross-cut first with Django who rides a horse, and then with the meeting between him and his wife. These instances of cross-cutting, together with flashbacks, flashforwards and shots of Django's imaginings, on the one hand underline Django's goal but on the other they often slow the narration, adding redundant information. The same occurs with montage sequences that are mainly used to shoot the travels of slaves and slave traders, of King and Django, and of many characters towards Candie's Land. Much like the shots of Broomhilda illustrating Django's imaginings seem to function both as a visual translation of his flux of consciousness, and as a description of his wife, montage sequences seem to adapt descriptions of landscapes, and of the difficulties of travelling. Tarantino seems to get closer and closer to the narrative structure of a classical novel.

As in the case of *Death Proof* and, especially, *Inglourious Basterds*, style rather than narrative structure and fabula development expands and compresses temporalities,

Table 5.9 The scheme of *Django Unchained*. The setting of the episodes (bold, first line), a brief description of each (subsequent lines) and the titles (bold, capital letters).

Old Man Carrucan's plantation	SOMEWHERE IN TEXAS	DAUGHTREY TEXAS	TENNESSEE		HEADING FOR… MISSISSIPPI	Calvin Candie's house	Towards Candie's Land	At Candie's Land
1858. TWO YEARS BEFORE THE CIVIL WAR.								
Django meets King								
	x							
King kills the Sheriff, Django and King around the fire								
		x						
Django's flashback about Old Man Carrucan								
		x						
x								
Django chooses his dress, and the Brittle brothers at Big Daddy's plantation								
			x					
Cross-cutting between Django's flashbacks								
	x							
	x							
	x							
	x							
	x							
			x					

Scene	1	2	3	4	5	6	7	8
The hooded men								x
Flashback about the hooded men		x						
The hooded men, Django and King around the fire, travelling, killing Smitty Bacall, training, working and travelling			x					
AND AFTER A VERY COLD AND PROFITABLE WINTER . . .								
Django's flashback of Broomhilda being burnt on her face	x			x		x		
Django and King meet Calvin Candie in his house				x	x			
Towards Candie's Land					x	x	x	
At Candie's Land								x

(Continued)

Table 5.6 Continued.

	Old Man Carrucan's plantation	SOMEWHERE IN TEXAS	DAUGHTREY TEXAS	TENNESSEE	HEADING FOR... MISSISSIPPI	Calvin Candie's house	Towards Candie's Land	At Candie's Land
King's flashbacks about D'Artagnan								
							x	
								x
							x	
								x
							x	
								x
EN ROUTE TO THE LEQUINT DICKEY MINING CO.								
								x
Django's flashback about training								
					x			
								x

playing mainly with suspense, shocking surprise and enjoyment of the present. When there is suspense, temporalities are either expanded or compressed. In the former case, long takes and montage that follows a peaceful rhythm are used during nonsense, amusing dialogue scenes, in which sentences can be pronounced quickly or slowly, but often delay the development of the fabula. Meanwhile, during action scenes, characterized by rapid editing and fast movement of characters and camera, details that announce an action or delete the development of the fabula, freeze-frames and slow motion expand temporalities. On the other hand, there is suspense and temporalities are compressed during action scenes characterized by rapid montage, quick movement of camera and characters. In these cases, a handheld camera is often used, and shots of details of arms or body parts are edited together during the fights, rather than preceding and delaying the action. When there is no suspense, and dialogue scenes are dominated by nonsense, funny dialogue, there are usually long takes and a montage that follows a slow rhythm, and new slowness is foregrounded.

Action scenes dominated by suspense are preceded by dialogue scenes during which temporalities are expanded to increase suspense, delaying the development of the action, and often end in the climax of shocking surprise through violent staged performances. This succession of dialogue scenes during which temporalities are expanded and the spectator either experiences suspense or pleasure in the present moment, suspenseful action scenes during which temporalities can be either compressed or expanded, and violent staged performances that provoke shocking surprise, also characterizes *Kill Bill*, *Death Proof* and *Inglourious Basterds*, and is exploited in *The Hateful Eight*. It is not a feature of previous Tarantino's films, especially *Reservoir Dogs*, *Pulp Fiction* and *Jackie Brown* where suspenseful scenes often do not reach their climax and violent staged performances come unexpectedly.

This play between suspense and shocking surprise, and the alternation of different rhythms is exemplified in the sequence in which Django and King visit Big Daddy's plantation to find and kill the Brittle Brothers. At the beginning, when the two protagonists meet Big Daddy, there is a dialogue scene dominated by nonsense and amusing dialogue, followed by another dialogue scene during which Django speaks with Betina (Miriam F. Glover) and enquires about the Brittle Brothers. These scenes, during which both camera and characters move slowly or remain still, and are characterized by long takes and leisurely montage, are followed, after Django recognizes one of the Brittle Brothers, by a close-up of Django that introduces the cross-cut enacted flashbacks discussed above. When he approaches Big John Brittle (M.C. Gainey), who is reciting the Bible before whipping a young girl, not unlike Jules in *Pulp Fiction* before shooting the boys in the apartment, a rapid montage links shots during which a handheld camera and characters move fast, there is a ping-pong effect during which the camera quickly tracks right and left, and a couple of zooms in. This compression of temporalities is followed by its expansion thanks to a series of shots in slow motion that sensationalize Big John's and Lil Ray Brittle's (Cooper Huckabee) deaths. At the end, there is a shot of Django from the dead Lil Ray's point of view, one of Tarantino's stylistic trademarks. When King reaches Django, before shooting Ellis

Figure 5.9 *Django Unchained* (Quentin Tarantino, 2012). Dr. King Schultz (Christoph Waltz) shoots Ellis Brittle (Doc Duhame).

Brittle (Doc Duhame) who is galloping away, there is humorous dialogue that retards the development of the action:

Dr. Schultz   Are you sure that's him?

Django   Yes!

Dr. Schultz   Are you positive?

Django   I dunno.

Dr. Schultz   You don't know if you're positive?

Django   I don't know what 'positive' means.

Dr. Schultz   It means you're sure.

Django   Yes.

Dr. Schultz   Yes, what?

Django   Yes I'm sure that's Ellis Brittle.

When King finally shoots Ellis, five shots shot in slow motion quickly succeed one another: blood gushes from Ellis' wound as a waterfall while he falls from his horse and stains white flowers (Figure 5.9). It is a splatter spectacle that becomes more gruesome thanks to the expansion of temporalities.

Like the previous three films, *The Hateful Eight* follows a source-path-goal schema and the development of the action is often retarded, as in *Django Unchained*, by shots and scenes that seem to translate novel descriptions. Moreover, like a novel and like *Kill Bill*, the film is divided into chapters (Table 5.10).

There are only two flashbacks. The first appears in 'Chapter 4. Domergue's Got a Secret', and Tarantino's voice-over explains that during Major Marquis Warren (Samuel L. Jackson) and General Sandy Smithers' (Bruce Dern) discussion, somebody poisoned the coffee and Daisy Domergue (Jennifer Jason Leigh) is the only witness. The enacted

Table 5.10 The scheme of *The Hateful Eight*. The time of the episodes (bold, first line), a brief description of each (subsequent lines) and the chapter titles (bold, capital letters).

EARLIER THAT MORNING	Subsequent four hours	John Ruth and Daisy Domergue enter the emporium		40 seconds before, coffee is poisoned	15 minutes before, General Sandy Smithers dies		Daisy is in-frame		
CHAPTER 1. LAST STAGE TO RED ROCK. CHAPTER 2. SON OF A GUN.									
	x								
CHAPTER 3. MINNIE'S HABERDASHERY.									
		x	x						
Major Marquis Warren's flashback about Chester Charles Smithers' death									
x									
			x						
x									
			x						
x									
			x						
x									
			x						
x									
			x						
x									
			x	x	x				
CHAPTER 4. DOMERGUE'S GOT A SECRET.									
						x	x		
Flashback									
				x	x				
							x		
								x	
CHAPTER 5. THE FOUR PASSENGERS.									
x									
	x	x							
LAST CHAPTER. BLACK MAN, WHITE HELL.									
									x

recounted analepsis ends with an enacted flashback of simultaneity that shows the shot of Daisy with which the previous sequence ended. This flashback provokes surprise because it fills a gap for the spectator, suspense because now they wait for somebody to drink the coffee and curiosity because they do not know who poisoned the coffee. The spectator realizes that a narration that they thought unrestricted, was and is restricted. 'Chapter 5. The Four Passengers' constitutes the second enacted flashback, and the spectator sees what occurred at the emporium before the arrival of John Ruth's (Kurt Russell) carriage. As the first analepsis ends with the same shot with which the previous sequence ended, this enacted flashback ends with the flashback of simultaneity during which John and Daisy enter the emporium by kicking the door and bolting it with nailed planks of wood. In 'Chapter 3. Minnie's Haberdashery', this scene is shot from John and Daisy's point of view, and from Joe Gage's (Michael Madsen), the General's and Oswaldo Mobray's (Tim Roth) point of view, much like the sequence of the money exchange in *Jackie Brown* and the head-on collision in *Death Proof*. This analepsis satisfies the spectator's curiosity.

The only enacted recounted flashback of a character is Major Warren's external analepsis about the death of Chester Charles Smithers (Craig Stark), the General's son. Images of what occurred in the past are cross-cut with shots of the Major in the diegetic present describing what happened and the General's reactions. This same technique was adopted in *Inglourious Basterds* to cross-cut between what occurred between the 'basterds' and Pvt. Butz and the latter's account of the events in front of Hitler. In *The Hateful Eight*, images of the past introduce curiosity about Chester's death and those of the present suspense about his father's reaction. Combined, these images make spectators doubt the truthfulness of the Major's tale because he leaves his gun near the General. Is the story true or false? Does the Major recount it only to encourage the General to shoot first and have the chance to kill him out of self-defence? Is the Major moved by the desire to avenge his companions slaughtered by the General in Baton Rouge? In this case, curiosity will never be satisfied and narration will remain restricted, as in the case of the content of the briefcase in *Pulp Fiction*.

In *The Hateful Eight*, much like in Tarantino's three previous films but unlike in *Reservoir Dogs*, *Pulp Fiction*, *Jackie Brown* and *Kill Bill*, suspense, shocking surprise and new slowness prevail, and temporalities are either compressed or expanded more through style than the development of action. Temporalities are dilated during dialogue scenes because there are long takes or the editing rhythm is slow and camera and characters move slowly. Unlike in the previous film, dialogue is often very slow and only sometimes amusing nonsense. Moreover, during dialogue scenes, the spectator often not only takes pleasure in the present moment, but he is also projected into the past or into the future because the content of dialogue increases curiosity or suspense, as in the scene between the General and the Major. Temporalities are extended also when the camera remains still, lingering on the effects of violence on characters' bodies or when slow motion is adopted for the same goal. This insistence, especially on bodily details, increasing empathy, is disturbing and the shots feel longer than they actually are. This discomfort is increased because dialogue is not as nonsensical as in the previous films, and violent actions are more believable, plausible, less spectacular than, for example, in *Kill Bill*. Much like in *Django Unchained*, temporalities are also expanded through digressions that seem to translate the descriptions of a novel and do not develop the action. There are montage sequences or single shots of John's carriage travelling, and a montage sequence of Jody's carriage travelling. There is a scene shot outside the emporium to show how frightening the snow storm is, and how difficult it is to plant the stakes in the snow to find the path after the snowfall; a montage sequence of O.B. (James Parks), who throws guns and bullets in the toilet; and a montage sequence of what happened after the General's death and before the arrival of John's carriage. More interestingly, John's and Daisy's arrival and the other characters' explanation of how to open and board up the door, are shown twice, but the instructions about the door are also repeated when O.B. and Sheriff Chris Mannix (Walton Goggins) enter the emporium. If at first the dialogue is amusing, and the second time it is enjoyably repeated, the third time dwelling on a witticism without variations ends up being redundant.

On the other hand, temporalities are compressed during action scenes characterized by rapid editing and fast movements of the camera and characters. These suspenseful scenes usually follow dialogue sequences during which temporalities are expanded and present gore-and-splatter shots that can either be emphasized, as discussed, or not. The spectator is shocked by violent action when a character unexpectedly shoots or hits another character, for example during the carriage journey when John hits Daisy on the head with his gun, or nudges her face, or when the Major shoots Bob (Demián Bichir), and at the end of the film Jody (Channing Tatum) and Oswaldo, and when Jody (Channing Tatum) shoots the Major from beneath the floor.

The narrative construction of *Once Upon a Time . . . in Hollywood* is more complex than that of *Grindhouse*, *Inglourious Basterds*, *Django Unchained* and *The Hateful Eight*. It seems to me a tribute to the narrative possibilities of cinema, and the content of the film is a homage to cinema in general and especially to the Hollywood films and spaghetti westerns of the 1960s. Tarantino's last film consists of three source-path-goal schemas and each is a part of the part-whole schema. It is a polyphonic or ensemble plot because, as explained in Chapter 1, each group of characters has an aim, but none of the characters' goals becomes the narrative's organizing principle, and each group acts at the same time and in neighbouring places and in the epilogue their lives intertwine. The three groups of characters are: the actor Rick Dalton (Leonardo DiCaprio), his stunt double, driver, and handyman Cliff Booth (Brad Pitt), who are joined at the end by Rick's new Italian wife Francesca Capucci (Lorenza Izzo); Roman Polanski (Rafal Zawierucha), his wife Sharon Tate (Margot Robbie), and their friend and Sharon's ex-lover Jay Sebring (Emile Hirsch), who all live together in the villa next to Rick's; and Pussycat (Margaret Qualley) and the other hippies who live at George Spahn's (Bruce Dern) Ranch and turn out to constitute the Manson family. Whereas Rick, Cliff and Francesca, and Polanski, Sharon and Jay are always surrounded by other people who work in the film industry, the hippies remain secluded from the rest of the diegetic world. Narration alternates between each group of characters mainly through flashbacks of simultaneity during which diegetic time goes back and forth to show the characters acting in different spaces at the same time, not unlike in Kubrick's *The Killing* and in the mall exchange sequence in *Jackie Brown* – although in *Once Upon a Time . . . in Hollywood*, the characters do not share a common goal. The parallel editing is further complicated by the numerous enacted and enacted recounted flashbacks, by inserts from films in which either Rick or Sharon played, by changes in the duration of represented time and by the play between extra-diegesis, diegesis and intra-diegesis.

From the point of view of narrative structure, the film can be divided into three parts: the first takes place during 8 and 9 February 1969; the second summarizes Rick's acting career in Italy and Spain from February to August 1969; and the third part takes place on 9 August 1969. The film opens with footage from *Bounty Law*, an imaginary western television series, in which Rick plays the role of the protagonist Jack Cahill, a bounty hunter, followed by an interview. Allen Kincade (Spencer Garrett), who in the extra-diegesis was a famous television interviewer in the 1950s and 1960s, questions Rick and Cliff about their relationship and work. This scene is followed by cross-cutting during which we see, alternately Rick and Cliff who are travelling to a bar by car, and Sharon and Polanski who are first on-board a plane and then at an airport. At the end of this parallel editing sequence, Rick and Cliff are seen inside the bar. There follows another shot of Sharon and her husband and finally the sequence in the bar begins, during which Rick speaks with Marvin Schwarzs (Al Pacino) – a publicist and producer probably inspired by the real Marvin Schwartz. During this sequence, dialogue between Rick and Marvin that plays in the diegetic present alternates with external enacted recounted or enacted flashbacks of Marvin who, the previous night, first with his wife and then alone, watched two films starring Rick – the western *Tanner* (Paul Wendkos) and the Second World War action adventure *The 14 Fists of McCluskey* (Paul Wendkos) – and who the next morning, in his office, watches two episodes of *Bounty Law* and a scene of a musical starring Rick. Together with Marvin's external enacted recounted and recounted flashbacks, there are inserts of the films cited above, Rick's external enacted recounted flashback of one of his car accidents and Rick's external flashback of his training with a flamethrower. After this sequence, there is a scene of Rick and Cliff who drive toward Rick's villa, followed by shots of a group of hippie girls who walk, alternating with shots of them scavenging for food in garbage. The sequence ends when the girls walk with the food they found and see Rick and Cliff stop at a traffic light. Rick and Cliff and the hippie girls act at the same time but in different spaces and at the end, they all meet in the same space-time: the scenes and shots involving different characters are flashbacks of simultaneity. Whereas the girls alternate between the diegetic past when they walk and the diegetic present when they look for food, external enacted flashbacks alternate with the diegetic present – as in *Inglourious Basterds* – and this parallel editing is embedded in another instance of cross-cutting, that between the girls and Rick and Cliff. The part that closes the first diegetic day, 8 February 1969, consists of a sequence of Cliff driving Rick home and one of Sharon and Polanski getting to their new villa, next to Rick's: they all arrive home at the same moment. At the end of this diegetic day, there is another ensemble of flashbacks of simultaneity during which Rick in his home studies his lines, Cliff reaches his caravan where he has

Table 5.11 The scheme of the first day of the first part of *Once Upon a Time . . . in Hollywood*. In bold on the first line the dates, on subsequent lines a brief description of each.

Unspecified Past			7 February 1969		Saturday, 8 February 1969					
Trailer of *Bounty Law*										
	x									
Rick's and Cliff's interviews										
		x								
Rick and Cliff by car										
					x					
Sharon and Roman by plane, at the airport, by car, at home										
					x					
Rick and Cliff										
					x					
Sharon and Roman										
					x					
Rick and Cliff										
					x					
Sharon and Roman										
					x					
Rick and Cliff										
					x					
Sharon and Roman										
					x					
Rick and Cliff at a bar										
						x				
Sharon and Roman										
						x				
Rick and Cliff at a bar										
						x				
External enacted recounted flashback of Rick's car accident										
x										
Rick and Cliff at a bar										
						x				
External enacted flashback of film reels										
			x							

(Continiued)

Table 5.11 Continued.

Rick and Cliff at a bar											
							x				
Enacted recounted flashback of Marvin and his wife watching *Tanner*											
				x							
Rick and Cliff at a bar											
							x				
Enacted recounted flashback of Marvin watching *The 14 Fists of McCluskey*											
				x							
Rick and Cliff at a bar											
							x				
Enacted recounted flashback of *The 14 Fists*											
				x							
Rick and Cliff at a bar											
							x				
Scenes from *The 14 Fists*											
				x							
Rick and Cliff at a bar											
							x				
External enacted flashback of Rick practising with a flamethrower											
x											
Rick and Cliff at a bar											
							x				
Scenes from *Bounty Law*											
					x						
Rick and Cliff in a bar											
							x				
Scene from a musical											
					x						
Rick and Cliff in a bar											
							x				
Rick and Cliff driving home											
										x	
Girls walking											
								x			
Girls looking for rubbish											
									x		

Event	1	2	3	4	5	6	7	8	9	10	11	12	13
Girls walking									X				
Girls looking for rubbish										X			
Girls walking									X				
Girls looking for rubbish										X			
Girls walking									X				
Girls looking for rubbish										X			
Girls walking									X				
Girls looking for rubbish										X			
Girls walking with rubbish											X		
Rick and Cliff meet girls											X		
Rick and Cliff get to Rick's												X	
Tate and Roman get to Roman's												X	
Rick studies dialogue													X
Cliff returns to his house and dog													X
Roman and Tate go to a party at Playboy Mansion													X

dinner with his dog and Sharon and Polanski join their friends at a party at Playboy mansion (Table 5.11).

A similar narrative structure is adopted to represent the next day, 9 February 1969. Flashbacks of simultaneity linking Rick, Cliff, Sharon, Pussycat and the Manson family are enriched with external enacted and enacted recounted flashbacks. There are a few exceptions. Cliff's auditory internal flashback of Rick telling him that it is useless to ask the stunt coordinator whether Cliff can act as his stunt double in the pilot episode of the western television series *Lancer* – a real western TV series – opens an external enacted flashback in which Cliff fights Bruce Lee (Mike Moh) and destroys a car. During this external enacted flashback, there is another of Rick's external enacted flashback of Cliff killing his wife. It is a flashback within a flashback. It seems to be Rick's flashback because it is him speaking with Randy Miller (Kurt Russell), the stunt coordinator, but Rick was not present during the murder. Thus, if it is Rick's flashback, it could be a representation of Rick's fantasy about the event or his fantasy mixed with Cliff's confession. Otherwise, it could be Cliff's flashback, although he was not present during Rick's and Randy's discussion. In the former case, the murder is only imagined and it leaves a permanent gap and curiosity. In the latter case, the killing is true but Cliff imagines the dialogue between Rick and Randy: in both cases, curiosity dominates. When Rick on the set of *Lancer* speaks with another actor, James Stacey (Timothy Olyphant) – Stacey was the name of a character in the real series – about his lost opportunity to play Steve McQueen's role in *The Great Escape* (John Sturges, 1963), there are shots of him acting in this film, shots that are not his flashbacks, but derive from his imagination (Table 5.12).

During the first part of the film, curiosity about the protagonists' pasts, introduced by dialogue and simple flashbacks, alternates with suspense about their futures and possible meetings between different groups of characters that is perpetuated by flashbacks of simultaneity. There is a climax, which ends in an action performance at the end of the sequence shot at George Spahn's Ranch, when Cliff fights a boy who sticks a nail in the tyre of his car, forcing him to change the tyre. This climax announces the end of the film when Cliff, Francesca and Rick have to fight to the death against three hippies.

When the title 'Six Months Later' appears, we know it is now August 1969. We see Rick and his new wife Francesca and Cliff on a plane: they are travelling back from Italy to California. The voice-over (Kurt Russell) explains that, after the lunch meeting between Marvin and Rick, six months before, the former found new roles in Italian films for the latter. The sequence alternates scenes shot on the plane with enacted recounted flashbacks of Rick's career in the last six months and inserts of his films and their posters (Table 5.13). The spectator's curiosity about the last six months is satisfied. It is interesting that in both the first and the second parts of *Once Upon a Time . . . in Hollywood*, films and television series starring Rick are shown through flashbacks, with the exception of the pilot episode of *Lancer* when Rick is shown acting on the set. The nostalgia for Hollywood films and television series and spaghetti westerns of the 1960s is emphasized by the narrative construction: these works are shown in flashbacks, often in black and white and in another format, thus the diegetic past is echoed in narrative choices. Furthermore, the diegetic past is evoked by Rick's and Cliff's concerns about their careers that seem to have petered out, and by the play of cross-references between extra-diegesis, diegesis and intra-diegesis.

As in the first part, the last proceeds mainly through flashbacks of simultaneity during which we see: Cliff and his dog, Rick and Francesca; Sharon, Jay and their friends Abigail Folger (Samantha Robinson) and Wojciech Frykowski (Costa Ronin);

Table 5.12 The scheme of the second day of the first part of *Once Upon a Time . . . in Hollywood*. The date (bold, first line) and a brief description (subsequent lines).

Unspecified Past			Sunday, 9 February 1969		
Jay and Tate at home					
			X		
Rick and Cliff drive to the set					
			X		
Cliff drives to meet Pussycat					
				X	
Ciff at Rick's					
					X
Tate at her home					
					X
Cliff's auditory internal flashback of Rick					
			X		
Rick speaks with Randy Miller					
	X				
Rick's external enacted flashback of Cliff killing his wife					
X					
Rick speaks with Randy Miller					
	X				
Cliff and Bruce Lee fight					
		X			
Cliff at Rick's					
					X
A man gets at Tate's house					
					X
Rick speaks with a girl					
					X
Tate in front of a theatre and in a bookstore					
					X
Rick speaks with James Stacy					
					X
Rick's fake external enacted flashback about him playing a part					
	X				

(*Contniued*)

Table 5.12 Continued.

Rick speaks with James Stacy						
						x
Rick plays a scene in a saloon						
						x
Rick in his caravan						
						x
Tate watching a film in which she plays						
						x
Tate's enacted external flashback of her training for the film						
	x					
Tate watching a film in which she plays						
						x
Tate's enacted external flashback of her training for the film						
	x					
Tate watching a film in which she plays						
						x
Tate's enacted external flashback of her training for the film						
	x					
Tate watching a film in which she plays						
						x
Tate's enacted external flashback of her training for the film						
	x					
Tate watching a film in which she plays						
						x
Tate's enacted external flashback of her training for the film						
	x					
Tate watching a film in which she plays						
						x
Tate's enacted external flashback of her training for the film						
	x					
Cliff drives to meet Pussycat						
						x
Rick plays a scene						
						x
Cliff arrives with Pussycat at the Ranch						
						x

Tate leaves the theatre					
					x
Cliff picks up Rick					
					x
Tate drives home					
					x
Cliff and Rick arrive at Rick's					
					x
Cliff's external enacted flashback of a girl who sold him a cigarette					
	x				
Cliff and Rick watch television					
					x
Marvin watches television in a bar					
					x
Cliff and Rick watch television					
					x
Marvin on the phone					
					x
Cliff and Rick watch television					
					x

and four hippies of the Manson family. The three groups of characters act in different spaces at the same time, but at first the first and third groups meet, and then the first and second meet. Suspense is increased by titles showing the hours and minutes passing: '12.30', '3:00', '5:00', '7:00', etc., as well as by the parallel editing and the extra-diegetic story of the Manson family. Indeed, anyone familiar with this tragic story knows that on the night of 9 August 1969, four members of the Manson family, Tex Watson, Susan Atkins, Patricia Krenwinkel and Linda Kasabian brutally murdered Sharon Tate, who was eight-and-a-half months pregnant, Jay Sebring, Abigail Folger, Wojciech Frykowski and a friend of the housekeeper. Aspiring to become a musician, Charles Manson in 1968 met the Beach Boys' drummer who helped him to record a demo that was presented to Terry Marker, a musician and record producer. Marker, who refused to produce Manson's music, sold his villa to the Polanskis and Tate was murdered together with her friends because they lived in the house previously owned by Marker. Thus, spectators familiar with the real events should expect that the diegetic events correspond to the real history, but they do not. Tex Watson (Austin Butler), Katie (Madisen Beaty) and Sadie (Mikey Madison) enter Rick's house where they find Cliff and his dog, Francesca and finally Rick. Cliff manages to kill them with the exception of Sadie who is killed by Rick with his flamethrower. The style of the slaughter

Table 5.13 The scheme of the second part of *Once Upon a Time . . . in Hollywood*. The dates of the episodes (bold, first line) and a brief description (subsequent lines).

February 1969							Six Months Later, 9 August 1969
Rick and Cliff on a plane							
							X
Marvin speaks on the phone with Rick							
X							
Nebraska Jim and Rick is with Sergio Corbucci and Francesca Capucci							
	X						
Uccidimi subito Ringo, disse il gringo (Clavin Jackson Padget)							
		X					
Red Blood, Red Skin (Joaquin Romero Marchent)							
			X				
Operazione Dyn-o-mite! (Antonio Margheriti)							
				X			
Rick, Francesca and Cliff on the plane							
							X
'On Location. Almeria, Spain, *Red Blood, Red Skin*'							
						X	
Rick, Francesca and Cliff on the plane							
							X

is consonant with other Tarantino performances of violence, and the events constitute a shocking surprise and a surprise for those spectators who are aware of the events that occurred in Cielo Drive on the evening of 9 August 1969. As in *Kill Bill* and the last four Tarantino films, in *Once Upon a Time . . . in Hollywood* violence is spectacularized at the end of a climax through gore-and-splatter shots.

Moreover, in *Once Upon a Time . . . in Hollywood*, there are several cross-references between extra-diegesis, diegesis and intra-diegesis that slow down temporalities, forcing the audience to draw interesting comparisons. Most of them are summarized in Table 5.14. To explain a few, Leonardo DiCaprio plays the role of middle-aged actor Rick Dalton, who seems to personify western actors who were famous in Hollywood during the 1960s. Rick plays the roles of: Jack Chill in *Bounty Law*, probably a spin-off of a future television series directed by Tarantino himself; Joe Tanner in *Tanner*, an imaginary western inspired by *Gunman's Walk* (Phil Karson, 1958), directed by Paul

Table 5.14 Table of the correspondences between extra-diegesis, diegesis and intra-diegesis in *Once Upon a Time . . . in Hollywood*.

Extra-diegesis	Diegesis	Intra-diegesis
Leonardo DiCaprio	Rick Dalton (mix of real and imaginary), an ensemble of real western actors, i.e. Steve McQueen, Ty Hardin, Ed Byrnes, Pete Duel	Jack Cahill (imaginary) in *Bounty Law* (imaginary), a western television series, may be a spin-off for a future series directed by Tarantino
Leonardo DiCaprio	Rick Dalton	Joe Tanner (imaginary) in *Tanner* (imaginary) (by Paul Wendkos, real) a western inspired by *Gunman's Walk* (Phil Karlson, 1958)
Leonardo DiCaprio	Rick Dalton	Sgt. Mike Lewis (imaginary) in *The 14 Fists of McCluskey* (imaginary) (by Paul Wendkos, real), a Second World War action adventure film
Leonardo DiCaprio	Rick Dalton	Caleb DeCoteau (imaginary, but inspired by Joe Don Baker) in *Lancer* (real), a western series
Luke Perry	Wayner Maunder (real)	Scott Lancer (real)
Timothy Olyphant	James Stacey (real)	Johnny Madrid (real)
Nicholas Hammond		Sam Wanamaker (real) actor-director who directed the pilot episode of *Lancer*
Leonardo DiCaprio	Rick Dalton	Guest star in *The F.B.I.* (real), a TV series (1965–74)
Leonardo DiCaprio	Rick Dalton	*Nebraska Jim* (imaginary) (Sergio Corbucci, real)
Leonardo DiCaprio	Rick Dalton	*Uccidimi subito Ringo, disse il Gringo* (imaginary) (Clavin Jackson Padger, real)
Leonardo DiCaprio	Rick Dalton	*Red Blood, Red Skin* (Joaquin Romero Marchent, real)
Leonardo DiCaprio	Rick Dalton	*Operazione Dyn-o-mite!* (Antonio Margheriti, real)
Spencer Garrett	Allen Kincade (real, television interviewer)	

(Contniued)

Table 5.14 Continued.

Extra-diegesis	Diegesis	Intra-diegesis
Al Pacino	Marvin Schwarzs (imaginary/ real inspired by Marvin Schwartz, publicist and producer)	
Margot Robbie	Sharon Tate (real)	*Dance of the Vampires* (Roman Polanski, 1967) (real)
Margot Robbie	Sharon Tate	Freya Carlson in *The Wrecking Crew* (Phil Karlson, 1968) (real)
Margot Robbie plays Sharon Tate who was murdered on 9 August 1969, together with Jay Sebring, Abigail Folger and Wojciech Frykowski by three of Charles Manson's followers – Charles Watson, Susan Atkins and Patricia Krenwinkel. These members of the Manson family, together with others, lived at George Spahn's Ranch	On 9 August 1969, Cliff Booth and his dog, Rick Dalton and Francesca Corbucci murdered three of Charles Manson's followers – Tex Watson (real, played by Austin Butler), Katie (played by Madisen Beaty) and Sadie (played by Mikey Madison). These members of the Manson family, together with others, lived at George Spahn's Ranch (real)	
Emile Hirsch	Jay Sebring (real, hairstylist and friend of Sharon Tate)	
Samantha Robinson	Abigail Folger (real)	
Rafal Zawierucha	Roman Polanski (real)	
Costa Ronin	Wojciech Frykowski (real, screenwriter)	
Bruce Dern	George Spahn (real)	
Lorenza Izzo	Francesca Capucci (there is an Italian actress named Francesca Capucci, unclear whether she is real or imaginary)	
Damian Lewis	Steve McQueen (real, actor)	
Rebecca Rittenhouse	Michelle Phillips (real, actress)	
Mike Moh	Bruce Lee (real, actor)	

Wendkos, a real director; and Sgt. Mike Lewis in *The 14 Fists of McCluskey*, an imaginary film, again directed by the real Wendkos, etc.

5.1.3 Conclusions about narrative schemas

Reservoir Dogs, *Pulp Fiction* and *Kill Bill* are characterized by jumbled plots. Towards the end, *Jackie Brown* presents a repeated event form. *Once Upon a Time … in*

Hollywood is a polyphonic or ensemble plot. In all of these films, the source-path-goal and the part-whole schema are intertwined. Whereas the former traces a horizontal path from beginning to end, allowing spectators to link characters and events in a chronological and strong causal chain, the latter delineates a vertical path focusing on different characters. On the other hand, all of the other Tarantino films are characterized by source-path-goal schemas. Except for *Jackie Brown* and *Kill Bill*, all of these films, notwithstanding the specific features of their narration, do not present one protagonist but a group of characters linked in strong causal succession.

In *Jackie Brown*, the part-whole schema characterizes its progression to the end of the film. Enacted flashbacks of simultaneity were already introduced in *Reservoir Dogs* and *Pulp Fiction*. This technique which, unlike cross-cutting, maintains the restricted narration, arousing curiosity, surprise or strong surprise together with suspense, is exploited in *Jackie Brown* and *The Hateful Eight*. Enacted flashbacks of simultaneity are also used in *Kill Bill* to emphasize Beatrix's goal, continuously showing shots of the massacre in the church. Similarly, in *Death Proof*, one of the accidents is shot from the four victims' points of view, emphasizing the violence of the scene.

Cross-cutting between episodes that occur at different times first appears in *Jackie Brown* and then in *Kill Bill*, *Inglourious Basterds*, *Django Unchained*, *The Hateful Eight* and *Once Upon a Time ... in Hollywood*. These instances of cross-cutting arouse curiosity, surprise, strong surprise or suspense, much like the repeated event form. With the exception of *Kill Bill*, they appear more often in *Death Proof*, *Inglourious Basterds* and *The Hateful Eight*. Indeed, while *Death Proof* consists of two parts linked by the presence of the protagonist and with a very similar fabula and style, and *Inglourious Basterds* and *The Hateful Eight* are divided into chapters, their narration follows a source-path-goal schema in which suspense prevails. Curiosity, surprise and strong surprise are mainly introduced through cross-cutting events taking place at different times.

On the other hand, Tarantino often deploys classical cross-cutting that alternates actions taking place at the same time, but in different or contiguous spaces, some camera movement and lingering on useless details to delay development of the action, increasing classical suspense. For example, in *Pulp Fiction*, when Vincent goes to Mia's for the first time, there is parallel editing between him waiting for her in the living room and her getting ready for the evening while watching him through monitors in the surveillance room. Similarly, when they return home, there is cross-cutting between Vincent in the bathroom who tries to persuade himself in front of the mirror to leave, and Mia in the living room dancing before she overdoses. This parallel editing expands temporalities, increasing suspense. The same effect is obtained through camera movement, for example before and after Butch shoots Vincent. When Butch approaches his apartment block in a long take, the camera first tracks forward following him, but when he stops to look around, the camera continues to advance until it reaches him. When he exits, having killed Vincent, in another long take the camera tracks forward to follow him but when he passes the gate of the building, the camera remains behind it. Camera movements seem to mimic the presence of somebody, and, indeed, Butch will find Vincent in his apartment and will meet Marsellus Wallace along the street.

Parallel editing is exploited in *Once Upon a Time ... in Hollywood* when camera movements, especially cranes, link different characters in the same long take, as when the camera moves from Rick repeating his lines in the swimming pool to Sharon and Polanski leaving for the party at Playboy mansion.

Moreover, Tarantino often lingers on details that most of the time are redundant, such as details of heroin and the instruments used to prepare and inject it when Vincent visits Lance for the first time – in this case, slow motion, extra-diegetic music and blurred images further extend temporalities. Feet and other, female, body parts often occupy the whole frame. Mia is presented through details of her lips and feet before her face is shown. Similarly, in *Jackie Brown*, Melanie's feet are seen before her face. Women's feet appear in *Death Proof*, too, whereas in *Django Unchained* there are several details of the bare bleeding feet of slaves. *Inglourious Basterds* seems to be a tribute to this part of the body. The boots of Landa and Nazi soldiers are in-frame before the slaughter of the Jewish family. The boots of the 'basterds' and Lt. Aldo Raine appear when they go downstairs to the main room of the tavern, before and after the slaughter, respectively. Before the massacre, a detail of Bridget's shoes is shown, and one of her shoes is found by Landa after the massacre and shown to her before he kills her. The camera lingers on her foot in plaster, and finally the scene of her choking is dominated by details of her feet.

In *Inglourious Basterds*, details are often useful clues to what will happen, increasing suspense and cross-referencing between scenes. For example, Landa orders for him and Shosanna a strudel with cream, and finally puts his cigarette out on the cream. Cream, together with the milk ordered by him for the girl and Landa's cigarette, evoke the milk offered him by LaPadite's family and the pipes smoked by him and Perrier before the latter tells him where Shosanna's family was hidden. In the tavern in Nadine, the camera lingers on the whisky poured into three glasses ordered by the 'basterds', blowing their cover. Interestingly, before the massacre in the theatre, we see the explosive that Donny and Omar hide on their shins (Figure 5.10). It is as if Tarantino mocks Hitchcock's famous example of how suspense can be aroused rather than

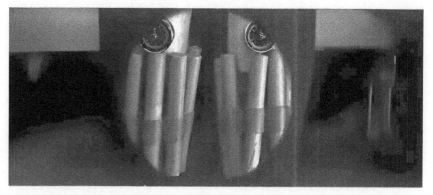

Figure 5.10 *Inglourious Basterds* (Quentin Tarantino, 2009). Spectators are shown the explosive hidden on the shins of Donny (Eli Roth) and Omar (Omar Doom).

surprise transforming a restricted narration in an unrestricted narration. Similarly, we see a detail of the explosive left by Landa under the seats of Goebbels and Hitler.

Whereas in *Inglourious Basterds* details are mainly adopted to increase suspense – with the exception of Bridget's wound and Lt. Aldo's finger pushing inside it – in *Kill Bill: Vols 1* and *2, Death Proof, Django Unchained, The Hateful Eight* and *Once Upon a Time . . . in Hollywood* details are often used to underline the effects of violence on human bodies and their parts. In *Django Unchained*, there are details of white flowers spattered with blood when the last of the Little Brothers is shot to death, an image evoked by Calvin Candie's white boutonnière before he is killed. In *Once Upon a Time . . . in Hollywood*, the bin containing Cliff's dog's food is shown in the first and last part of the film before being used to smash the face of a member of the Manson family. Similarly, Rick's flamethrower is shown twice in the first part of the film before being used to kill one of Manson's followers.

In *Pulp Fiction, Jackie Brown, Kill Bill* and *The Hateful Eight*, suspense often ends in shocking surprise when, instead of progressively increasing till a final climax, an act of violence takes place unexpectedly. It is as if Tarantino plays with the spectator, downplaying curiosity and suspense, and giving answers and violent staged performances all of a sudden, without making them wait. On the other hand, in *Reservoir Dogs*, when suspense comes to a climax, violence often occurs out of frame, whereas in *Kill Bill* and in the last five Tarantino films, violence is often exhibited in gore-and-splatter shots.

As discussed in Chapter 4, spectators can watch one or more of Bay's *Transformers* saga, but if they watch all of them, and if they also know comic books, animated television series, stories underpinning toy lines and video games, their enjoyment and knowledge of the pentalogy increases. Similarly, in Tarantino's oeuvre, each film refers directly or indirectly to other films by Tarantino or other filmmakers. As to genre, they are hybrid films, according to Ira Jaffe's definition adopted in Chapter 2 to describe the last six Kubrick films – creating a play for cinephiles, fans and scholars interested in film genre and aesthetics. The audience is not only actively involved in reconstructing the chronological order of the fabula, in filling in temporary gaps and proposing hypotheses about permanent ellipses, but also in catching references and quotations that break the boundaries of the diegesis, laying bare the extra-diegetic level and the self-referentiality.

According to Simona Brancati, the postmodern style, in literature and cinema, breaks the chronological development of the fabula, and privileges circularity and repetition – what I have called 'flashbacks of simultaneity', but also all the stylistic cross-references within one film or among different films. Playing with the features of genres, and with more or less explicit references to other films, Tarantino's postmodernism surprises and destabilizes spectators who have to continually revise hypotheses that are often drawn from their knowledge of genre conventions (Brancati 2004: 11, 85–6). Tarantino's style changes the cause-and-effect order and its meaning through the spatialization of time that, according to Jameson, is one of the characteristics of the postmodern social experience (Buccheri 2009: 64–5). Both Brancati (2004: 11) and Vincenzo Buccheri link Tarantino's narrative style to pulp literature, a comparison suggested by the director himself in the title *Pulp Fiction*, and the explicative title at the beginning of this film:

pulp/'palp/n. 1. A soft, moist, shapeless mass of matter. 2. A magazine or book containing lurid subject matter and being characteristically printed on rough, unfinished paper.

This is a definition taken from the *American Heritage Dictionary*. Pulp literature evokes a random and careless reading, and its reader par excellence is represented in *Pulp Fiction* by Vincent, who reads sitting on the toilet. When Honey Bunny and Pumpkin begin to rob the restaurant, and when Vincent is shot to death by Butch, he is reading *Modesty Blaise* (1965) by Peter O'Donnell, a spy novel in which the protagonist is a female with several talents. Moreover, the editing, in particular that of jumbled plots, can be compared to channel surfing, as well as to the narrative structure of television series that are either interrupted by advertisements or by the end of an episode (Buccheri 2009: 64). Both through the combination of the source-path-goal and part-whole schema, and through cross-references within one film or several films or genres, Tarantino plays with and challenges his spectator with what Dana Polan calls a 'guessing game' (Buccheri 2009: 64).[7]

Interestingly, in *Pulp Fiction*, Tarantino refers not only to cinema's past but also to its future, paradoxically choosing to do so in a setting that clearly evokes the past, for example at Jackrabbit Slim's, a restaurant that imitates the style of the 1950s, in which waiters and waitresses are dressed as Marilyn Monroe, Buddy Holly and Mamie Van Doren, and in which Ed Sullivan plays the host and Rick Nelson performs on stage. During dinner, Vincent asks Mia about her role in a pilot episode of a series entitled *Fox Force 5* that in the end was not produced. She should have been one of the protagonists, an expert with knives, who recounts a joke at the end of each episode. The other four protagonists should all have been female: the blonde girl was the leader; the Japanese girl the kung-fu master; the black lady the demolition expert; and the French fox should have used sex as her weapon. This is not only a story within the story, but also a spin-off in which Tarantino seems to refer to a future project that he will develop in *Kill Bill*. Similarly, but less explicitly, when Butch manages to free himself in the basement of the shop, he runs upstairs. In a long take, he carefully looks for a suitable weapon, and he picks up in this order a hammer, a bat, a chainsaw and finally chooses a long sabre. Beatrix in *Kill Bill* faces a long and challenging journey to obtain the right sabre to carry out her revenge. Moreover, when Wolfe is asked by phone to help in the Bonnie situation, he takes notes and, on a white sheet, under Jimmie's address, writes:

Jules (black)
Vincent (white)
Jimmie (white)
Bonnie (black)
No head body

[7] See Zagarrio (2009: 7–32), Brancati (2004), Gandini (1996) and Morsiani (2016) for references in Tarantino's oeuvre to other films and genres.

It is a ridiculous list for a roll call with an absurd end: who would forget that there is a headless corpse? Similarly, Beatrix in *Kill Bill* keeps a list of the five people that she wants to kill – an apparently childish and useless memo for her but an extremely helpful device for spectators. In *Once Upon a Time . . . in Hollywood*, Rick plays the role of Jack Cahill in *Bounty Law*, a western series, which should be a spin-off of a future Tarantino project.

5.2 New slowness

New slowness dominates when dialogue is amusing nonsense, and rather than developing the action it creates a pause in the narration, allowing viewers to take pleasure in it. Tarantino himself admitted that he imitated the Hollywood scriptwriters Ben Hecht and Charles MacArthur's technique of overlapping dialogue, which finds its best expression in *His Girl Friday* (Howard Hawks, 1940; Morsiani 2016: 49). These new slowness dialogue sequences are shot with different stylistic features. Characters pronounce their sentences more or less quickly during long takes, or in the context of more classical, usually slow editing, with a still or moving camera that sometimes turns around them but usually they remain still or move slowly.

In *Reservoir Dogs*, there are several long takes, but in only a few do both the camera and characters remain still, and in all of them characters speak. This is the case when the gang members are having breakfast in a diner, when Joe assigns them names of colours and, especially, during Mr. Orange's long flashback about the commode story. As discussed, the sequence that features more long takes, together with funny dialogue, is that about the torture, but in this case new slowness also increases suspense, delaying the conclusion of the scene.

Much like in *Reservoir Dogs*, in *Pulp Fiction*, there are several long takes, and in all of them characters speak and the camera or characters move. The ASL is slower than that of *Reservoir Dogs*,[8] and the majority of long takes can be found during 'Vincent Vega and Marsellus Wallace's Wife' and 'The Gold Watch', the parts that feature the highest ASL.[9] In particular, Butch's flashback about his father's gold watch, much like Mr. Orange's analepsis about the commode story, appears like gags, amusing digressions. This effect is emphasized by their place in the editing. The enacted flashback comes unexpectedly, preceding the arousal of curiosity about the importance of the watch, as much as Mr. Orange's analepsis follows curiosity about the spy's

---

[8] The ASL of *Reservoir Dogs* is 8.9 seconds (Cinemetrics, data submitted by Eric T. Jones on 7 September 2009. Last accessed 30 September 2019), whereas that of *Pulp Fiction* is 7.9 seconds (Cinemetrics, data submitted by Charley Leary on 12 November 2006. Last accessed 30 September 2019).

[9] The ASL of the scenes shot in the diner is 6.3 seconds, that of the sequence during which Jules and Vincent go to collect the suitcase from the boys' apartment is 7.3 seconds, 'Vincent Vega and Marsellus Wallace's Wife' is 8 seconds, 'The Gold Watch' is 8.9 seconds, and 'The Bonnie Situation' is 7.9 seconds (Cinemetrics, data submitted by Charley Leary on 12 November 2006. Last accessed 30 September 2019).

identity. Spectators are no longer engaged in making hypotheses about the past and can enjoy the present. Unlike in *Reservoir Dogs*, in *Pulp Fiction* new slowness dominates almost all the scenes, with the exception of those that precede and follow the scene staged at Jackrabbit Slim's, Vincent's death and the last scene of 'The Gold Watch'.

In the segment 'The Man from Hollywood' in *Four Rooms*, Tarantino explicitly plays with the expansion of temporalities, generating extreme results out of new slowness. Amusing dialogue accompanies the whole segment that almost completely lacks action. Moreover, there are no ellipses, 60 per cent of the film is constituted by three long takes and the remaining 40 per cent has an ASL of nine seconds. During long takes, the camera mainly moves in a circular fashion, tracking and panning. These virtuoso camera movements, together with Tarantino's presence, playing the role of a director, and with characters who often look directly into the camera, lay bare the film's self-referentiality, thus decreasing suspense and further expanding temporalities. During the first long take, the camera moves around the room to frame the characters that Chester (Quentin Tarantino) introduces to Ted (Tim Roth), as if he is presenting them to the spectator, and evoking both the first sequence of *Reservoir Dogs* when the gang members are framed in slow motion, accompanied by their names, and the end credits of *Pulp Fiction* when each of the main actors' names appear together with a shot of each.

While the narrative schema of *Jackie Brown* is more classical than that of *Reservoir Dogs* and *Pulp Fiction*, new slowness dominates the film. When the spectator first sees Ordell and Louis, they are watching a recorded commercial of girls in bikinis with guns. Ordell varies the volume or switches it off, rewinds and fast-forwards the cassette to comment on the girls, guns, black men's taste in guns and which guns are used by the most famous criminals. Long, slow dialogue, enriched with colourful curse words, also dominates the sequence during which Ordell goes to meet Beaumont and tells him about his future: everything is made up because Ordell will soon kill him. And in this sequence, unlike in the previous, there are also three long takes during which neither the camera nor the characters move so that dialogue is emphasized. A couple of long takes and useless information about Melanie's life entertain the spectator in the scene during which she and Louis have sex in the kitchen. Similarly, when Jackie meets Ray and Mark in the parking lot before the trial run of the money exchange, Ray describes what he finds in Jackie's bag to record the information, and they all lose time indulging in a description of the bag in which money will be put. In these cases, temporalities are extended and the development of the action suspended.

In *Kill Bill*, especially in *Vol. 1*, unlike in the previous Tarantino films, temporalities are extended more to increase suspense or create staged violent performances than to entertain spectators with nonsense dialogue, opening amusing parentheses in the development of the story. This dialogue *à la* Tarantino is adopted when the Bride first meets Hattori Hanzo before telling him that she is looking for him, and when Sheriff Earl McGraw (Michael Parks) comments to his son about the slaughter at the church. In the latter case, temporalities are further expanded thanks to a long take during which the camera tracks backwards to precede them. In *Vol. 2*, amusing dialogue usually occurs before action scenes and only in two cases does it create funny scenes that break the development of the action. For example, before the massacre at the church, before Budd and Elle's fight and before the last combat between Beatrix and Bill. This contrasts with the scenes during which Budd is scolded by his boss at the nightclub, and the Bride speaks with Esteban (Michael Parks) about Bill initiate amusing digressions.

Unlike *Kill Bill*, *Death Proof* indulges in much play with new slowness, although in both cases, temporalities are sometimes also extended to emphasize violence. Interestingly, as in *Kill Bill*, the scene in which Earl and Edgard McGraw talk about the slaughter constitutes a funny digression that does not add important information. In most of the dialogue scenes, there are long takes and dialogue is nonsensical and funny, although when Stuntman Mike appears, the dialogue not only entertains the spectator, but also delays development of the action, increasing suspense.

In *Inglourious Basterds*, much like in *Kill Bill*, temporalities are extended to increase both suspense and the violence of scenes. Long takes are mainly used during dialogue sequences when amusing dialogue is adopted to increase suspense. For example: 31 per cent of the long takes occur in the first sequence when Landa enquires of Perrier LaPadite about Shosanna's family; 19 per cent of long takes are used before the tavern shooting in Nadine; and 12 per cent occur before the massacre at the theatre. In the scene in which Shosanna meets Goebbels and Landa at the restaurant, dialogue *à la* Tarantino is adopted to increase suspense, but the scene contains only one long take, while the montage is slow. Much like in *Inglourious Basterds*, in *Django Unchained* and *The Hateful Eight*, long takes are mainly used during nonsense dialogue sequences to increase suspense. In *Django Unchained* this is the case in 79 per cent of long takes, and in *The Hateful Eight* in 67 per cent of sequences.

In *Inglourious Basterds*, new slowness is mainly used to increase suspense, although there are scenes that appear as digressions, descriptions that interrupt suspense, but do not involve an amusing dialogue scene. This trend is exploited in *Django Unchained* and *The Hateful Eight*. Indeed, in *Inglourious Basterds*, pauses in development of the action can be considered: the shot of Goebbels having sex with Francesca which, thanks to montage, can be attributed to Shosanna's imagination; Sgt. Hugo's enacted flashback, in which he imagines himself tied up and whipped; Landa's enacted flashback about an ambush of the 'basterds'; the narrator's digressions about Sgt. Hugo's fame and silver nitrate; and the montage sequence of Shosanna getting ready for the premiere; and of her and Marcel during the production and post-production of their film. Similarly, in *Django Unchained*, many of Broomhilda's shots that seem to be his husband's imagination, and Django's flashbacks are pauses, like the montage sequences about travel, but also the brief dialogue between Django and Amerigo Vessepi (Franco Nero), an explicit homage to Sergio Corbucci's *Django* (1966), in which Franco Nero played the role of Django. As in *Django Unchained*, in *The Hateful Eight* montage sequences and flashbacks of simultaneity often become digressions that, more than entertaining the spectator, open 'visual descriptions' between dialogue and action scenes, not unlike descriptions in novels. On the other hand, in *Once Upon a Time . . . in Hollywood*, new slowness does not prevail: much of the dialogue between characters is about films and the film industry. As discussed, a mix of information and cross-references between extra-diegesis, diegesis and intra-diegesis slows the development of the fabula, involving the audience in a guessing game between reality and fiction, and past, present and future films, rather than in nonsensical funny dialogue entirely experienced in the present.

5.3 Conclusion

I believe that Tarantino's achievements cannot be summarized in the expression 'the Tarantino effect'. Jumbled and repeated event plots, enacted flashbacks and enacted flashbacks of simultaneity due to aesthetic or thematic choices that make the narration more complex dominate. This type of narration is enriched with shocking surprise and violent staged performances, new slowness and a self-referentiality that implicitly or explicitly evokes other films and genres. The temporalities of the main line of action, of the source-path-goal schema, is often slowed down, and sometimes stopped by the part-whole schema and by the very features that characterize Tarantino's oeuvre. Whereas in his early films, *Reservoir Dogs, Pulp Fiction, Jackie Brown* and *Kill Bill: Vol. 1* and *Vol. 2,* Tarantino plays with montage, in *Death Proof, Inglourious Basterds, Django Unchained* and *The Hateful Eight,* he almost abandons the complexity of the jumbled and repeated event plot – with the exception of the polyphonic or ensemble plot of *Once Upon a Time … in Hollywood.* Rhythm slows down, narration seems to progressively approach that of a classical novel, with fewer violent staged performances and overlapping dialogue, especially in the case of *The Hateful Eight.* But in Tarantino's oeuvre as a whole, he seems to adapt some features of the written medium to cinema, with the exception of violent staged performances.

Tarantino compares his films to novels, claiming, for example in the case of *Reservoir Dogs,* that, together with the main line of action, he sought to introduce his characters through a series of chapters, as in a novel, where the chain of events is broken to introduce a character's description and then resumes (Bernard 1996: 146; Gatti 1995: 24).[10] Comparing Tarantino's film to Kubrick's *The Killing,* Tarantino emphasizes that, whereas both films can be considered heist movies that oscillate in diegetic time, the structure of Kubrick's film imitates that of a newsreel, while in *Reservoir Dogs* that of a novel (Bernard 1996: 146). Moreover, Kubrick uses a voice-over and the narration focuses on the hold-up and the precise role of each member, whereas Tarantino does not even show the robbery (Gandini 2009: 37–8, 49, 51) – although Chapter 2 considers the complexity of style and narration, and the mistakes in diegetic time that seem to announce the final slaughter. Regarding *Pulp Fiction,* Tarantino states that he wished to embed three stories, each with its own protagonists, into one film and at the same time, using the characters of a story for another story, just as a writer uses a character of a novel for another book (Gatti 1995: 33–4).[11] He refers to *Franny and Zooey* by J. D. Salinger (1961), in which the characters link all the episodes (Gandini 1996: 27). I discuss this method, claiming that the source-path-goal and the part-whole schema are

---

[10] Interview with Graham Fuller (1990) *American Movies,* nr. 90, Milan, reported in (Gatti 1995).
[11] Statements collected by Michel Ciment and Hubert Niogret (1994) *Positif,* nr. 405, reported in Gatti (1995).

intertwined, and emphasized that this narrative structure, together with that based on flashbacks of simultaneity, often creates surprise and strong surprise, or shocking surprise in the case of violent staged performances. According to Tarantino, nine out of ten spectators start to lean to the left as soon as the film is going to turn left because they predict what is going to happen, and he uses this mechanism against the audience to provoke surprise (Gatti 1995: 11).[12] Dialogue in *Pulp Fiction* seems to clarify this anti-climax in favour of surprise. At the restaurant with Mia, Vincent asks her to tell him the joke she recounted at the end of the pilot episode:

Mia   It's corny.

Vincent   Don't be that way, tell me.

Mia   No, you wouldn't like it. I'd be embarrassed.

Vincent   You've already told fifty million people. And you can't tell me? I promise I won't laugh.

Mia   That's what I'm afraid of.

Vincent   That's not what I meant.

Mia   I'm not telling you, we built it up too much.

Not building too much suspense around a clue and surprising the audience is one of the techniques adopted by Tarantino, as well as freezing suspense – as he literally does when Honey Bunny and Pumpkin begin the hold-up, but a freeze-frame suspends their action until the last sequence of the film. Mia tells Vincent her joke at the end of the part dedicated to their date when he accompanies her home, after the spectator, and Vincent himself, shocked about the injection into her heart, have completely forgotten about it.

---

[12]   Interview by Graham Fuller (1994) *American Movies*, nr. 90, Milan, reported in Gatti (1995).

Conclusion

As in a time loop, I return to the Introduction where I argue that, while time does not exist according to quantum mechanics and it is only a metaphor for Conceptual Metaphor Theory, it is a self-determining prophecy deriving from relations among different variables. We are imprisoned in circadian rhythms, as well as in our life reviews that follow chronological and cause-and-effect links. For the majority of us, our lives are source-path-goal schemas that we plan and strive to follow, enveloped in the container schemas defined by birth and death. We can change the schema or we can sometimes be doubtful about our aims, but we can neither avoid Newtonian time nor that of our container schema. The price we pay to escape these schemas is, at least in most modern societies, that of being considered insane. Nevertheless, we can still experience fleeting moments, during which we forget the past and the future, as well as the very flow of time, in which we neither feel time moving – as in the time-moving metaphor – nor do we move along its path – as in the ego-moving metaphor. During these intense moments, when strong emotions dominate, we are free. The magic is that we do not have to include these moments in our live reviews because they do not need to coincide with the achievement of a goal: they are intense emotions which prompt us to burst out laughing or crying, or scream with pleasure, or to be fascinated by a work of art, or just by eyes staring at us.

Similarly, when we watch a film, representational time has a well-defined beginning and end, as does our life span, and when we enjoy the screening we wish that the spectacle will never end, as when we are satisfied with our lives we would like to be immortal. In a film, the screening and diegetic time and their relation, along with narrative and stylistic techniques, determine what I have called 'temporalities': times within the times of our life, with their own rules and exceptions. Chapters 2–5 closely analyse both the overall 'dominating' time of a film, and that of some or all of a director's films, and the moments during which this 'ruling' time is disrupted and spectators momentarily forget the trajectory towards the diegetic future – suspense – or the past – curiosity and surprise. It is in these very moments, as much as in our lives generally, that the prison of time through which the film is constructed and that is constructed by the film, crumbles, exposing our role as spectators, our deepest relations with the film.

Thanks to his still photography and his first three shorts, Stanley Kubrick develops a play of cross-references among shots, scenes and sequences, but also among films and genres, creating a complex web of stylistic, thematic and narrative features. From *Fear and Desire*, he crafted implicit temporalities that call attention to themselves. Through the film noir *Killer's Kiss* and *The Killing*, he overcomplicates the chronological and causal chains, trapping his characters in the narrative and stylistic features, going beyond the conventional rhythms of classical Hollywood style. This entrapment continues in *Paths of Glory* and *Spartacus*, through a virtuoso style in the former and massive configurations in the latter. Moreover, during the final battle in *Spartacus*, the rhythms of music, editing, *mise-en-scène* and cinematography coincide for the first time in Kubrick's oeuvre. But in *Lolita* and *Dr. Strangelove*, the director disrupts the represented time of characters and events through moments in which comedy, tragedy and eroticism prevail in the former case, and comic gags come to the fore in the latter. Subverting completely the classical rhythm of Hollywood style, in his last six hybrid films Kubrick can be considered a Hollywood Renaissance director who creates temporalities that imprison characters and spectators either in its slowness or in its syncopated rhythm.

In Adrian Lyne's films, suspense alternates with staged musical performances in *Flashdance*, and staged erotic performances in *Nine ½ Weeks, Fatal Attraction, Indecent Proposal, Lolita* and *Unfaithful*. During these performances, the source-path-goal schema and its suspense – often fostered at the beginning by a play of gazes among characters, and carried on by a narration based on love triangles and various characters' knowledge of events – is either suspended or slowed down. Whereas in the impossible puzzle film *Jacob's Ladder*, the filmmaker plays directly with the characters' diegetic time, challenging our hypotheses.

Meanwhile, in the majority of Michael Bay's films, suspense alternates with staged action performances and gags. Whereas during staged action performances temporalities are either accelerated or slowed down and almost frozen, during gags they are usually decelerated. But in both cases, the accumulation of suspense towards the end is not completely halted – as occurs in some staged musical performances of *Flashdance*. The rhythm of suspense of the source-path-goal schema is instead speeded up, mainly through countdowns, parallel editing and a different ratio between diegetic and screening time that usually, towards the end of the films, almost coincide. The pentalogy of *Transformers* offers instead the possibility of a diegetic time that goes beyond the boundaries of a single film to encompass the whole saga.

More than all the other directors discussed in this book, Quentin Tarantino plays most explicitly with temporalities, with the order of represented and representational time and their duration, using jumbled and repeated event plots, regular flashbacks and flashforwards, and flashbacks and flashforwards of simultaneity, through cross-cutting not only among actions occurring in different spaces at the same time but also at different times. Classical suspense, curiosity and surprise are often substituted by strong and shocking surprise, by staged violent performances during which temporalities are frozen, or by the new slowness through nonsense and funny dialogue during which temporalities slow down.

The difference between these directors' temporalities, created and sustained by different narrative and stylistic features, enables us to appreciate their uniqueness, independent of the scholarly literature about them, and calls for new terms and expressions to name their achievements. Far from discriminating between these filmmakers, I have chosen to adopt a more neutral stance – close analysis sustained by formalism, structuralism, embodied cognition and cognitive linguistics – to highlight their peculiarities. Their creation of different temporalities mirrors these directors' different approaches to cinema and its possibilities, together with the chance of escaping from its habitually represented and representation time, in much the same way as each of us constructs a different life review, but can temporarily break free of it.

Films

Anderson, Paul Thomas (1999) *Magnolia*.
Antonioni, Michelangelo (1966) *Blow-Up*.
Ardolino, Emile (1985) *Dirty Dancing*.
Badham, John (1977) *Saturday Night Fever*.
Bay, Michael (1995) *Bad Boys*.
Bay, Michael (1996) *The Rock*.
Bay, Michael (1998) *Armageddon*.
Bay, Michael (2001) *Pearl Harbour*.
Bay, Michael (2003) *Bad Boys II*.
Bay, Michael (2005) *The Island*.
Bay, Michael (2007) *Transformers*.
Bay, Michael (2009) *Transformers: Revenge of the Fallen*.
Bay, Michael (2011) *Transformers: Dark of the Moon*.
Bay, Michael (2013) *Pain & Gain*.
Bay, Michael (2014) *Transformers: Age of Extinction*.
Bay, Michael (2016) *13 Hours: The Secret Soldiers of Benghazi*.
Bay, Michael (2017) *Transformers: The Last Knight*.
Bay, Michael (2019) *6 Underground*.
Bress, Eric and J. Mackye Gruber (2004) *The Butterfly Effect*.
Cameron, James (1984) *Terminator*.
Chabrol, Claude (1969) *La femme infidèle*.
Corbucci, Sergio (1966) *Django*.
Cousins, Mark (2011) *The Story of Film*.
Edwards, Blake (1961) *Breakfast at Tiffany's*.
Figgis, Mike (2000) *Timecode*.
Fincher, David (1999) *Fight Club*.
Foley, James (2017) *Fifty Shades Darker*.
Foley, James (2018) *Fifty Shades Freed*.
Gaghan, Stephen (2005) *Syriana*.
Gilliam, Terry (1995) *Twelve Monkeys*.
Hawks, Howard (1940) *His Girl Friday*.
Hitchcock, Alfred (1948) *Rope*.
Howitt, Peter (1998) *Sliding Doors*.
Huston, John (1941) *The Maltese Falcon*.
Huston, John (1950) *The Asphalt Jungle*.
Jarmusch, Jim (1984) *Stanger than Paradise*.
Jarmusch, Jim (1995) *Dead Man*.
Kelly, Richard (2001) *Donnie Darko*.
Kubrick, Stanley (1951) *Day of the Fight*.
Kubrick, Stanley (1951) *Flying Padre*.
Kubrick, Stanley (1953) *Fear and Desire*.

Kubrick, Stanley (1953) *The Seafarers.*
Kubrick, Stanley (1955) *Killer's Kiss.*
Kubrick, Stanley (1956) *The Killing.*
Kubrick, Stanley (1957) *Paths of Glory.*
Kubrick, Stanley (1960) *Spartacus.*
Kubrick, Stanley (1962) *Lolita.*
Kubrick, Stanley (1964) *Dr. Strangelove or: How I Learned to Stop Worrying and Love the Bomb.*
Kubrick, Stanley (1968) *2001: A Space Odyssey.*
Kubrick, Stanley (1971) *A Clockwork Orange.*
Kubrick, Stanley (1975) *Barry Lyndon.*
Kubrick, Stanley (1980) *The Shining.*
Kubrick, Stanley (1987) *Full Metal Jacket.*
Kubrick, Stanley (1999) *Eyes Wide Shut.*
Kurosawa, Akira (1950) *Rashomon.*
Lynch, David (2006) *Inland Empire.*
Lyne, Adrian (1973) *The Table.*
Lyne, Adrian (1976) *Mr. Smith.*
Lyne, Adrian (1980) *Foxes.*
Lyne, Adrian (1983) *Flashdance.*
Lyne, Adrian (1983) *Michael Sembello: Maniac.*
Lyne, Adrian (1986) *Nine ½ Weeks.*
Lyne, Adrian (1987) *Fatal Attraction.*
Lyne, Adrian (1990) *Jacob's Ladder.*
Lyne, Adrian (1993) *Indecent Proposal.*
Lyne, Adrian (1997) *Lolita.*
Lyne, Adrian (2002) *Unfaithful.*
Noé, Gaspar (2002) *Irréversible.*
Nolan, Christopher (2010) *Inception.*
Ozon, Francois (2004) *5x2.*
Porter, Edwin Stanton (1903) *Life of an American Fireman.*
Preminger, Otto (1960) *Exodus.*
Ramis, Harold (1993) *Groundhog Day.*
Rodriguez, Robert (1996) *From Dusk till Dawn.*
Rodriguez, Robert (2005) *Sin City.*
Rodriguez, Robert (2007) *Planet Terror.*
Schwentke, Robert (2009) *The Time Traveler's Wife.*
Shyamalan, M. Night (1999) *The Sixth Sense.*
Scorsese, Martin (1990) *Goodfellas.*
Société Lumière (1986) *L'Arrivée d'un train en gare de La Ciotat.*
Soderbergh, Steven (2000) *Traffic.*
Sturges, John (1963) *The Great Escape.*
Tarantino, Quentin (1992) *Reservoir Dogs.*
Tarantino, Quentin (1994) *Pulp Fiction.*
Tarantino, Quentin (1995) *The Man from Hollywood of Four Rooms.*
Tarantino, Quentin (1997) *Jackie Brown.*
Tarantino, Quentin (2003) *Kill Bill: Volume 1.*

Tarantino, Quentin (2004) *Kill Bill: Volume 2.*
Tarantino, Quentin (2007) *Death Proof.*
Tarantino, Quentin (2009) *Inglourious Basterds.*
Tarantino, Quentin (2012) *Django Unchained.*
Tarantino, Quentin (2015) *The Hateful Eight.*
Tarantino, Quentin (2019) *One Upon a Time . . . in Hollywood.*
Tarr, Béla (2000) *Werckmeister Harmonies.*
Tarr, Béla (2011) *The Turin Horse.*
Taylor-Johnson, Sam (2015) *Fifty Shades of Grey.*
Van Sant, Gus (2003) *Elephant.*
von Sternberg, Josef (1930) *The Blue Angel (Der blaue Engel).*
Wachowski, Lana and Lilly Wachowski (1999) *The Matrix.*
Wachowski, Lana and Lilly Wachowski (2003) *The Matrix Reloaded.*
Wachowski, Lana and Lilly Wachowski (2003) *The Matrix Revolutions.*
Welles, Orson (1941) *Citizen Kane.*
Welles, Orson (1958) *Touch of Evil.*
Wells, Simon (2002) *The Time Machine.*
Zemeckis, Robert (1985) *Back to the Future.*
Zinnemann, Fred (1952) *High Noon.*

References

'1990 Director Adrian Lyne Talks with Patty Spitler about "Jacob's Ladder"' (2018 [1990])
YouTube, 30 August. https://www.youtube.com/watch?v=Y-PEOavL0sI. Last accessed
15 March 2022).

'Adrian Lynn Interview' (1998) YouTube, 28 July. https://www.youtube.com/watch?v=
ACi2JdJBM44. Last accessed 15 March 2022.

Aristotle (2012) *Poetica*. I classici del pensiero libero. Greci e latini – 11. Milano: BUR
Rizzoli, RCS Media Group Divisione Quotidiani.

Barthes, Roland (1994) *Sul cinema*. Genova: Il melangolo.

Barthes, Roland (2003) *La camera chiara. Nota sulla fotografia*. Torino: Giulio Einaudi
Editore.

Bernard, Jami (1996) *Quentin Tarantino. L'uomo e i film*. Torino: Lindau.

Biltereyst, Daniel (2015) '"A Constructive Form of Censorship". Disciplining Kubrick's
Lolita'. In Tatjana Ljujic, Peter Krämer and Richard Daniels (eds) *Stanley Kubrick: New
Perspectives*, pp. 136–49. London: Black Dog Publishing.

Bordwell, David (1986) 'Classical Hollywood Cinema: Narrational Principles and
Procedures'. In Philip Rosen (ed.) *Narrative, Apparatus, Ideology. A Film Theory Reader*,
pp. 17–34. New York: Columbia University Press.

Bordwell, David (2001) *Narration in the Fiction Film*. New York: McGraw-Hill.

Bordwell, David (2002) 'Film Futures'. *SubStance, Issue 97: Special Issue: The American
Production of French Theory*, vol. 31, nr. 1, pp. 88–104.

Bordwell, David (2006) *The Way Hollywood Tells It*. Berkley and Los Angeles, CA:
University of California Press.

Bordwell, David and Kristin Thompson (1998) *Storia del cinema e dei film. Dal dopoguerra
a oggi*. Milano: Editrice Il Castoro.

Bordwell, David and Kristin Thompson (2001) *Film Art. An Introduction*. New York:
McGraw-Hill.

Borgna, Eugenio (2015) *Il tempo e la vita*. Milano: Feltrinelli.

Brancati, Simona (2004) *Kill Tarantino. Quentin Tarantino: istruzioni per l'uso*. Roma:
Pericle Tangerine Editrice.

Branigan, Edward (2002) 'Nearly True: Forking Plots, Forking Interpretations: A Response
to David Bordwell's "Film Futures"'. *SubStance, Issue 97: Special Issue: The American
Production of French Theory*, vol. 31, nr. 1, pp. 105–14.

Broderick, Mick (2017) *Reconstructing Strangelove. Inside Stanley Kubrick's 'Nightmare
Comedy'*. New York: Columbia University Press, Wallflower.

Buccheri, Vincenzo (2009) 'Pulp Fiction'. In Vito Zagarrio (ed.) *Quentin Tarantino*,
pp. 52–71. Venezia: Marsilio.

Caprara, Valerio (2007) *Erotico. Dizionari del cinema*. Milano: Eletta Accademia
dell'Immagine.

Carocci, Enrico (2012) 'L'emozione condivisa. La parte dell'empatia nell'esperienza
spettatoriale'. In Enrico Carocci and Giorgio De Vincenti (eds) *Il cinema e le emozioni.
Estetica, espressione, esperienza*, pp.331–51, Roma: Fondazione Ente dello Spettacolo.

Carocci, Enrico (2018) *Il sistema schermo-mente. Cinema narrativo e coinvolgimento emozionale*. Roma: Bulzoni Editore.

Ciment, Michel (2003) 'The State of Cinema'. *Unspoken Cinema*. http://unspokencinema. blogspot.com/2006/10/state-of-cinema-m-ciment.html. Last accessed 18 June 2019.

Cinemetrics (2016) http://www.cinemetrics.lv/index.php. Last accessed 10 May 2018.

Cobb, Humphrey (1935) *Paths of Glory*. New York: Viking Press.

Coëgnarts, Maarten (2017) 'Stanley Kubrick and the Art of Embodied Meaning-Making in Film'. *Cinergie*, nr. 12, pp. 53–71.

Coëgnarts, Maarten and Peter Kravanja (2012) 'The Visual and Multimodal Representation of Time in Film, or How Time is Metaphorically Shaped in Space'. *Image & Narrative*, vol. 13, nr. 3, pp. 85–100. https://www.academia. edu/2039619/2012_-_The_Visual_and_Multimodal_Representation_of_Time_in_ Film_or_How_Time_is_Metaphorically_Shaped_in. Last accessed 19 October 2016.

Coëgnarts, Maarten and Peter Kravanja (2016) 'Perceiving Emotional Causality in Film: A Conceptual and Formal Analysis'. *New Review of Film and Television Studies*, vol. 14, nr. 4. https://www.academia.edu/23152789/2016_-_Perceiving_Emotional_Causality_in_ Film_A_Conceptual_and_Formal_Analysis. Last accessed 3 October 2016.

Cohen, Annabel J., Kelti MacMillan and Robert Drew (2006) 'The Role of Music, Sound Effects & Speech on Absorption in a Film: The Congruence-Associationist Model of Media Cognition'. *Journal of the Canadian Acoustical Association*, vol. 34, nr. 3, pp. 40–1. http://jcaa.caa-aca.ca/index.php/jcaa/article/view/1812/1559. Last accessed 19 October 2016.

Connolly, Julian W. (2009) *A Reader's Guide to Nabokov's 'Lolita'*. Brighton, MA: Academic Studies Press.

Conrich, Ian (2006) 'Musical Performance and the Cult Film Experience'. In Ian Conrich and Estella Tincknell (eds) *Film's Musical Moments*, pp. 115–31. Edinburgh: Edinburgh University Press.

Conrich, Ian and Estella Tincknell (2006) *Film's Musical Moments*. Edinburgh: Edinburgh University Press.

Cook and Bernink (1999) *The Cinema Book*. London: BFI.

Curti, Roberto (2007) *Stanley Kubrick. Rapina a mano armata*. Torino: Lindau.

D'Aloia, Adriano and Ruggero Eugeni (2016) 'Connecting (and Dis-connecting) Events. A Neurofilmological Approach to Narrative Time'. Working paper presented at in/ between: cultures of connectivity, The NECS 2016 Conference (Potsdam, Germany, 28–30 July 2016).

Daniels, Richard (2015) 'Selling the War Film: Syd Stogel and the *Paths of Glory Press Files*'. In Tatjana Ljujic, Peter Krämer and Richard Daniels (eds) *Stanley Kubrick: New Perspectives*, pp. 80–97. London: Black Dog Publishing.

Day, Ingeborg [Elizabeth McNeill] (1978) *Nine and a Half Weeks: A Memoir of a Love Affair*. New York: E.P. Dutton.

de los Rios, Riccardo and Robert Davis (2006) 'From Hollywood to Tokyo: Resolving a Tension in Contemporary Narrative Cinema'. *Film Criticism*, vol. 31, nr. 1–2, pp. 157–72.

Dogliani, Mario (1997) *Spartaco. La ribellione degli schiavi*. Milano: Baldini & Castoldi.

Douglas, Kirk (2013) *Io sono Spartaco! Come girammo un film e cancellammo la lista nera*. Milano: Il Saggiatore.

Eugeni, Ruggero (2017) *Invito al cinema di Kubrick*. Milano: Mursia.

Eugeni, Ruggero (January–June 2018) 'What Time Is In? Subjective Experience and Evaluation of Moving Image Time'. In *Reti, saperi, linguaggi – Italian Journal of Cognitive Science*, nr. 1, pp. 81–96.

Falsetto, Mario (2001) *Stanley Kubrick. A Narrative and Stylistic Analysis.* Westport: Praeger.

Fast, Howard (1951) *Spartacus.* New York: Howard Fast/Blue Heron Press.

Forster, E.M. (1927) *Aspects of the Novel.* New York: Harcourt, Brace & Company.

Frenzel, Leif (2008) 'Narrative Patterns in Time Travel Fictions'. https://www.yumpu.com/en/document/view/6668315/narrative-patterns-in-time-travel-fiction-leif-frenzel. Last accessed 16 May 2018.

Gallese, Vittorio and Michele Guerra (2015) *Lo schermo empatico. Cinema e neuroscienze.* Milano: Raffaello Cortina Editore.

Gandini, Leonardo (1996) *Quentin Tarantino. Regista pulp.* Roma: Fannucci Editore.

Gandini, Leonardo (2009) 'Le iene'. In Vito Zagarrio (ed.) *Quentin Tarantino*, pp. 33–51. Venezia: Marsilio.

Gatti, Francesco (ed.) (1995) *Quentin Tarantino.* Roma: Dino Audino Editore.

Genette, Gérard (1986) *Figure III.* Torino: Einaudi.

Genette, Gérard (1997) *Palimpsests: Literature in the Second Degree.* Lincoln, NE: University of Nebraska Press.

Ghislotti, Stefano (2012) *Film Time. Le dimensioni temporali della visione.* Bergamo: Bergamo University Press, Sestante.

Girard, René (2012) *Geometrie del desiderio.* Milano: Raffaello Cortina Editore.

Gorbman, Claudia (1987) *Unheard Melodies: Narrative Film Music.* Bloomington, IN: Indiana University Press.

Grant, Barry Keith (2007) *Film Genre: From Iconography to Ideology.* London: Wallflower.

Hengelhard, Jack (1988) *Indecent Proposal.* New Jersey: Donald I. Fine and E. Rutherford.

Hughes, David (2000) *The Complete Kubrick.* London: Virgin Books.

Hunter, I. Q. (2015) 'Introduction: Kubrick and Adaptation'. *Adaptation, Special Issue: Kubrick and Adaptation*, vol. 8, nr. 3, pp. 277–82.

Hutto, Daniel (2016) 'Memory and Narrativity'. *Revised Version to Appear in the Routledge Handbook of Philosophy of Memory.* https://www.academia.edu/25340514/Memory_and_Narrativity. Last accessed 19 October 2016.

Jaffe, Ira (2008) *Hollywood Hybrids. Mixing Genre in Contemporary Films.* Lanham, MD: Rowman & Littlefield Publishers.

Jaffe, Ira (2014) *Slow Movies. Countering the Cinema of Action.* New York: Columbia University Press, Wallflower.

Jess-Cooke, Carolyn (2009) *Film Sequels.* Edinburgh: Edinburgh University Press.

Kiss, Miklós (2015) 'Film Narrative and Embodied Cognition: The Impact of Image Schemas on Narrative Form'. In Maarten Coegnarts and Peter Kravanja (eds) *Embodied Cognition and Cinema*, pp. 43–62. Leuven: Leuven University Press.

Kiss, Miklós and Steven Willemsen (2017) *Impossible Puzzle Films. A Cognitive Approach to Contemporary Complex Cinema.* Edinburgh: Edinburgh University Press.

Koestler, Arthur (1949) *The Gladiators.* London: Jonathan Cape.

Krämer, Peter (2015) 'Complete Total Final Annihilating Artistic Control: Stanley Kubrick and Post-War Hollywood'. In Tatjana Ljujic, Peter Krämer and Richard Daniels (eds) *Stanley Kubrick: New Perspectives*, pp. 48–61. London: Black Dog Publishing.

Krämer, Peter (2017) 'Stanley Kubrick and the Internationalisation of Post-War Hollywood'. *New Review of Film and Television Studies*, vol. 15, nr. 2, pp. 250–69. http://www.tandfonline.com/doi/abs/10.1080/17400309.2016.1208993. Last accessed 24 November 2017.

Lakoff, George and Mark Johnson (1998) *Metafora e vita quotidiana*. Milano: Strumenti Bompiani.

Lash, Dominic (2017) 'Distance Listening: Musical Anachronism in Stanley Kubrick's *Barry Lyndon*'. *Cinergie*, nr. 12, pp. 83–93.

Leonard, Elmore (2004 [1992]) *Jackie Brown [Rum Punch]*. Milano: Il Saggiatore.

Lewis, David (April 1976) 'The Paradoxes of Time Travel'. *American Philosophical Quarterly*, pp. 145–52.

LoBrutto, Vincent (1997) *Stanley Kubrick. A Biography*. London: Faber and Faber.

Mamber, Stephen (1998) 'Simultaneity and Overlap in Stanley Kubrick's *The Killing*'. *Postmodern Culture*, vol. 8, nr. 2. http://pmc.iath.virginia.edu/text-only/issue.198/8.2mamber. Last accessed 24 November 2017.

Mather, Philippe D. (2013) *Stanley Kubrick at Look Magazine. Authorship and Genre in Photojournalism and Film*. Bristol: Intellect Ltd.

Mather, Philippe D. (2015) 'A Portrait of the Artist as a Young Man. The Influence of Look Magazine on Stanley Kubrick's Career as a Filmmaker'. In Tatjana Ljujic, Peter Krämer and Richard Daniels (eds) *Stanley Kubrick: New Perspectives*, pp. 20–47. London: Black Dog Publishing.

McAdams, Dan P. (2001) 'The Psychology of Life Stories'. *Review of General Psychology*, vol. 5, nr. 2, pp. 100–22. https://www.sesp.northwestern.edu/docs/publications/430816076490a3ddfc3fe1.pdf. Last accessed 19 October 2016.

Mee, Laura (2017) *The Shining*. Leighton Buzzard: Auteur.

Menarini, Roy (2009) 'Kill Bill Voll. 1 e 2'. In Vito Zagarrio (ed.) *Quentin Tarantino*, pp. 91–110. Venezia: Marsilio.

Menarini, Roy (2015) *Il corpo nel cinema. Storie, simboli e immagini*. Milano: Mondadori.

Metz, Christian (1989) *Semiologia del cinema. Saggi sulla significazione nel cinema*. Milano: Garzanti.

Moore, Kevin Ezra (2014) *Spatial Language of Time*. Amsterdam: John Benjamins Publishing Co.

Morsiani, Alberto (2016) *I film di Quentin Tarantino. Il regista che ha reinventato il cinema*. Roma: Gremese.

Nabokov, Vladimir (1955) *Lolita*. Paris: Olympia Press.

Nabokov, Vladimir (1997) *Lolita: A Screenplay*. New York: Vintage Books.

Nabokov, Vladimir (2000) *Lolita*. London: Penguin Books.

Nelson, Thomas Allen (2000) *Kubrick. Inside a Film Artist's Maze*. Bloomington, IN: Indiana University Press.

Palmer, Lorrie (2012) '*Cranked* Masculinity: Hypermediation in Digital Action Cinema'. *Cinema Journal*, vol. 51, nr. 4, pp. 1–25.

Pezzotta, Elisa (Winter 2011) 'Personal Time in Alternative and Time Travel Narrative: The Cases of *Groundhog Day*, *Twelve Monkeys* and *2001: A Space Odyssey*'. *Alphaville: Journal of Film and Screen Media*, nr. 2, pp. 1–13.

Pezzotta, Elisa (2013) *Stanley Kubrick: Adapting the Sublime*. Atlanta, GA: Mississippi University Press.

Pezzotta, Elisa (2015) 'The Magic of Time in *Lolita*: The Time Traveller Humbert Humbert'. *Adaptation*, vol. 8, nr. 3, pp. 297–320.

Pezzotta, Elisa (2016a) 'Adapting Time in Robert Schwentke's *The Time Traveler's Wife*'. *Cinergie*, n. 9, pp. 117–27.

Pezzotta, Elisa (2016b) 'Time Anxiety in Burgeois Couples: *Voyage to Italy*, *The Night* and *Eyes Wide Shut*'. *Elephant & Castle*, nr. 14, pp. 5–38.

Pezzotta, Elisa (2017) 'Slowness and Time Expansion in Long Takes: *2001: A Space Odyssey*, *Barry Lyndon*, and *Eyes Wide Shut*'. *Cinergie*, nr. 12, pp. 41–52.

Pirandello, Luigi (1986) *L'umorismo*. Milano: Arnoldo Mondadori.

Plantinga, Carl (1999) 'The Scene of Empathy and the Human Face on Screen'. In Carl Plantinga and Greg M. Smith (eds) *Passionate Views. Film, Cognition, and Emotion*, pp. 239–56. Baltimore, MD: Johns Hopkins University Press.

Pramaggiore, Maria (2015) *Making Time in Stanley Kubrick's* Barry Lyndon: *Art, History, and Empire*. New York and London: Bloomsbury.

Prévost-Balga, Antoine (2017) 'Three Kubrickian Machinic Characters and their Technical Malfuncion'. *Cinergie. Il Cinema e le altre Arti, Special Issue: Stanley Kubrick: A Retrospective*, nr. 12, pp. 9–19.

Radford, Fiona (2015) 'Having His Cake and Eating It Too: Stanley Kubrick and *Spartacus*'. In Tatjana Ljujic, Peter Krämer and Richard Daniels (eds) *Stanley Kubrick: New Perspectives*, pp. 98–115. London: Black Dog Publishing.

Ramírez Berg, Charles (2006) 'A Taxonomy of Alternative Plots in Recent Films: Classifying the "Tarantino Effect"'. *Film Criticism*, vol. 31, nn. 1/2, pp. 5–61.

Recalcati, Massimo (2012) *Ritratti del desiderio*. Milano: Raffaello Cortina Editore.

Recalcati, Massimo (2019) *Mantieni il bacio. Lezioni brevi sull'amore*. Milano: Feltrinelli.

Regosa, Maurizio (2002a) 'Max Ophuls, nel gioco della seduzione e dello sguardo'. In Maurizio Regosa (ed.) *Il sorriso di Dioniso. Cinema e psicoanalisi*, pp. 56–71. Firenze: Alinea Editrice.

Regosa, Maurizio (2002b) 'Una rappresentazione della passione: L'angelo azzurro'. In Maurizio Regosa (ed.) *Il sorriso di Dioniso. Cinema e psicoanalisi*, pp. 36–55. Firenze: Alinea Editrice.

Resnik, Salomon (2007) *Il teatro del sogno*. Torino: Bollati Boringhieri.

Rodriguez, Rene (2005) *Morning Call*, 23 July.

Rovelli, Carlo (2017) *L'ordine del tempo*. Milano: Adelphi Edizioni.

Ryan, Marie-Laure (Winter 2006) 'From Parallel Universes to Possible Worlds: Ontological Pluralism in Physics, Narratology, and Narrative'. *Poetics Today*, vol. 27, nr. 4, pp. 633–74.

Salinger, J. D. (1961) *Franny and Zooey*. New York: Little, Brown.

Salt, Barry (2006) *Moving into Pictures*. London: Starword.

Salt, Barry (2009) *Film Style and Technology: History and Analysis*. London: Starword.

Singer, Jefferson A. and Susan Bluck (2001) 'New Perspectives on Autobiographical Memory: The Integration of Narrative Processing and Autobiographical Reasoning'. *Review of General Psychology*, vol. 5, nr. 2, pp. 91–9. http://self-definingmemories.homestead.com/Singer___Bluck__2001.pdf. Last accessed 19 October 2016.

Smith, Greg M. (1999) 'Local Emotions, Global Moods, and Film Structure'. In Carl Plantinga and Greg M. Smith (eds) *Passionate Views. Film, Cognition, and Emotion*, pp. 103–26. Baltimore, MD: Johns Hopkins University Press.

Stam, Robert (2005) 'The Metamorphoses of Lolita'. In Robert Stam (ed.) *Literature through Film: Realism, Magic and the Art of Adaptation*, pp. 223–42. Oxford: Blackwell Publishing.

Sternberg, Meir (1978) *Expositional Modes and Temporal Ordering in Fiction*. Bloomington, IN, and Indianapolis, IN: Indiana University Press.

Sternberg, Meir (1992) 'Telling in Time II: Chronology, Teleology, Narrativity'. *Poetics Today*, vol. 13, nr. 3, pp. 463–541.

Stuckey, Karyn (2015) 'Re-Writing Nabokov's *Lolita*. Kubrick, the Creative Adaptor'. In Tatjana Ljujic, Peter Krämer and Richard Daniels (eds) *Stanley Kubrick: New Perspectives*, pp. 116–35. London: Black Dog Publishing.

Telotte, J. P. (2006) 'The New Hollywood Musical: From *Saturday Night Fever* to *Footloose*'. In Steve Neale (ed.) *Genre and Contemporary Hollywood*, pp. 4–61. London: BFI.

Terrone, Enrico (2017) 'On Time in Cinema'. In Ian Phillips (ed.) *The Routledge Handbook of Philosophy of Temporal Experience*, pp. 327–38. New York: Routledge.

Tincknell, Estella (2006) 'The Soundtrack Movie, Nostalgia and Consumption'. In Ian Conrich and Estella Tincknell (eds) *Film's Musical Moments*, pp. 132–45. Edinburgh: Edinburgh University Press.

Todorov, Tzvetan (1975) *The Fantastic: A Structural Approach to a Literary Genre*. New York: Cornell University Press.

Tomaševskij, Boris (1968 [1925]) 'La costruzione dell'intreccio'. In Tzvetan Todorov (ed.) *I formalisti russi. Teoria della letteratura e metodo critico*, pp. 305–50. Torino: Einaudi.

Truffaut, Francois (1967) *Hitchcock*. New York: Simon and Schuster.

Tsivian, Yuri (n.d.), 'Films and Statistics: Give and Take'. In *Cinemetrics*. http://www.cinemetrics.lv/dev/fsgt_q1a.php. Last accessed 10 May 2018.

Ulivieri, Filippo (2017) 'Waiting for a Miracle: A Survey of Stanley Kubrick's Unrealized Projects'. *Cinergie*, nr. 12, pp. 95–115.

'*Unfaithful* Interview' (2016) '"Unfaithful" Interview, YouTube, 19 January. Available at: https://www.youtube.com/watch?v=UXRysIgQiT4. Last accessed 15 March 2022.

Yacavone, Daniel (2008) 'Towards a Theory of Film Worlds'. *Film-Philosophy*, vol. 12, nr. 2, pp. 83–108.

Walker, Alexander, Sybil Taylor and Ulrich Ruchti (1999) *Stanley Kubrick, Director. A Visual Analysis*. New York: Norton.

White, Lionel (1955) *Clean Break*. New York: E.P. Dutton & Company.

Zagarrio, Vito (2009) 'La grande mall dell'immaginario. Il cinema di Quentin Tarantino'. In Vito Zagarrio (ed.) *Quentin Tarantino*, pp. 7–32. Venezia: Marsilio.

Index